DEATH TRAP

"A chilling tale of a sociopathic wife and mother willing to sacrifice all those around her to satisfy her boundless narcissism . . . a compelling journey from the inside of this woman's mind to final justice in a court of law. Fair warning: for three days I did little else but read this book."

—Harry N. MacLean, *New York Times* bestselling author of *In Broad Daylight*

I'LL BE WATCHING YOU

"Skillfully balances a victim's story against that of an arrogant killer as it reveals a deviant mind intent on topping the world's most dangerous criminals. Phelps has an unrelenting sense for detail that affirms his place, book by book, as one of our most engaging crime journalists."

—Katherine Ramsland

IF LOOKS COULD KILL

"M. William Phelps, one of America's finest true-crime writers, has written a compelling and gripping book about an intriguing murder mystery. Readers of this genre will thoroughly enjoy this book."

—Vincent Bugliosi

"Starts quickly and doesn't slow down. . . . Phelps consistently ratchets up the dramatic tension, hooking readers before they even know they've been hooked. His thorough research and interviews give the book a sense of growing complexity, richness of character, and urgency."

—Stephen Singular

MURDER IN THE HEARTLAND

"Drawing on interviews with law officers and relatives, the author has done significant research and—demonstrating how modern forensics and the Internet played critical, even unexpected roles in the investigation—his facile writing pulls the reader along."

—*St. Louis Post-Dispatch*

"Phelps expertly reminds us that when the darkest form of evil invades the quiet and safe outposts of rural America, the tragedy is greatly magnified. Get ready for some sleepless nights."

—Carlton Stowers

"This is the most disturbing and moving look at murder in rural America since Capote's *In Cold Blood*."

—Gregg Olsen

SLEEP IN HEAVENLY PEACE

"An exceptional book by an exceptional true crime writer. Phelps exposes long-hidden secrets and reveals disquieting truths."

—Kathryn Casey

EVERY MOVE YOU MAKE

"An insightful and fast-paced examination of the inner workings of a good cop and his bad informant, culminating in an unforgettable truth-is-stranger-than-fiction climax."

—Michael M. Baden, M.D.

"M. William Phelps is the rising star of the nonfiction crime genre, and his true tales of murderers and mayhem are scary-as-hell thrill rides into the dark heart of the inhuman condition."

—Douglas Clegg

LETHAL GUARDIAN

"An intense roller coaster of a crime story . . . complex, with a plethora of twists and turns worthy of any great detective mystery, and yet so well-laid-out, so crisply written with such detail to character and place, that it reads more like a novel than your standard nonfiction crime book."

—Steve Jackson

PERFECT POISON

"True crime at its best—compelling, gripping, an edge-of-the-seat thriller. Phelps packs wallops of delight with his skillful ability to narrate a suspenseful story and his encyclopedic knowledge of police procedures."

—Harvey Rachlin

"A compelling account of terror . . . the author dedicates himself to unmasking the psychopath with facts, insight and the other proven methods of journalistic legwork."

—Lowell Cauffiel

Also by M. William Phelps

Perfect Poison

Lethal Guardian

Every Move You Make

Sleep in Heavenly Peace

Murder in the Heartland

Because You Loved Me

If Looks Could Kill

I'll Be Watching You

Deadly Secrets

Cruel Death

Death Trap

Kill for Me

Failures of the Presidents (coauthor)

Nathan Hale: The Life and Death of America's First Spy

The Devil's Rooming House: The True Story of America's Deadliest Female Serial Killer

The Devil's Right Hand: The Tragic Story of the Colt Family Curse

Love Her to Death

Too Young to Kill

The Dead Soul: A Thriller (available as ebook only)

Never See Them Again

KISS
OF THE
SHE-DEVIL

M. WILLIAM PHELPS

PINNACLE BOOKS
Kensington Publishing Corp.
http://www.kensingtonbooks.com

PINNACLE BOOKS are published by

Kensington Publishing Corp.
119 West 40th Street
New York, NY 10018

All Kensington Titles, Imprints, and Distributed Lines are available at special quantity discounts for bulk purchases for sales promotions, premiums, fund-raising, and educational or institutional use. Special book excerpts or customized printings can also be created to fit specific needs. For details, write or phone the office of the Kensington special sales manager: Kensington Publishing Corp., 119 West 40th Street, New York, NY 10018, attn: Special Sales Department, Phone: 1-800-221-2647.

Pinnacle and the P logo Reg. U.S. Pat. & TM Off.

ISBN-13: 978-0-7860-2487-2
ISBN-10: 0-7860-2487-9

First Printing: March 2013

10 9 8 7 6 5 4 3 2 1

Printed in the United States of America

*This book is dedicated to Kensington Publishing Corp.—
and all those who have supported me throughout the
years, including Michaela Hamilton, Doug Mendini,
and publisher Laurie Parkin, with a special thanks to the
Zacharius family and Kensington's late founder,
Walter Zacharius.*

I

THE MURDER

1

IT WAS JUST about nine o'clock. Time for the library to close. Barbara "Barb" Butkis, a veteran librarian supervisor for fifteen years, planned on staying late. Barb needed to work on a few things related to the library's computer system. This type of work had to be done after hours. Barb had told Martha Gail Fulton, one of her library aides, that there was no reason for her to stick around. Martha, who went by her middle name, Gail, was always asking how she could do more. Barb explained that she and another employee could take care of the extra work. Gail's home life wasn't so stable lately, anyway; in fact, it was no secret to most employees at the library that home was probably the best place for the forty-eight-year-old married mother of three grown children. Gail had recently taken her husband back after he had an extended and tumultuous affair. But that was Gail: the forgiving, devout Catholic, always willing to pardon for the sake of souls.

All the employees generally met near the staff door heading out into the parking lot at the end of a shift. Barb and another coworker, librarian Cathy Lichtman, stayed behind.

"Computer backup," Barb said to the others as they gathered, ready to leave.

It sounded boring and tedious. The only plus for Barb was that it would take maybe ten or fifteen minutes, tops.

The Orion Township Library, on Joslyn Road, was a central point in the quaint Michigan town of Lake Orion, "where living is a vacation," the town's website claims. Lake Orion is about forty-five minutes due north of the more well-known and popular home of the Tigers and Pistons, the Motor City, Detroit. By small-town standards, the landmass of Lake Orion is infinitesimal: 1.2 square miles, 440 acres of which are eaten up by water. On that cool October night, when Barbara Butkis and Gail Fulton's lives outside of books collided, there were fewer than two thousand residents registered in Lake Orion. So, without overstating it, one could say this was a town, literally, where not only did everybody know everyone else's business, but nothing much beyond bake sales, PTA meetings, and bingo games happened. Lake Orion was as charming and dainty as any fabricated plastic town in the middle of a child's train set: perfect and pleasant and quiet. Maybe even boring, too—just the way townies liked it.

Gail's work imitated her life—she was flexible. Gail worked every Monday night (tonight) from five to nine, but she would come in on additional, alternate days and nights at different hours. Those Monday nights were Gail's, though, and had been since she'd taken the job eighteen months earlier. The job Gail did—and did it very well— was what one would have expected from a librarian's assistant. Throughout everybody's time inside libraries, patrons have all come in contact with these everyday, average women and men. They push carts of books from one aisle to the next, quietly, in solitude, depositing each into its respective, numerically placed slot. Once in a while, they will answer a patron's question. If a person loved books, this was a dream job.

Gail walked out with the others. "Good night," she said. "See you soon." In the inflection of Gail's voice, there was an unremarkable (yet unmistakable) Texas drawl. Gail and her husband and kids had been in Michigan only a few years, transplants from Corpus Christi.

Gail's maroon van was parked in the lot just out the door, about twenty-five yards straight ahead. Gail walked to her van and immediately noticed something different about it. The way it sat. She couldn't put her finger on what, exactly, but something didn't seem right.

Gail shook off what was an odd feeling before placing her pocketbook on the passenger seat and getting in on the driver's side.

Inside, she turned the key, backed out of her parking space, and drove away.

She got about ten yards from her parking space before realizing one of the tires on her van was flat. So she turned, driving around a small island of mulch and shrubs, before pulling back into the same space she'd just left.

Then she got out and had a look.

Gail stood staring at her flat tire, then turned back toward the library. All of her coworkers, save for Barb and Cathy (still inside finishing up that computer work), were gone by now, on their way home to another peaceful night in paradise.

So Gail walked toward the employee entrance.

Not yet out of the immediate area where she had parked, Gail noticed a car, with its lights bright and shining in her face, pull up. There was a man and woman in the front seat. A second man dressed in a black leather jacket, black gloves, black ski mask, and a do-rag sat in the back.

Gail didn't like the look of this. It didn't appear that they were there to help.

The man dressed in black got out.

No one said anything.

Gail grew concerned; she kept eyeing the library's employee entrance, no doubt hoping someone would walk out.

2

WITH CATHY LICHTMAN'S HELP, Barbara Butkis finished the computer backup. Both women got their things together and proceeded to leave. It was October 4, 1999, at 9:10 P.M., when they walked out the door, Barbara later recalled.

Outside, it was dark and crisp. Cooler than normal temperatures had forced the brittle, colorful leaves of fall to settle like feathers on the ground. A slick sheen of drizzle moistened the pavement. All the doors to the library were locked. Nobody could walk in off the street. A person would have to know what Barb later described as a special "key code" in order to open the door.

Gail knew this code.

Barb and Cathy stood near the employee exit. Barb punched the alarm code number to set it, watched Cathy walk out in front of her, and soon followed behind.

When she was outside the building, Barb made sure the exit door was secure. She pulled on it, hearing that click of the lock, feeling resistance.

They could go home.

"Have a good night, Cathy," Barb said.

"You too. See you tomorrow."

Barb and Cathy walked toward the parking lot. As Barb

later explained, "We usually kind of look back and forth, because it is evening, to see if there is anything in the parking lot before we start approaching our cars. . . ."

Two women, alone in the night, were being vigilant and careful, mindful of their surroundings. This was the kind of world they lived in—even there, in what many would have deemed the safest place on earth.

After making that routine gaze into the night, looking for anything out of the ordinary, Barb peered straight ahead—and then stopped.

Something caught her eye.

It was on the ground. Maybe about fifty feet ahead.

Fabric?

It looked like a piece of clothing. However, neither Cathy nor Barb could tell what it was because, as Barb later explained, who expects to see clothing on the ground as you leave work?

Barb and Cathy walked toward the fabric.

A pile of clothes?

Strange, someone's clothes spread out on the ground like that. Here. At night. In the parking lot of a library.

Kids? Maybe a pre-Halloween prank?

No. Couldn't be.

Barb noticed what she called "breath or steam coming from the object"—and that's when things began to make sense.

Walking up next to the fabric, Barb and Cathy noticed something else.

"It was a person," Barb remembered.

"Gail!" Barb yelled, recognizing her coworker lying on the tar.

Cathy was just as shocked to see Gail, barely moving, on the ground, on her back, motionless, moaning in a whisper. ("She was very still," Barb said later. "I could not tell at that moment what had happened to her, if she had fainted or—I couldn't tell because she was lying on the ground.")

Barb knelt down beside Gail. "Honey? Gail? Talk to me!"

No response.

Cathy stood beside Barb; then she, too, knelt down.

Barb grabbed Gail's wrist to check for a pulse.

"I'm going to call 911," Cathy said, standing up, turning, and running for the library.

"Gail?" Barb said, with her fingers applied gingerly to the back side of Gail's wrist. (Later, Barb remarked: "Her eyes were just staring. . . .")

Gail Fulton was slipping away.

Cathy had the phone in her hand; the door to the library was open. She yelled to Barb, who could not find a pulse, "Is Gail diabetic, Barb?" Obviously, Cathy was speaking to a 911 operator, who was directing her on which questions to ask.

Barb knew this was no diabetic coma or fainting spell, she could see what she thought was blood coming from the top of Gail's forehead. As Cathy continued to yell questions, Barb noticed a large pool of "liquid" surrounding the back of Gail's head, tacky to the touch, seemingly growing in size as Barb focused on it. The fluid was dark, thick, and spreading in a halo pattern around Gail's head.

Oh, my, Barb thought.

"Is she breathing?" Cathy yelled.

Barb looked. That growing pool of fluid had to be blood—lots of it, in fact, pouring out from the back of Gail's head.

"She's been hurt bad!" Barb yelled. "Someone hurt her *very* bad."

Cathy hung up with 911 and grabbed a blanket. Barb met her at the door, took the blanket, ran back to Gail, and placed it over her body.

"Gail, honey . . . can you hear me?" Barb said as she consoled her friend, trying to keep her warm and awake.

Cathy then walked up with a towel, which she applied with firm pressure to the back of Gail's head. The tears came when Barb realized Gail had been shot in the head, maybe a few other areas of her body, too. There could be no other explanation.

Gail was still alive, though. She was breathing laboriously, and her pulse was weakening.

She had a heartbeat. She was fighting.

Sirens pierced the night as Barb and Cathy did their best to let Gail know she was not alone. They would not let her die out here by herself, in the dark, on her back, lying on the cold parking lot pavement in a pool of her own blood.

3

GUY HUBBLE HAD been with the Oakland County Sheriff's Department (OCSD) since 1985. As the call came in that a woman was hurt at the Lake Orion Public Library, road patrol officer Hubble, nearing the end to his generally carefree and quiet three-to-eleven shift, realized he was right down the street. The Township of Orion had been under Hubble's patrol. Looking at his watch—9:14 P.M. on the nose—Hubble sped toward the scene.

"I was already northbound on Joslyn Road, coming up to [West] Clarkston Road," Hubble recalled. "I was approximately a quarter mile away, maybe half, at the most."

From his scanner Hubble had gleaned basic details of what was going on: *injured party . . . a medical emergency.*

The patrol officer hit his lights and siren, passing Square Lake Cemetery on the right, several residential houses on the left. Coming up to the library's driveway a few moments after receiving the call, Hubble raced into the backward J-shaped entrance toward the employee parking lot and spied "two white females . . . standing above another white female that was [lying] on the ground."

Hubble parked, flung his door open, and approached

the women. Understandably so, they were upset, a bit manic, and did not know what else they could do for Gail.

"What is the nature of the situation?" Hubble asked.

"We think she's fallen," Barb said. She held a "paper cloth" to Gail's forehead. After thinking about it, Barb figured Gail had fallen and hit her head. She was confused and traumatized, not thinking clearly. She didn't want to believe her friend had been shot in the head.

Hubble walked closer. "Please remove the cloth," he said, wanting to see the extent of Gail's injuries, maybe try to discern what had happened, and if he could do anything to help.

As soon as Barb removed the cloth, it was clear to the veteran cop what happened: Gail had not fallen, as the women had now suspected. "I noticed a large hole in the upper part of the forehead," he explained. It was obvious that Gail had been shot.

Emergency personnel and another officer pulled up at the same time, chirping to a stop. The lights on each vehicle flashed strobes of red and blue, brightening the parking lot, making a scene out of what was, on any other night, a place of peace and quiet, where nothing much of anything happened.

"Back away, please," the officer said, approaching. "They need to administer help."

Gail was slipping; that white light approaching fast. She had been shot in the head and torso four times. She had stood, looked into the eyes of her killer, turned away instinctively, knowing, it seemed, the end was near. Anyone who knew Gail would agree that in those crucial moments after she was shot, as she fell to the ground, this pious woman, undoubtedly, began to recite the Catholic prayers she had breathlessly said thousands of times throughout her life. Gail was known to say a rosary every night; maybe tonight she was saying that same prayer as she lay dying.

Hubble noticed Gail was "moaning and moving" slightly. "I was trying to keep her from moving her neck area," he recalled, "[when] shortly after that, fire [rescue] arrived and [she] took her last breath."

As he knelt beside her, Hubble heard a *whoosh* of air from Gail's lungs, so subtle and unexpected and yet eerily normal. Then there was total quiet.

Gail had given up her fight. She was gone.

With a volunteer emergency medical technician (EMT) now helping, Hubble got to work performing cardiopulmonary resuscitation (CPR). As they prepared Gail's body for CPR, undoing her clothing, Hubble noticed "what appeared to be multiple gunshot wounds . . . above and to the left of the right breast, and one below."

The EMT continued CPR, but Hubble felt Gail wouldn't respond. There was no bringing her back. While she had moaned previously, Hubble leaned down and asked Gail if she could relate any information about what had happened. It was then that Hubble "could hear the air leaving her lungs. It was just a—all I could hear was a *'hough,'* a deep *huff* type of sound as the air left."

This was Gail's final breath.

Hubble got together with those officers who were now responding to the scene in droves. "Close down the entrance to the township [library]," he ordered, "so nobody can enter." Hubble wanted the area cordoned off. If Gail had been shot, there must be some sort of trace evidence around, maybe even a few spent projectiles.

"Ladies, go back into the library," Hubble told Barb and Cathy, who were wandering around in a daze, unaware—in shock, perhaps—of what had actually taken place, yet understanding that something horrible had happened right before their eyes.

More rescue personnel arrived, all of them now working on trying to revive a dead woman.

Hubble saw that Gail held a set of keys in her hand. He walked over and took them. Then he opened the passenger-side door to her vehicle and found her pocketbook, where he quickly located her identification. The bag was sitting on the passenger seat, as though she had just set it down. He took a quick look around the van and did not see anything out of place or disturbed. Then he gave a once-over to the outside of the van. Save for the flat tire, nothing seemed suspicious.

As Hubble walked the scene, surveying what he could, Barb came out and mentioned what she thought might be of some help. "Cameras," Barb said. "We record what goes on out in the parking lot and around the building."

"You do?" Hubble said.

"Yes," Barb reiterated. She pointed to a camera on the building that faced the exact spot in the parking lot where Gail lay dead.

Gail Fulton's murder has been caught on tape, Hubble thought.

This murder of a local housewife and librarian would send the OCSD to call on Oak Force, a multiagency crime-fighting organization. As luck would have it, that very same week this super police force had been formed as a team of lawmen. Comprised of local Federal Bureau of Investigation (FBI) agents, members of the Michigan State Police (MSP), and OCSD—on top of police officers from the nearby towns of Pontiac, Southfield, and Troy—the agency investigated major crimes. Good thing. Because from the moment Hubble and his colleagues arrived and found Gail Fulton—a harmless librarian's assistant, whose father, Noe Garza, and uncle, Margarito Garza, were former federal judges—it was clear that she had been targeted. Gail's mother, Dora Garza, was also a well-known figure in the community and a church leader in her native home of Corpus Christi.

These could be people, law enforcement concluded, that others might hold grudges against.

4

PATROL OFFICER HUBBLE asked Barb where the videotapes from the night were kept.

She showed him the closet, saying, "Right in there."

As Barb further explained, she was unaware of how the "video machines" worked. She suggested they call in the library's maintenance man.

Not too long after, Hubble followed the guy with all the keys clipped to his belt and watched him take the videotape out of the video player. By now, Hubble had called in his sergeant, Alan Whitefield, who had arrived at the library by nine-thirty to help secure the scene and make sure a chain of custody with regard to the videotape was maintained.

Sergeant Whitefield took control of the scene, directing Hubble to give him the videotape and head back outside, where he could watch over things until the crime scene unit arrived. From there, Whitefield called in the crime lab and dispatched several additional officers to keep watch on the library and its surrounding area. There was a shooter somewhere in town, after all—likely, not too far away. It had, by Barbara's estimation, been only twenty minutes (at most) since Gail had been shot.

Detective Chris Wundrach (pronounced Won-Drack) showed up in Whitefield's wake—the situation extremely fluid by now—and took possession of the videotape, suggesting to Whitefield that they go into the library and have a look at it right away. It could yield an important clue to the killer's identity, like perhaps a car license plate number.

"Right," Whitefield said.

The tape contained a view from four different video cameras recording in one-second intervals, so, as Whitefield later explained, "it was very quick." More than a film of the events, it looked like a bundle of snapshots flipped into action. The cameras were posted over the employees' entrance, the main entrance, toward the rear of the parking lot, and looking down at a loading dock in the back of the building. At best, the portion of the tape depicting the murder was grainy and blurry and fuzzy. As they sat and watched, a car pulled up to Gail's van after she walked around to the passenger side; they could see the car's headlights clearly. Then someone got out from the backseat after the car stopped. Wearing what appeared to be a white shawl, Gail came out toward the car from around the back side of her van. The man from the car (his back to the camera) approached. Without warning, there were several white blasts of light, disturbing in the context of which they now knew. Gail, who was standing in one frame, was on the ground in the next; then the man, her killer, headed back toward the waiting vehicle. It was clear from the video that there were other people in the car. The remainder of the video showed the car pulling out of the driveway and disappearing into the night. Without enhancing the video (zooming in on different sections of each frame), there was no way to make out a license plate number—if, in fact, the license plate itself wasn't covered up with something. The only fact they could be certain of without sending the video to the lab to be enhanced was that they were dealing with three people inside a contemporary-looking vehicle that had pulled into the parking lot for one reason.

To kill Martha Gail Fulton.

While additional police arrived and the parking lot became an official crime scene, Barb decided she needed to make a call and let Gail's husband know what was going on.

A young man answered. It was Gail's son. "Is your father home?" Barb asked. The urgency in her voice was aggressive and apparent.

Moments later, George Fulton said, "Hello? What is it?"

"Something happened to Gail in the parking lot," Barb said.

"I'll be right there."

Barb told one of the officers at the scene that she had called George.

"How long since the time you found Mrs. Fulton, did you call Mr. Fulton?"

"Twenty minutes," Barb said.

He wrote it down.

"Several weeks ago," Barb added, "I overheard Gail telling another employee that she was having marital problems. So I asked her later on that day if everything was okay."

"What'd she say?"

"She told me that she and her husband were going to counseling, and she thought things were going to be all right."

As Guy Hubble worked the action outside, some time

had passed and a colleague notified him that George Fulton and his son had arrived.

"Do not allow them on the scene."

"What should we tell them?"

"Have them escorted to the Orion substation so we can conduct interviews."

By 9:27 P.M., the doctor on scene had pronounced Gail Fulton's death, making it official. All efforts to revive her were stopped. Someone had murdered this devout Catholic housewife and librarian. The police were already suspicious of Gail's husband. At first, from all outward appearances, George wasn't the least bit torn up over his wife's sudden death. No tears. No urgency to find the perp. Either George held his emotional cards close to the vest, or he had things to hide.

5

THE LIBRARY WAS not quite surrounded by woods, but there was a section of thickly settled weeds and pines. As one officer walked the perimeter of the parking lot near this area, flashlight in hand, searching for what he did not know, he "heard movement."

The officer keyed his radio: "I need another unit . . . for search."

Two additional officers ran up. They went into the wooded area with flashlights and looked around.

It took about ten minutes, but they found nothing.

Officer Robert Timko, one of the cops conducting this search, was told to give George Fulton and his son a ride to the substation.

"I'm not going anywhere," George said defiantly, suddenly becoming concerned, "until I find out what happened to my wife."

Timko told George to relax. He called Sergeant Alan Whitefield over.

Whitefield was busy. He had a crime scene unfolding. There were medics and doctors and cops all over the place. Yellow crime-scene tape was going up. Passersby were beginning to gather at the entrance. Neighbors across from the library were beginning to wonder what in the world was going on.

"What's up?" Whitefield asked Timko.

They stood out of earshot from George and his son. Timko explained the situation, noting how he believed George had been acting strange, irate and not wanting to cooperate.

Whitefield walked over and told George, "Look, your wife has been shot, and we need your complete cooperation."

Timko showed George and Andrew Fulton to his patrol car and they left for the substation.

Officers went out and canvassed the neighborhood, both facing the library and in back of the building, through the woods. Just about every neighbor within earshot of the library reported the same thing: gunshots heard at 9:00 P.M. In this part of the country, most are accustomed to what a gun going off sounds like. There's not too much mistaking a gunshot with a car backfiring or some other noise. People here know the sound of a gun firing because it is a place where residents hunt and fish and participate in all sorts of outdoor activities. The only difference in the five reports neighbors gave was the number of shots heard: Some said three; some said four; one said five.

Sometime after midnight, several library employees, George Fulton and his son, Andrew, along with their youngest daughter, Emily, waited at the OCSD Substation in town. Whitefield had instructed detectives from the sheriff's department to head over to Talon Circle, George and Gail's home, to collect evidence and see what they could figure out about the life and times of George and Gail Fulton. George had already admitted to owning several handguns, but he had said little else. He seemed a bit hostile and uncooperative, even angry—not the response cops generally get from a grieving spouse. Investigators had interviewed George briefly, but nothing of value came out of it.

"George was very unemotional," said one investigator. "*Very* hard to read."

George Fulton's weapons would have to be confiscated and taken to the lab. Also, police wanted swabs of DNA from George, Emily, and Andrew. Gail's maroon 1992 Plymouth Grand Voyager van was impounded and towed from the crime scene; the flat tire was removed from the vehicle and sent off to the crime lab for further processing. There was protocol to follow now: steps to take in order to find out if Gail's murderer had left behind that one clue that could break the case open. It was likely there, investigators knew, somewhere in all of the interviews going on and the evidence collected. No killer is flawless. They all leave behind a mark or clue—no matter how trivial or, conversely, significant. An investigator knows this and follows his training and instincts; sooner or later, that one piece of evidence will emerge.

A man who left the library right about the time of Gail's murder had heard what happened and came forward to tell police this story: "I think I seen two cars, one larger, maybe a four-door. There may have been two gentlemen, one in each car; but it was unusual because [there's] always some cars there when I was leaving . . ."

Maybe this was something. Maybe not. The officer took the statement and placed it with what was a growing number of witness testimonials.

The one person, however, investigators were just sitting down with—alone and away from his father's grasp—was a boy who could tell police where George was, and what he was doing at the time of his wife's murder. Spouses are always suspects in murders of one another; but George, with his unusual behavior, inconsistent and erratic as the night progressed, was judged a bit more quickly by police. Something—maybe just a cop's instinct—told law enforcement to look closely at George.

6

HIS BIRTH NAME is George Andrew Fulton, but everyone in the family called him Andrew. It was near eleven o'clock on the night of his mother's murder when Andrew sat down with Detective Chris Wundrach at the Lake Orion Township Substation. According to a family member, Andrew was "a very social person . . . and caring [individual], as he will go out of his way to do nice things for the people he cares about."

Andrew and his mother were close. Her death was devastating to him.

"You're not under arrest or anything like that," Wundrach explained. Andrew was going to be turning eighteen in two months. "We're just looking for your help in our investigation."

"Okay," Andrew said.

Start with the basics: "Tell me what you did tonight."

The boy seemed nervous, which was expected. This was a tense and alarming situation. Still, as one family member recalled, Andrew "can also have a temper on him," which he acquired from his *"papu"* (grandfather on his mother's side). Saying Andrew and his mother were tight was a gross understatement; Andrew was not afraid to tell his mother anything.

"My dad was always very critical of [Andrew] and didn't have a kind word for him, but my mom was always very loving and understanding of whatever my brother did," Emily Fulton later observed.

"Near six o'clock," Andrew said, "me and my girl-friend, Alicia Caldwell (pseudonym), left my house to go over her house for dinner. My dad was just getting home from work as we were leaving."

Andrew spent much of the night over at Alicia's, which Wundrach would soon verify. Alicia dropped her boyfriend back off at home around eight-thirty that night. The library, Wundrach knew, was about a ten-minute ride—at most—from home.

"How did you know your dad was home, Andrew?"

"I heard him working in the basement."

"Did your father leave the house at any time that you know of?" It was not hard to tell where this line of questioning was headed.

"No," he said.

"How do you *know* that?"

"I was watching television in our den, so I would have seen him come up from the basement and leave."

There was always the possibility—and as a cop, Wundrach had to consider every potential scenario plausible—that Andrew was covering for his father, or for himself. And the way to get that out of the boy, Wundrach knew, was to dig into the day-to-day dynamics of the family.

Sins and secrets. Every family walked casually around them every day. Some emerge and cause a breakdown within the unit, while others are able to work through them.

"Tell me how your mom and dad's relationship was?" Wundrach asked.

Andrew looked down at his hands. This was not a tough question, and he was upfront: "It was stressed."

"How so?"

"My dad had an affair last year with his boss, while he was working in Florida."

This interested Wundrach, of course. Love, money, and revenge were three potential reasons behind *any* murder. More than that, why hadn't George mentioned anything about his mistress while being interviewed at the substation earlier? Why was George holding this fact back?

"Can you tell me anything about it?" Wundrach pressed.

Andrew said the affair dated to "last December 1998," as far as he knew. "My dad ended the affair and was going to counseling with my mom to work on their marriage." Gail was a firm believer in the sacrament of marriage and saw it as a vocation, as she had been taught since childhood through Catholic school and church teaching. She was a devoted parish member of St. Joseph's Catholic Church, on the north side of Lake Orion, where Barb Butkis had explained that she saw Gail at mass often. So working on the marriage, although it had suffered the hammering blow of adultery, was something Gail had been bred to do, an observer could say. There had been times— *boy, had there ever*—when Gail was ready to pack it in and head to divorce court, but she was willing to forgive George and move on, especially since he had broken it off with his mistress.

"Do you know your father's boss's name, Andrew?"

"Donna," he said. "She lives in Florida." He didn't have a last name.

"You ever see Donna?"

"No."

"Andrew, let me ask you, have you *ever* heard of any threats made against your mom?"

Andrew thought about this. "My mom told me once that Donna had threatened her, telling her she was going to 'drag her out in the street and beat her.'"

That was pretty significant. There wasn't a lot of wiggle room there to speculate what this Donna person wanted to do.

"When was that?" Wundrach asked.

"It was a few months ago that [my mom] told me. Donna came here to Michigan to see my dad."

"Donna ever call your house?"

"Yeah, of course. My dad still works for her."

"When was the last time she called?"

"Around nine-twenty—tonight."

"Really. How'd you know it was her?"

"I heard my father say, 'Bye, Donna.'"

After being asked, Andrew explained that they had two phone lines in the house: one for George's business and another for the family, adding, "As my dad was saying, 'Bye, Donna,' on one line, the library people were calling on the home line to tell us something had happened."

How ironic!

Or maybe not.

Were Donna and George discussing Gail's murder?

"Your dad have any weapons in the house, Andrew?"

"He owns three handguns. One's a twenty-two—and two are nine millimeters."

"When was the last time you saw the guns?"

"My dad was cleaning all three of them, just three days ago in his bedroom."

"Have *you* ever shot the weapons?"

"Yes . . . but when I was in fifth grade."

"When was the last time—and we're almost done here, okay—you shot a gun, Andrew? Do you recall?"

"A week ago. I shot my BB gun at a friend's house."

"Think about this, son. Is there anyone that you can think of who would want to harm your mother?"

Andrew took a breath. "No."

7

IT STARTED FOR Emily Fulton earlier that morning, October 4, 1999. She called it intuition, a paranormal "ability" of some sort she'd had since childhood.

"I was extremely agitated."

Of course, she had no idea that her mother was going to be murdered, but there was something tugging at Emily—relating to her mother—all day long. She had a feeling that was nagging and pulling at her emotions.

"I had no reason to be mad at my mother," Emily added, "but I was mad at her all day long."

Gail was one of those mothers—wives—who had a meal on the table every night. Didn't matter if she had to work that night or not. If Gail had a shift at the library, she'd prepare the meal and have it ready in the refrigerator.

Throughout that day Emily had a sense that she needed to go to her mother; yet she felt she wasn't supposed to intervene in the situation in any way. Whatever was to be would be, and Emily had a strange "knowing" of having to step aside on this one and allow fate to run its course. The feeling became stronger that night—possibly, according to Emily, right around the time Gail was being slain—as Emily sat at a friend's Pampered Chef party. Not normally someone who needs to be prodded into socializing or talking, Emily wasn't herself. Her friend walked up and asked why she was so quiet. Emily had sat around during the party; there was something heavy weighing on her mind.

"I didn't feel right. I had a headache. I kept getting that feeling that I needed to go see my mom and be with her, but that I *wasn't* supposed to, at the same time."

Emily had been to several of these sales parties—be it jewelry, food, cooking supplies, Amway, whatever. She always had made purchases, both to support her friend and to get something for her mother.

"But on that day, I knew," Emily recalled. "I was going to buy something for my mom, but I knew. I needed to wait. I wasn't going to buy anything for her."

Why the hesitation?

Because she felt that her mother wasn't going to need it, she added.

"When she died, the moment she died," Emily said, "I must have felt it."

After the Pampered Chef party, Emily should have gone home. It was the thing to do. She'd have to get some sleep so she could get up and go to class in the morning.

"But something told me not to. I didn't want to face what was there."

Inside that house, Emily sensed, was bad news. She knew it. She understood that what was waiting for her might change her life in some way. She just didn't know how.

"I was avoiding going home, at all costs."

So Emily went over to her boyfriend's house.

It was near eleven at night when she dredged up the nerve to drive home.

"I put it off as long as I could. Then I showed up and the police are there."

All those feelings throughout the night—the connection with her mother, the aura of something dark that was hovering around like a ghost following her—were now in her face. She had been right, after all.

"There's been an accident," one of the cops at the house told Emily after she walked in. It was late now, well after midnight. "Could you come down to the substation with us?"

Emily had just started her sophomore year of college. Same as her brother, Emily lived at home. (Their older sister had stayed in Texas and lived with Gail's mother, Dora Garza, and finished up college before marrying and moving to Virginia.) Emily was the outspoken one of the bunch. She had graduated high school in Michigan in 1998. This was after changing schools two years before, in 1995, when George Fulton had decided—against Gail and all the kids' wishes—that the family was moving north to Michigan from Texas.

"Sure," Emily said, responding to the OCSD's request to go down to the substation.

Emily stepped into the police cruiser. They took off.

"What happened?" Emily asked as the cop drove.

"Well, we'll explain it all when you get to the substation."

Emily thought about it. "What's wrong with my mom?" she pressed. "I can't feel her. Something's happened to my mom. . . . I cannot feel her with me."

This statement shocked the police officer. "Why do you think that?"

"Because I have not felt right all day about my mom, so it must be about her."

"Don't worry," the police officer said, "your family is there [at the substation]. We'll explain when you get there." Then the cop broke into what Emily described as "small talk," and the officer started to ask her all sorts of questions.

"What's wrong?" Emily asked again. "You're nervous. You're repeating the same questions over and over. You're also just saying 'family.' You're not mentioning who's there at the substation. What's going on? What happened to my mom?"

Some time passed. "Let's just not talk," the cop suggested.

When Emily arrived at the substation, the first family member she spied upon entering the building was Andrew.

"Where's Dad?" Emily asked. "What happened?"

Cops were standing around everywhere.

"I got into trouble for stealing something," Andrew said with a troubled, mocking smirk, likely more out of nervousness than trying to be funny. ("Although I do believe that the police told him to say this," Emily recalled.)

"You didn't *steal* anything," Emily said. She was the middle child, the type A of the three, the one willing to speak her mind (her truth) and let the chips fall. Emily was a doer. She got things done. She had been through a lot this past year with her mother and father, and the affair George had had with Donna. There were times when Emily had found herself in the middle of the affair, observing, asking questions, even confronting her father's lover, and trying to talk her mother into divorcing her father and moving back home to Texas.

"Where's Dad?" Emily asked for a second time.

"Well," Andrew said, looking down and away from his sister, "I got into some trouble, and this is why we're all here."

"No, you didn't!" Emily shouted. "You didn't do *anything* wrong. Now I know something happened to Mom. I need to know *what*!"

They were surrounded by police, who were coming in and out of the room, standing around, listening to the conversation. What Emily meant by "I know" was that she'd had that premonition earlier in the night.

One police officer pulled Emily aside and explained

that she needed to go with him into another room. They sat her down in a chair, she said, and the room was "full of cops." A female police officer, with a look of despair on her face, walked over to Emily. She knelt down on bended knee in front of Gail's middle daughter. Andrew came in and stood nearby. The room was quiet. "I'm sorry," the female officer explained somberly, "but your mother . . . She has been in an accident."

"That bitch! That bitch killed my mom," Emily blurted out through tears, without another word.

It was as if everyone in the room had frozen. The officers looked at each other. Andrew put his hand on his sister's shoulder and squeezed. The world had stopped.

"What was that, Emily?" the cop asked.

Emily looked into the female officer's eyes. Everything else in the room, Emily recalled, faded. She was focused on this one moment.

"Accident"? she said to herself. *There was no* accident.

"I knew," Emily said later, "that was *not* the case."

Emily felt the police had likely said this—calling it an "accident"—on purpose to see what type of reaction they would get from Emily and Andrew.

She was right. Emily, Andrew, and George were all suspects at this point.

"That bitch murdered my mom!" Emily blurted out again. She was crying more dramatically now. The entire complexity and totality of her day and night had come into focus. Emily knew why she had felt so strange all day long, why she had never bought her mother a Pampered Chef gift. Emily believed she had felt her mother's presence leave as Gail died in that parking lot.

As news of her mother's death settled on Emily, she began to make sense of what had occurred.

"I need to tell you what happened," Emily explained to the police officer.

"What do you mean by that?" an investigator asked.

"I am seeing in my mind what happened."

There was silence in the room again.

"You are going to blame my father," Emily added. "I need to tell you what happened. It's *not* my father. *She* did it with other people."

She . . . meaning the lover.

"My sister here, Emily"—Andrew piped in, explaining in a halfhearted fashion, almost to imply that his sister had no idea what she was saying, that it was the trauma of losing their mother—"thinks she's psychic!"

8

THIS SKILL EMILY Fulton described as intuitive, instinctual, and even supernatural perception hadn't come to her overnight. It wasn't something Emily pulled out of the air one day after watching a marathon of *That's So Raven* (a Disney sitcom for teens with a supernatural slant) episodes, and then decided to take it on as some sort of protection against emotional trauma. It was not a wall she put up to defend against the broken home of dysfunction that she believed to be living in over the past several years. To downplay it all as trickery, or as a Sylvia Browne–inspired "gift," would not bother Emily. Rather, it would prove to her how much skeptics *didn't* know. Emily wasn't about explaining herself. She didn't need approval from anyone or, for that matter, to prove herself and her ability. It was a gift she knew she had—and that's all that mattered to her.

"It has served me correctly," Emily commented, "and saved my life in some instances. So I just go with it."

Her memories of this celestial insight go back as far as the late 1980s, when Emily was seven years old. Emily's grandfather died right before she turned seven. At the moment he died, Emily and her family lived in Virginia; her grandfather and grandmother resided in Texas. She was too young, Emily said, to understand the gradual decline a slow death can sometimes bring. She didn't even know that her grandfather was sick at the time.

While her grandfather endured an illness at home, some 1,400 miles away, Emily began to receive what she described as "visions."

"I don't know how else to explain what they were."

She began to see her grandfather lying on a couch at home, a "very specific afghan blanket" covering him. She didn't know it then, but her grandmother had crotched this blanket at the time of her grandfather's illness.

"It was red, gray, and black." Emily could see this blanket as clear as if it were in front of her. "I saw my grandmother feeding him soup."

She had no idea the man was dying. She had no idea (or conception, really) of his being sick in any way.

"Mommy," Emily said to her mother one day, "Grandpa is dying."

"No, no. Your grandfather is okay, Emily. Nothing's wrong. He's okay."

How many families are afraid of death and shield the youngest members of the clan from the details and ebb and flow of watching a loved one die?

Emily had no way of knowing that her grandfather had been on a list of cardiac patients waiting for a heart.

Not long after she had that vision (her grandmother feeding him, that afghan blanket covering him, keeping the old man warm as he faded), Emily's grandfather died of a heart attack. There was no way to hide it anymore from the kids.

"I think," Emily concluded, "that as children, we all have that ability to see *things*. Yet we lose it over time—especially if it's not developed or cultivated."

This episode taught Emily a hard lesson—one she didn't come to understand until much later in life. Still, it was something she often went back to. She never questioned what she saw, or the strong feelings that sometimes came over her. For instance, she would stare at her father and sense a strong presence of turmoil and distrust and darkness brewing inside the man. The stress the guy lived under had manifested itself, according to Emily's readings and feelings, into an aura that she could see and feel. This was why, when she told police she knew what had happened to her mother, she was saying it with not only a straight face, but with a logic rooted in that "gift" she had developed and learned to embrace over the years. And this ability Emily had would soon help Gail's youngest daughter cope with this enormous loss and get her through what would become the most shocking and alarming allegations Emily had ever heard.

It was near midnight when George Fulton sat with OCSD investigators David Ross and Chris Wundrach at the Lake Orion Township Substation. George had been interviewed once already, briefly, but he had not said much of anything. Investigators had more information now. They could ask pointed questions. Because George had been acting standoffish and not wanting to talk, not to mention that he failed to tell police at first that he had cheated on Gail, he became a person of interest cops were looking at very closely.

"You're not under arrest," Wundrach explained. "We want to make that clear. But we need to talk to you about the shooting."

George shook his head in agreement. "I understand. I want to cooperate."

"Good. Begin by telling me what you were doing tonight."

George did not hesitate. He said he arrived home from work about six in the evening. As he walked in the door, it seemed Andrew was just walking out to go over to his girlfriend's. "I had to cook for myself because Emily was at some cooking party." The way he made it sound was as if a married man with daughters should never have to cook; it was not his duty. But on this night, with his wife working and his daughter out, George said he made spaghetti. Gail had not left dinner, as she generally did. "I then went down into the basement office and did some work until around eight-thirty, when Andrew came home."

"What happened next?"

"Andrew came down the stairs about nine-thirty and told me I had a phone call. It was Barbara Butkis from the library. She said Gail was hurt . . . that I should come down to the library. Andrew and I left immediately. When I got there, no one would tell me anything."

George was getting excited and antsy as he felt a lingering finger being pointed directly at him.

"Relax, Mr. Fulton," one of the investigators said. This was not an interrogation; they were trying to develop information and see if George knew anything that might be helpful in finding his wife's killer.

After a brief pause Wundrach asked, "Are you and your wife having any marital problems, Mr. Fulton?"

"No!" George answered quickly.

"Did you have an affair with your boss?"

"I did have an affair, and at one point wanted a divorce. But I am Catholic. I wanted to work things out. Gail and I were counseling with a priest from our parish. We went twice. I said I didn't want to go anymore. I counseled personnel in the military, and counseling is not something that would work on me."

"What is your relationship with your boss currently?"

"I still work for Donna Trapani." He gave the name of the company. "But the company is going under and I am not getting paid for my work."

"Okay, when did you end your relationship with Miss . . . What was her name again? . . . Oh, yeah, Trapani?"

"I was living with her in Florida and moved out in October 1998 to my own apartment. I moved back in with Gail in April of . . . let me see . . . 1999. Donna took that very hard. She came here during the weekend of July 4, 1999. I set up a meeting between Donna and Gail at a hotel—the ConCorde Inn in Rochester Hills. I left the room. . . . Gail soon left. . . . I stayed . . . with Donna and talked to her."

Things were getting more interesting as George Fulton talked through it: How many guys would set up a sit-down with his mistress and his wife? There had to be more to it than just the two of them getting together to talk things out.

"Do you think that Donna could be responsible for your wife's shooting?" Wundrach asked, quite curious about this new fact.

"No!" George said. "She could *never* do anything like that."

"Did Gail have any enemies?"

"Gail had no enemies. . . ." For George, it was ridiculous even to say something like that. "I have no idea who could have done this." George had a tone that indicated he wanted to leave.

"When was the last time you spoke to Donna?"

"I talked to Donna about four or five times today because of my work. I was on the phone with Donna when my son came down the stairs to tell me something happened at the library and Barbara was on the phone."

David Ross asked George, who might have killed Gail?

"I. Don't. Know." He said these words angrily. "She was a sweet person and had *no* enemies."

"Did you have any knowledge or involvement in your wife's death?" Ross asked.

"No."

"Listen, Mr. Fulton, would you be willing to take a

polygraph—you know, a lie detector test—to help clear your name from our investigation?"

George became even angrier. He stood up. "No! I will not. I do not believe in polygraphs! And you know what," he added, heading toward the door, "I'm all done talking here. I need to leave."

Ross and Wundrach looked at each other.

They had rattled George Fulton's cage.

But how?

9

THE SHERIFF'S DEPARTMENT kept Emily and Andrew at the substation for quite some time that night and well into the next morning. It wasn't until the sun seemed to be peeking its shine over the nearest mountain range, casting a hue of banana yellow across the lake, that Andrew and Emily finally went home. That statement Emily had given regarding knowing who did it, accusing "that woman"—on top of Emily talking about seeing how "it" happened—sparked some interest within the rank and file of the sheriff's department. Before taking Gail's kids back to the house on Talon Circle, investigators separated Andrew and Emily and checked their hands and clothes for gun residue, a common galvanic skin response (GSR) test sometimes referred to by cops as the "invisible clue." If either had shot a weapon within the past twenty-four hours (and had not been wearing gloves), this test would show traces of blow-back powder and residue from the gun going off in their hands.

Both Emily and Andrew tested negative.

"I'm sure they thought I was cuckoo," Emily said later, referring to her paranormal statements.

Before they were taken home, Emily said, "I want to see

my dad." An investigator was taking a complete statement from her. "Where is he?"

"You cannot see your father until you're finished here," Emily claimed the investigator told her.

When they returned to the house, Emily and Andrew were emotionally and physically exhausted. What a night. As the fog of what had happened began to clear, the impact of Gail's death settled. Their mother was gone. Gail was the kids' rock, the anchor of the household. She was the go-to parent—the person they could depend on to be there for whatever the reason. Now she was gone. They'd have to call family and friends. Make arrangements. What a word—"arrangements"– to describe a death, as if you were setting up a dinner or meeting with school officials. There'd be a funeral. A mass. Tears. Questions. Anger. It was coming in waves, Emily felt, like a car heading into a busy intersection.

A collision course.

Yet, for Emily, when she speaks about that night and the following days, one gets a sense that it was almost as if days or weeks before it had occurred, she had seen a film of this night—and she had been expecting it.

"He was crying," Emily said, discussing her father's response. "He seemed really upset." The magnitude of his wife's murder had, apparently, just hit George Fulton.

After they had a moment together, Emily, with Andrew by her side, sat down next to George and said, "Dad, you know Donna did this, right?"

"What! No way! Not a chance."

"How can you say that? That was the first thought that came to my mind without even thinking! How can you *deny* otherwise, Dad?"

George had his head in his hands. "No way. . . ."

Emily had a background with Donna Trapani, George's boss and former mistress. They had spoken on several occasions over the phone and even met once at a nearby hotel. Emily felt she knew Donna. It all seemed to fit. Donna came up to Michigan—as she had in the past—from her home in Florida and took out the competition. The woman was crazy and insane. According to one former coworker, Donna Trapani was "extremely bipolar." This was it. Donna had snapped and Gail paid the price. Gail had expressed an issue with Donna that might lead to one of them killing the other. Emily thought about this as George tried to talk her out of blaming Donna. Now it had come to pass. Mom was dead. What additional proof did any of them actually need?

"No, no . . . no!" George repeated, as if speaking from some sort of firsthand knowledge. "Not a chance. No, she didn't, Emily."

"I know my mom, with her own mouth, had talked about knowing what would happen to her."

Gail's exact words to Emily—spoken just a few months before her murder—stung Emily's thoughts as she listened to her father protect his former lover: "This will not end until one of us is dead," Gail had said, speaking about the tension and hostility between her and her husband's mistress.

Back at the OCSD in Pontiac, the main hub of the investigation, Sergeant Alan Whitefield called Donna Trapani, the woman George said he had worked for, and the kids said—George later admitting reluctantly—he had also had a tumultuous affair with at one time. It was near one o'clock on the morning after Gail's murder. Now was as good a time as any to get an idea, if possible, from "the other woman" regarding where she stood in the relationship with George, and, maybe most important, where she was at nine o'clock the night before. Logistically speaking, it was probably impossible—if Donna was in Florida—for her to fly into Pontiac, kill Gail, and fly back home (especially without leaving a paper trail). Still, Whitefield needed to find out what Donna was doing at the time of Gail's murder, and if she was, in fact, in Florida. Anyone can feign where they're calling from and roll over calls to another line. Just because George had said Donna was calling from Florida, it didn't mean it was so. Donna Trapani could have been at a nearby hotel, for all the OCSD knew.

Donna lived in the Panhandle of Florida, outside Panama City. During his second interview George had claimed to be talking to Donna between the hour of nine and nine-thirty that night—that's why he had been so adamant about Donna having had nothing to do with killing Gail.

But then maybe the guy just didn't want to believe it.

Whitefield needed to verify George's "alibi." Maybe they were covering for each other? After all, George had had the opportunity to kill his wife. And the wife in the way of an affair was one of the oldest motives for murder. Phone records would take some time, so the next best thing was an interview.

"Mrs. Trapani, this is Sergeant Alan Whitefield with the Oakland County Sheriff's Department in Michigan."

"Yes . . . yes," Donna said in her scratchy I-just-woke-up voice. She sounded groggy and tired. It was late, about 1:00 A.M., Panama City, Florida, time. Donna claimed to have been awoken by the ringing telephone. "What is it—who is this?"

"Do you know George Fulton?" Whitefield asked right out of the box.

"Yes . . . yes. He works for me."

"When was the last time you spoke with Mr. Fulton, ma'am?"

Donna thought about it a moment. "Earlier tonight. He paged me and I returned the call." Then she added—

without being asked, Whitefield wrote in his report of the phone call—"I spoke to him maybe four to six times last night all together."

"What is the nature of your relationship with Mr. Fulton?"

"We work together in the health care business. I own the company. It's about to go bankrupt. George is helping me with the books."

Whitefield asked when they had last spoken.

Donna didn't hesitate: "Between eight and eight-thirty." (That meant nine to nine-thirty in Michigan because of the time difference.) "He paged me about seven forty-five and I called him back as soon as I could."

As they spoke, it was clear to Whitefield that there still may have been more to the relationship than employee and employer. When he broached the subject, Donna said flat out: "Yes, I had an affair with George. Hell, we even lived together for three months!"

"What happened?"

"He left me and got his own apartment [in Florida]. He wanted to save his marriage, so he then moved back to Michigan in April [1999]. We have remained close friends."

But there was more—plenty. Whitefield asked Donna to explain.

"Well, he asked me to come to Michigan in July. The Fourth [of July]. He wanted me to talk to Gail." Donna didn't explain why George had requested Donna fly up to Michigan, meet him and Gail at a hotel, and have a little powwow: the mistress, the wife, and the husband. It seemed odd if the affair was over. (Donna didn't mention it here, but this meeting involved a baby and a terminal illness.) "I told George to get Gail some counseling. He told me she would talk to a priest if she needed to speak with someone."

"When was the last time you were with George?" Whitefield asked, meaning sexually.

"August seventeenth," Donna said. How could she forget? "It was my birthday. He broke it off with me that night." She never mentioned if they had started up the relationship again or why; but it was clear that the affair was reignited after that Fourth of July meeting with Gail— if only for that one birthday night celebration in August.

Whitefield knew there would come a time when the sheriff's department conducted a formal, longer, much more detailed interview with Donna, likely in person. Talking to Donna, nearing the end of their conversation, Whitefield realized she had not once asked why the sheriff's department in Michigan was asking her such pointed questions in the middle of the night. It was as if Donna knew something she wasn't sharing.

"Thanks," Whitefield said. He didn't want to broach the subject now.

Then Donna spoke up, suddenly, as if she'd had a second thought: "What is this about, anyway?"

"George's wife has been killed."

"Oh, no . . . not Gail," Donna said. "How are George and the kids doing?"

Whitefield didn't know how to answer.

"Well," Donna said, "thank you for calling."

10

THE MORNING OF October 5, 1999, now almost twelve hours after police had found Martha Gail Fulton barely breathing in the parking lot of the Orion Township Library, investigators were certain of a few things: One, George Fulton had several reasons to want his wife taken out; and two, George, whom investigators knew to be a smart man, West Point–educated and a military officer at one time, had left out the crucial fact that he had a mistress in Florida during their first conversations with him. It wasn't until Andrew Fulton, George and Gail's son, dropped that bombshell that investigators knew about Donna. George had been interviewed at the substation briefly, but he had failed to talk about his relationship with Donna Trapani. Investigators saw this as a sign of George hiding something.

"Surveillance," said one of the sergeants in charge, James A'Hearn. "Let's follow him." From the moment he met George Fulton, A'Hearn did not like him.

It was a good idea to watch George's house.

In the meantime Chris Wundrach, who was taking over a pivotal role in the case along with other members of the sheriff's department, got in touch with a coworker of Gail's who seemed to shed some light on a few personal issues. Cops liked to hear several witnesses—who did not know each other and had never met—reveal the same basic facts. There was credibility in numbers and independent, similar facts being corroborated.

It was 8:30 A.M., and Wundrach was sitting in the substation across from a woman who had heard about what had happened the previous night and wanted to share a conversation she'd had recently with Gail. Word of her murder had traveled through town like a chain e-mail. Gail's coworkers began to think about her unstable and tenuous situation at home with George.

"Gail told me about an affair her husband was having with a woman in Florida," the woman reported to Wundrach. Gail's coworker made it clear that she was personally appalled by this. Gail was the most loving, caring, kindhearted person this woman had ever met. Everything Gail did, she had done for her family—or for others. Gail was a churchgoing wife who *respected* the sacrament of marriage and did everything possible to work it out with George—even against her better judgment of knowing that a "playa" hardly ever changes his style of play.

"Did she say anything about the affair—any details?" Wundrach asked.

"Well, she did. Gail told me she had even met the woman once at a hotel in Rochester Hills."

"Did Gail talk about the meeting?"

"Yeah, yeah," the woman explained. "Gail told me [George's mistress] had claimed to be terminally ill and she wanted George to move to Florida to take care of her. Gail explained how the woman had looked her in the eyes and said, 'You've had him for twenty-five years. Now it's *my* turn!'"

Wundrach realized this was something Donna Trapani

had left out of her conversation with Alan Whitefield the previous night.

"When was the last time you spoke to Gail?" Wundrach pressed.

"We talked several times. . . . Um, a few weeks ago was the last time we *really* talked."

"What'd she say?"

"She said, actually"—the woman thought about it a moment, hesitated, almost embarrassed for Gail to have to admit it, then continued—". . . she and George were trying to work things out."

Surveillance on George Fulton and his residence by a detective from the sheriff's department started as George arrived home that morning at eleven thirty-eight. George pulled into his driveway on Talon Circle and drove into the garage, unaware that the OCSD was watching him, recording his every move. The neighborhood was a nice middle-class suburb, a cookie-cutter subdivision of new homes owned by good, wholesome, hardworking people, just a twenty-minute ride north of Pontiac. The Fulton house was a 5.4-mile drive from the library where Gail had been murdered, a straight shot north on M-24, then left onto West Clarkston Road, right onto Joslyn. No one disputed the fact that George Fulton worked hard and took care of his family materially and monetarily, giving them the finer things life could offer a middle-class family in suburban America.

"Although my dad," Emily commented, "made it clear to me that he was *not* paying for college."

It was George's character and his behavior that had gotten him to this point and put his actions under a law enforcement microscope.

The surveillance was based on the notion that George

had failed to tell investigators he'd had an affair until after he must have figured out that his kids had let the proverbial "cad" out of the bag. Why would he hide that fact? If he had withheld one piece of vital information, the investigators wondered, what else was the guy holding onto?

Cars came and went, in and out of the driveway. People, young and old, walked in and out of the Fulton house all morning long. One might guess friends were stopping by and comforting the family. By early afternoon, however, George was back on the road, and the undercover investigator watching him followed close behind as Gail's husband took off from the house and traveled north on M-24 toward Broad Street and West Clarkston Road, heading in the direction of the lake.

11

DR. R. ORTIZ-REYES was the deputy forensic pathologist with the Oakland County Medical Examiner's Office on the day Gail Fulton's body was brought in for autopsy. A doctor since 1976, Ortiz-Reyes had performed, he later estimated, somewhere in the neighborhood of over one thousand autopsies. The man knew his way around an autopsy suite—no doubt about it. Had Gail died of something other than those obvious gunshot wounds, Ortiz-Reyes would find it.

The first thing Ortiz-Reyes did was to conduct an external exam of Gail's nude body. Ortiz-Reyes noted several "abnormalities" as he found them. Then he got to work opening (his word) Gail's body to see what, in fact, had caused her death. It would be unethical (not to mention unprofessional) to assume that the shots alone had killed Gail. There were cases, any medical examiner (ME) can say, that baffle the mind after autopsy, whereby an obvious cause of death—i.e., a blast to the head—was a front for something else that had the potential to give away the killer's identity. So heading into an autopsy, any medical examiner worth his or her weight never presumed anything; he simply allowed the dead to speak from beyond.

Gail was forty-eight years old at the time of her murder.

She was a petite woman at five feet four inches, 114 pounds, with a thick mane of dark black hair (a trait she would pass on to her three children with George Fulton). Gail was pretty and beautiful and charming in a Mary Tyler Moore way—circa *The Dick Van Dyke Show*—and her appearance reflected how she had changed over the years from a hopeful, wholesome military wife into a woman struggling to keep a drowning marriage afloat. There were periods during her life with George—and these had taken a toll on her—when Gail refused to take care of herself and would not eat sufficiently. She'd beaten herself up emotionally and starved herself so often that even her hair had fallen out at times. Periodically her eyes had sunk into dark circles, and her skin had become pale and emaciated. She could come across as anorexic, withdrawn, and weak during these episodes. It was generally when George was traveling "for work" that sent Gail into an abyss of self-loathing. Before George had even met Donna Trapani, Gail's health had gone downhill. It was a gut feeling Gail had, and it had never lied to her over the years, she told friends. A wife of Gail's caliber—educated and smart and intuitive—listened to that inner voice telling her not to trust the man she had given her life to. It didn't mean she acted on it; just that there was no denying a feeling that the man she loved was stepping out on her. The fact that she internalized these feelings showed, mostly, on her body: noticed by her kids, her friends, her coworkers. Yet the remarkable aspect of Gail Fulton was that at the time of her death, she looked as though she had come back to life. She had color in her face, a bounce in her step. She understood that sometimes there was no way to plug a sinking ship and a person had to walk away, swim to shore, and start over.

"She was so close to leaving him," said an old friend. "So, *so* close . . . right before she died. Poor Gail."

Dr. Ortiz-Reyes recorded his findings as he made them: *Multiple gunshot wounds to the body.* The shot to Gail's forehead Guy Hubble had seen first was one of two potential life-ending wounds—that much was clear from the moment Ortiz-Reyes peeled back Gail's scalp and buzz-sawed her skull open.

It (that bullet) went down to the brain separating all the bones of the face and ending on the left side of the cheek . . . , Ortiz-Reyes reported.

The good news for investigators was that Ortiz-Reyes had been able to retrieve the bullet from Gail's head.

The second shot—although Ortiz-Reyes was not certain the shots had been fired in this particular sequence—was to Gail's upper-right breast. It had gone in through the skin and—not surprisingly, if you understand how projectiles fly at such a high rate of speed—exited an inch away from the entrance wound, reentering the skin and traveling through her stomach, liver, bowels, stopping on the left side of Gail's pelvis.

This had to have been a painful shot, if it struck Gail first.

Ortiz-Reyes was able to retrieve this projectile also.

The third and final shot Gail took in the back, no doubt because she had turned away instinctively from her murderer, or fell to the ground. This shot entered her upper-left back area, through the soft tissue (muscle), but not penetrating or passing through any organs, exiting through her chest.

Gail's killer was an accurate shooter. Head and chest are money shots, per se, if murder is the endgame. The anomaly here was that it was likely Gail's murder had not been a paid hit in the sense of, say, organized crime, the work of a professional hit man. In that respect this murder was far too sloppy. Hit men like to sneak up on their targets (maybe pop a cap into the back of the head just below the ear), or kill from a distance (vis-à-vis a sniper shot). This murder was more or less in the lines of something quite a bit more personal. Gail was shot in the breast and head. This, any armchair profiler could determine, suggested an intimate connection to the victim: anger, hatred, payback. Gail's murderer knew her or had been told things about her that would, for investigators, place her death under a heading of personal and incidental.

It looked like George Fulton had some explaining to do.

12

TURNED OUT THAT George Fulton wasn't running off to meet Donna Trapani, toss his weapons in the lake, or go pay a tab on a murder he had contracted. At least not at this stage. As George was being followed that morning, the undercover behind him watched as Gail's hubby pulled into Sparks-Griffin Funeral Home. George was on his way to make arrangements for Gail's body to be transported to Texas for burial.

No sooner had he parked, run in and out of the funeral home, and then taken back off, did a second car, with four people inside, which George, alone in his car, had met at the funeral home, beckoned to follow him. They drove in a small caravan directly to the library, the employees' parking area, to be exact, where Gail had been gunned down the previous night. As George parked near the spot where Gail had been killed, "two males and two females" walked out of the building, but did not approach or say anything.

It was 2:00 P.M. when George got out of his car and hugged the others. They chatted for a few minutes. Then, before walking away, all of them bent down and placed the palms of their hands on the tar where Gail had died, as if reaching out to her spirit.

Gail's cousin, Pricilla Salanas, had left a message with

dispatch for someone at the OCSD to call her as soon as possible. She wanted to know what was happening with the release of Gail's body back to the family.

The sergeant on duty called Gail's cousin and explained that Gail was being examined by the medical examiner. "Tell the funeral home to contact the ME's office and they can work it out."

"George had called Dora Garza and told her what happened," Pricilla explained to police.

"Listen, we're so sorry for your loss. We know this is a difficult time. But we will be calling on you and Gail's mom later today. We need to ask you some questions."

They hung up.

A few moments later, Pricilla Salanas called back. "Gail's mother has some information that she wants you to know about."

She handed the phone to Dora Garza. "Hello," Dora said. "Yes, ma'am?"

"I wanted to tell you about an affair between George and a woman named Donna from Florida," Dora explained. "But that Gail and George, I was told, were working things out."

"Thank you for that information, ma'am."

"Oh, there's more," Dora Garza said. "When George finally told Donna it was over, Donna called me several times to tell me that my daughter needed help. She called so often, Officer, that I stopped answering my telephone. When I told George about these phone calls, he didn't believe me! He said, 'Oh, Donna would never do something like that.' Melissa (George and Gail's oldest daughter, who was living in Texas with Dora at the time, but was now in the navy and living in Virginia Beach) was here and can verify the calls. We even recorded them."

Dora stopped and took a breath.

Then she said, "Gail once told me that Donna had

called and left some horrible—just horrible—messages on the phone machine. My daughter could not believe the mouth on that woman. George should have those tapes."

Another important point George had failed to mention.

"Do you think George could have been involved?"

"Oh, no. . . . I don't think George could ever do anything like this," Dora said.

"Mrs. Garza, a detective will be in touch with you later today to talk some more."

"That's fine."

"Can we have Melissa's number and address, please?"

Dora gave the address to the police officer and hung up.

13

THE OCSD FOCUSED its investigation on a few important leads it could confirm without question: There had been no sexual assault and no robbery; George Fulton had an alibi and was now willing (and going) to take a polygraph; and that grainy video, the one cops confiscated on the night of the murder, had produced an important clue—the car used in the murder, a dark-colored Chevy Malibu, had a damaged left taillight. This could potentially be as important as a fingerprint.

Find the car; look at the light.

Detectives had checked with the local airlines and confirmed that there were no direct flights out of Michigan to Florida after ten o'clock on the night of the murder. The airlines would not release manifests of passenger lists without a court order. What stood out to investigators looking into this thread of the case was that although there had not been any direct flights to Florida, Delta Airlines had flights into Atlanta and Cincinnati. So they put in a request with airport security to view the videotapes of the concourse near the time of those flights.

"Copies cannot be released," the airport said, "at this time due to a terrorist threat. . . ."

Another roadblock.

The next step was to check out all the rental-car agencies in the area and see if any familiar names turned up, or if a Chevy Malibu had been rented and returned with a broken taillight.

After a check, no luck there, either.

Another friend of Gail's came forward and explained that Gail had confided several things about her marriage that seemed significant now that Gail had been murdered: "The woman [Donna] had come here . . . and had met with Gail at a motel in Rochester. She (Donna) told Gail she was terminally ill and she wanted [George] to come and take care of her. She had a letter from a doctor stating this, Gail told me."

Further, Gail's friend told police that Gail was certain George had broken off the relationship with Donna by July 1999, and that Donna had then turned around and called Gail's mother in Texas and told her that Gail was suicidal!

"Anything else?"

"Well, Gail told me that either she or George had contacted the doctor and he said he had never written that letter."

What it looked like to Sergeant James A'Hearn and Detective Chris Wundrach, the more they studied the interviews the OCSD had conducted, along with the evidence as it presented itself thus far, was that the OCSD needed to put together a team and head down to Florida. There were answers there somewhere, for certain. Donna Trapani needed to be interviewed in person.

After a few days to clear her head and wrap her mind around what was the worst situation life could throw at a person, Emily Fulton was back at the Lake Orion Township Substation sitting with investigators, searching for answers. Emily had had some time to think about things in a more coherent manner. She was somewhat impassive and lucid, now that she'd had nearly two days to process her mother's untimely, violent death. The past twenty-four hours had been rough, but Emily was determined to convince the police that she knew who had murdered her mother, why, and how it was done. What were they waiting for? Why wasn't a team of cops heading to Florida to grab Donna Trapani?

"Come in," the detective said, greeting Emily at the door. "Sit, please. Thank you for coming."

Emily looked tired and, at the same time, manic. She was determined to get her point across and make some noise about how she felt.

"Donna is responsible for my mother's death," Emily said. "She's a psycho!"

Emily felt she had been saying this for the past twenty-four hours—why wasn't anyone *doing* anything about it? The impatience of a college sophomore. It was something Emily knew she had to get a handle on. In the due course of time, she was confident that if she pounded the drum loud enough, the OCSD would hear.

"I really think it was a professional hit," Emily added.

"Why would you say that?"

"Whoever did this knew what they were doing. They waited for my mother. They knew her schedule. They flattened her tire and shot her in the body and in the head. No kid could have done this. A kid wouldn't be able to shoot like that!"

It all made sense. But when the "kid" of the victim was telling cops that someone else did it, and she was providing very *specific* details of the crime, not yet released to the public, she was essentially pointing a finger back at herself—or, in this case, at her brother and father.

"Look, if Donna didn't do it, she paid someone to."

The investigators interviewing Emily kept looking at each other.

"She wanted my mother out of the picture."

It was as simple as that, according to Emily. Donna Trapani was behind this murder.

"I have met this woman," Emily said, explaining briefly how she and Donna met at the ConCorde Inn back in July. "She told me she wants to be my mother. She told me she had a photo of me she took from my father's wallet . . . that she showed it to people and told them I was her daughter. My *dad* even thinks she's a psycho. He told me."

The investigator encouraged Emily to talk more about Donna Trapani.

"My mom had the locks changed on the house after Donna came by once, unannounced. . . . Donna wanted to take my mother's place."

Investigators told Emily to stay in touch. If anything else came up, she should get ahold of the police immediately.

Emily left the substation. Getting into her car, she sat for a moment.

That's it*? Why are they not going to Florida right now?*

Investigating a murder of this type boils down to checking the obvious off a list, while moving forward on the evidence that the police have in front of them—not on the speculation and advice of family and friends. OCSD investigators took pride in the fact that in order to uncover what happened to Gail Fulton, and by whom, a victimology chart had to be established in the most benign, cautious manner. Part of this investigatory approach involved a search warrant served to George Fulton at his Talon Circle home. It was time to get into the house and have a look at the paper trail and evidence—if any—Gail (and maybe George) had left behind.

George was not thrilled about opening up his home to the cops and allowing them to search through his most intimate possessions. But what could the man do? Investigators had interviewed Barbara Butkis again, Gail's boss, the woman who had found Gail in the parking lot. Still shaken considerably by the death of her friend and employee, Barb had called the OCSD and reported that George had left "a harassing telephone" message on the library's answering machine. In her report to police, Barb did not go into detail regarding what George had said, but it had scared her enough to call them. A report of the incident said that Barb thought it was "odd" that Mr. Fulton had called. She had never met the guy before Gail's death. But here he was, according to her, harassing them at the library for no apparent reason.

It was strange.

Beyond those common domestic items every household has lying around, not much of anything was uncovered inside George's house that was going to help move the investigation into a checkmate position. George kept meticulous financial records, which was part of what he did for a living. Gail had kept a calendar, which would have to be read through painstakingly. The financial papers would be helpful as investigators checked George's records against withdrawals and deposits. If George had paid someone to whack his wife, he had probably made a few mistakes along the way. Many would-be murder-for-hire masterminds make mistakes financially—money leaves an imprint everywhere in the banking industry. There potentially could be an odd withdrawal here, or a deposit that doesn't make sense there.

Next, the OCSD Crime Lab came in with its report of the crime scene, which yielded no clues that jumped out at investigators. It did, however, lend a hand to moving the investigation in the right direction. A spent projectile was uncovered underneath Gail's body; a set of "inked finger impressions" were found on Gail; the lab collected clippings from underneath Gail's fingernails, hairs, all of Gail's clothes, which contained blood and additional trace evidence. The lab also had collected three weapons (George's) from the substation: a Browning 9mm handgun, a Spanish semiautomatic .380/9mm handgun, and a Ruger .22 caliber. These were rounded up, along with a six-shot .22-caliber cartridge and four .380 cartridges, along with—perhaps more important than any other find—one *empty* gun clip.

Then word came of an interesting discovery, especially here within the first forty-eight hours: a 1998 Honda Accord LX, silver, a vehicle located and photographed inside George's garage.

The lab report stated: *Collected from the vehicle . . . 1— suspected blood from rear driver's side door frame; 1—suspected blood from rear quarter near gas tank, driver's side; [and] 1—disposable camera from front passenger floor.*

Why did a car in George's garage have blood inside it? And whose blood was it? Had George shot his wife, rushed to her side after feeling guilty, gotten blood all over himself, panicked, and then taken off? After all, he had an alibi—his mistress. But that was only a phone call. Couldn't George and Donna have planned Gail's murder together? They could have connected via telephone; then George could have left the phone on a desk while he speedily drove to the library, shot his wife, and rushed back home. By reporting that his dad was downstairs during the entire time period Gail had been murdered, Andrew could be either covering for his father—under the duress and threats of dear old dad—or been fooled into thinking George was home.

There was plenty for investigators to think about. And every time the OCSD turned around, another piece of the puzzle was backed up with factual evidence. For example, several interviews had yielded information that Donna Trapani was in town during July 1999. Two detectives were sent over to canvass the hotels and motels in the "M-59 and Opdyke corridors of Auburn Hills and Rochester Hills." They were looking for the names George Fulton and Donna Trapani. This was an area from Lake Orion south, down toward Mosteiro and Pontiac, east and west, heading toward Otter Lake, Elizabeth Lake, Loon Lake, Shelby Township, and several other areas where a majority of the hotels were located. It took some time, but during an inquiry at the ConCorde Inn in Rochester Hills, investigators made a discovery. Someone going by the name of Donna Kaye Trapani, from Fort Walton Beach, Florida, had checked in on July 3, 1999, and checked out on July 7, 1999. Telephone records indicated that Donna had made an obsessive number of phone calls, not only to George's house, but several additional numbers in Oakland County.

"You have any information about the type of car she was driving?" investigators asked the hotel manager.

After a complete search the manager said, "No."

So Donna was either picked up and driven to the hotel, or she hid the type of vehicle she had rented.

14

GEORGE FULTON TOOK A ride over to the sub-station to pick up a few of Gail's personal belongings, which the OCSD was ready to release. It was 3:00 P.M., October 6, 1999, almost forty-eight hours after Gail's murder. The embattled husband, about whom the town was now whispering and gossiping behind his back, sat in the lobby by himself. His right palm was supporting his chin.

Detective Chris Wundrach walked into the room and greeted George. "Come on in," Wundrach said, beckoning George to follow him.

George stood. He didn't say much of anything unless prompted.

"Would you like something to drink?" Wundrach asked cordially.

"Some water would be fine," George replied.

No sooner had they settled into the empty interview room than George broke down and, as Wundrach later put it, began to "tear up."

"I have been so busy," George explained, almost as if issuing an excuse, "that I have not had time to grieve the loss of my wife."

Wundrach guessed George meant making arrangements for Gail's funeral was keeping him busy, although George never said what had kept him so consumed that he had not felt much sorrow for a woman he had been married to for twenty-three years.

Was this some sort of act?

When George was finished with his brief meltdown, and "regained his composure," he said, "I hope when you catch the person who did this, the justice system does its job!"

"Yeah. . . ."

"Because if not," George continued, without paying mind to what Wundrach was about to say, "I will be sure to finish it myself!"

"We're doing everything in our power to catch whoever is responsible, Mr. Fulton."

Wundrach stood. He told George to hang on a moment. He had to leave the room.

When the detective returned after going to his office to retrieve Gail's purse, he handed it and its contents (in a separate bag) to George, saying, "You'll have to sign a receipt for the purse and contents.

"Where?"

George got up to leave. Wundrach considered they were done.

Before walking out the door, George stopped, turned to Wundrach, and said, "I need a favor."

"What's that?" Wundrach answered, his attention piqued.

"If there comes a time when you have to arrest me, I hope that you do not do it at the airport or in front of my children. I will come in here anytime you want me to."

Police officers for the OCSD started off, as Chris Wundrach later explained, in corrections, serving the needs of the prison system. It was 1992 when Wundrach made the move from corrections to the OCSD road patrol division in Lake Orion Township. He had been promoted to detective just a year before Gail Fulton's murder.

Wundrach was a local boy. He grew up in Oakland County and went to college in the area. He earned a bachelor's in criminal justice, never intending to go into police work. He had entered college with accounting as his major, but he soon found the math and all those numbers buzzing in his head to be boring and cumbersome. "I hated it." One thing led to another, and after several entrance exams, Wundrach went through avionics and a few other career choices before settling on criminal justice.

The thing about being an Oakland County substation detective, Wundrach explained humbly, is that a person works on everything. It's not just murder cases, as one might be led to believe by the glorifying way popular culture and television promote the gold shield aspect of law enforcement. There are retail fraud cases, assault, rapes, robberies, burglaries, drug cases—or, as Wundrach put it, "all crime."

In the thirty-six-square-mile township of Lake Orion (the county, in other words), there are about 55,000 to 60,000 residents at any given time, so the detective bureau of the OCSD is busy all the time.

"It's not as bad as the inner cities," Wundrach remarked, "but we get our share of everything."

Within all of that crime on any given day, week, or month, however, murder is "pretty rare." It's not as though the OCSD was running around the county investigating one murder after the next, as they do in Detroit or Pontiac. For Wundrach, Gail Fulton's murder was his first.

At the time of Gail's murder, Sergeant James A'Hearn was in charge of the fugitive and investigative unit of the OCSD. He ran the show. A'Hearn was that brassy, deep, baritone-speaking type of cop you wanted on any case that demanded results. Murder—and death—was an aspect of life that A'Hearn had had a long history with as both a police officer and veteran of the Vietnam War. He had been drafted right out of high school into the military. Once in, A'Hearn gave it his all, choosing to stay an additional year to enter into the military police (MP) division. Once out of the army, A'Hearn was immediately hired by the Birmingham (Michigan) Police Department, where he spent the next five years. From there, A'Hearn walked into a job at the Oakland County Prosecutor's Office as an investigator. He was soon promoted to chief investigator. Then, in 1996, "after a political change," as A'Hearn referred to it, within the Oakland County community, he was offered a job within the OCSD as a sergeant by the then-sheriff John Nichols.

A'Hearn's interest in law enforcement is an interesting one. His father was a news editor for a major Detroit news station for many, many years. "And watching him interact with police over all those years" sparked a desire in him to want to be a cop, A'Hearn revealed.

When A'Hearn was asked to come up with a case, off the top of his head, that has bothered him for a lot of years, he didn't hesitate.

"We had a series of child killings that date back to the late seventies," A'Hearn recalled. "Unsolved. I was assigned to that task force. It's probably the most important case that has ever happened here and remains unsolved . . . and . . . it's kind of like a burr under my sweater. Depending on who you talk to, there are twelve kids involved, four of whom they attribute [connect] to one [killer]."

What a case. Some twenty thousand tips have been collected over the years; there are file cabinets full of documents and reports. It's one of those cases cops cannot stop looking at—it has to be solved. Society can never allow child killers to get away with the most horrible of crimes. Monsters cannot win.

A'Hearn is the embodiment of a man's man; he's a guy who has the tough skin it takes sometimes to weather investigations that at first might seem a bit complicated, branching out into other states and involving additional perps. Perhaps more than anyone else who was working the Gail Fulton case, he knew that time was on law enforcement's side in this case, unlike it generally is in many other murder cases. There was a conspiracy to commit murder in that adulterous marriage, A'Hearn reckoned. And George Fulton, a guy A'Hearn had little use for, had been involved in adultery for what the OCSD knew to be years. Donna Trapani was involved in this crime, and maybe even George, too; A'Hearn was certain.

Be patient. Hit the brick. Keep knocking on doors, tracking down the paper trail. A recipe for murder would surface sooner or later.

A'Hearn and Wundrach talked about Gail's murder as it unfolded. A dead librarian found murdered in the parking lot of the library. It sounded so . . . well, Lifetime Television . . . so salacious. So intriguing. The media was on it right away, salivating, waiting for any little morsel or crumb to feed on.

Wundrach and A'Hearn kept coming back to one point that aggravated the two of them: Why had George not mentioned that affair when they first spoke to him? Why hadn't he come clean with that? Why hide such an important fact and motivating factor in many murders?

"You don't want to go right off the bat, 'It's you. It's you. It's you,' pointing at George," Wundrach explained. "You want to befriend him, keep him at ease, lock him into a story. But, you know, we found out about his mistress through his kids. That told us a lot."

They had asked George about Donna and his reaction was, "Oh, yeah . . . her."

"So we began to focus a little bit more on him," Wundrach said.

The fact that George had been emotionless (A'Hearn and Wundrach's description) was significant. Now, A'Hearn knew from experience that all they needed was a break—some sort of witness to come forward and begin talking. Whenever several people were involved in a murder—and the OCSD knew from watching the video that there were at least three people who knew the specifics of this murder—one of them will eventually get drunk, high, or feel safe enough to open his or her mouth.

It was inevitable.

15

THE WOMAN LYING in the casket "did not look like my mother," Emily Fulton recalled years later, thinking back to that day she and her family had a chance to view her mother's body for the first time. It was the look on Gail's face: plastic, stiff, contorted.

Fake.

Gail's lips were pulled taut; her forehead was "furrowed"; her eyes (which had not been shut yet) had, quite shockingly, a look of surprise on them. What was more than obvious to Emily as she stood and stared was the wax the mortician had used to cover the bullet hole in her mother's forehead.

"The hole . . . the size of a fifty-cent piece," Emily recalled, "looked beyond painful and made me cry all the harder. I could not believe that that bastard did this to my mom—my mom that weighed [about] one hundred pounds and was [just over] five feet. Her long beautiful nails were chopped off and were not still quite jagged, [but] the mortician painted them a pinkish color. My mom *never* wore nail polish."

That shell of a person, lying dead before her, "did not look like my mother," Emily said. More than that, all the lines etched in Gail's face—that expression frozen by her death—told Emily that "this person went through terrible pain and suffering" as she died.

"This person" might have seemed an odd choice of words. Yet for Emily, her mother was gone. This body left behind—a cocoon, really—had nothing in common with the woman Gail Fulton was, or the mother she had been to her children. For Emily, regardless of what the body displayed, or the pain and suffering her mother endured while dying in that parking lot, Emily was convinced of something that was more important to her than anything else at this point: "I also believe that God does not want innocent people to suffer and that the soul leaves the body prior to feeling any real pain." Emily thought later she might have read that theory somewhere, but nevertheless, "I hope [it] is true."

After seeing this, "needless to say, we decided to have a closed casket," Emily recounted.

It was early evening, October 6, 1999. Emily and her family wanted a private viewing before the funeral home in Michigan readied Gail's casket for a trip south to Texas.

Corpus Christi, Texas, is a 1,500-plus-mile trek south from Lake Orion, Michigan. But that's where Gail's mother and her children wanted this wonderful woman laid to rest. The funeral was set for October 8. The funeral mass was held at St. Theresa's Church in Corpus, the same parish the family had been members of when they lived in Texas.

"I understand the cultural significance of having funerals, as it helps to make the death of your loved one a reality for the survivors, and I think this is a good thing," Emily remarked. "However, when the family member who dies is so significant in your life, funerals are draining on so many levels."

Hallelujah. Saying a final good-bye to someone close sucks the life out of you.

From the moment Emily stepped back into the church, the building of St. Theresa's itself brought on a flood of memories. Masses weren't generally packed at this parish, but the church had good attendance from week to week. It felt like home to Emily as she entered through the front doors. When they lived in Texas, Emily, George, Andrew, and Gail had been involved in the church on many different levels. Emily and George were lectors. Gail and George were Eucharistic ministers (helping the priest and deacons give out Holy Communion every week). Andrew was an altar boy. Emily volunteered at church events, including bingo and other fund-raising festivities, along with Gail's mother, who, with Gail, was part of the Altar Society. In many ways this was a homecoming for the family. Everyone in the church knew the Fultons. Gail's untimely death was a punishing blow to this community—many of whom had known Gail personally and adored her immensely.

"And, of course, they knew my grandma," Emily added, "as she is basically a pillar of the community. And then you add the fact that my *papu* was so well regarded, even though he had died so many years before."

The OCSD needed to send a team down to good old boy country so it could work with Texas authorities to set up surveillance at the funeral and conduct one very important interview. There was always the outside chance Gail's killer would attend the funeral and take part in the sick satisfaction of enjoying the fruit of his or her labor—and, heck, maybe he was even part of the mourning crowd of attendees. A photo of Donna Trapani was distributed among investigators, who were told to be on the lookout for the woman who, authorities believed, had had the most to benefit from Gail's demise. Of course, at the same time there would be many eyes on George Fulton. His every move scrutinized and recorded.

"The sexual revolution sort of bypassed us here in South Texas during the late sixties and early seventies," an old friend of Gail's said with a laugh.

Gail was a junior and her friend Jeanette Cantu-Bazar was a sophomore when they met at an all-girls school outside Corpus Christi. This was a time in Gail's life when coming of age was innocent and clean; it was something to enjoy without much fear of the dangers and social pitfalls that kids face today. Both Gail and Jeanette had come from traditional American-Hispanic Catholic homes, where Mary, the Virgin Mother, and the seven sacraments played key roles in everyday life. Gail's father was a federal judge. All of her family members were educated and popular within this large, predominantly Catholic community. They had friends, same as everyone. They gave to local charities. They went to church more than just on Sundays. They took to raising their kids with the utmost sincerity, seriousness, love, and care. They gave of themselves. Life was full of promise and peace. The American dream was a reality for Dora and Noe Garza, Gail's parents, who had worked extremely hard and raised great kids.

"Gail was a lot of fun in high school," Jeanette remembered. "The word that comes to me as I think back is 'prim-and-proper.' Our school uniforms [consisted of modest] hemlined skirts, cardigan sweaters." Every part of the body was covered. This was quintessential Catholic school attire. "The sisters that taught us were all in their full habits, and most of us, at one time or another, talked about and wanted to be nuns."

It was a good time to be a teenager. The United States—if not the world—was in a state of continuous transformation and innovation. When social commentators talk about Texas during the sixties, the space program comes to mind, as well as JFK's assassination and the rise of the Republican party. Strong family ideals. An iron-clad economy.

The kids went to church every day while in school. Religious instruction was mandatory teaching.

"We also participated in the Catholic Youth Organization for our parish, and that's where we met George," Jeanette recalled.

George Fulton was one of Jeanette's neighbors; he and his family lived down the block. George hung out at Jeanette's house because she had three brothers. Gail took to George, a cross-country runner and senior class president, almost from the moment that she met him. In high school George was considered "Mr. It," according to several classmates. He was first-chair clarinet and all-around pretty boy whom the girls chased. "George's dad had worked at a newspaper." George had the makings of a potentially perfect husband. During an era when girls were looking for boys to run off and get married to before the war took the men away, George was a catch. Marriage was much more of an expected aspect of life for a young girl then, especially in devout Catholic homes. For a young Catholic woman, there were two vocation choices: marriage or religious life. Being single was not an option that parents or the Church pushed. Gail, who prayed the rosary every night (right up until her death), had grown up with strong family values. She wanted to have a family of her own and pass on that legacy to her own kids.

George's father had died when he was young, and his mother had raised nine kids on one income, so it was hard for them, a friend later explained. They did not have it easy. And then George's mother died. This, some later suggested, hardened George.

The one thing George wanted out of life as he entered into his senior year of high school was to be a career officer in the military. He knew the military could pay for his education and allow him the opportunity to excel in whatever career choice he made. If he was going to be drafted, why not jump in headfirst and take control of a presumed destiny himself?

As Gail and George spent time together, talking, hanging out, it was a period in their lives when Gail and Jeanette loved nothing more than going to the local revival movie house and watching old films. They had those actors they bit their palms over and became rubbery at the sight of: Randolph Scott, Tyrone Power, James Dean. They adored the likes of Maureen O'Hara and Elizabeth Taylor. The movie *West Point* was a favorite of the girls. So when George was appointed to go to West Point, a romantic dream—a manifestation of Hollywood—came into focus for this conservative Catholic schoolgirl. As George left and went off to West Point, Gail graduated high school and enrolled at Baylor University, which was a family legacy. Baylor was a Christian university located in Waco. The school was in the same state as her home, but it was a 320-mile, near six-hour drive from her house. It seemed George and Gail's paths had crossed and separated. The white-picket-fence dream quashed before it had a chance to blossom. Gail was one of those who believed that if God wanted it to be, the relationship with George would find its way. The next several years were about studying, anyway. She could wait.

They lost touch and did not write much as George pursued his dream of becoming an officer. Gail sank herself into her major, speech therapy. But when George returned from West Point and Gail came home from Waco as a college graduate, they ran into each other again and started dating. The dream of a house filled with kids was back on.

"George was the first guy Gail was really attracted to," said a friend. But he wasn't the first guy she'd ever dated. "Definitely the first serious relationship, though."

Gail had heard that Jeanette had dated George once. "But it was more like we went to a movie together," Jeanette corrected. George and Jeanette had been like brother and sister because George had spent so much time at Jeanette's house. Yet before Gail could ever consider a serious relationship with George—and this showed the type of person Gail was—she approached Jeanette and asked her if she was still interested. It bothered Gail that perhaps she was stealing her friend's man.

"Oh, my," Jeanette responded, "if you want him, Gail, you can _have_ him!"

And they laughed about it.

Jeanette had been at the funeral home the night before the funeral mass, "arranging flowers, setting chairs straight . . . just hanging around, paying my last respects to Gail." It was her way of spending a final few moments alone with her onetime best friend.

As she was doing this, George happened to "burst into the viewing room." Jeanette could tell he was not in a good mood. He had fire in his eyes. Something was on George's mind, and it had everything to do with Jeanette.

"Get out of here," George said loudly, according to Jeanette.

Jeanette was appalled. The mouth on the guy—in front of his dead wife!

The nerve.

"What is your _problem,_ George?"

"I need some time *alone* with my wife!" George snapped.

Jeanette was about to say something ("Well, if you hadn't been screwing around, this would have never happened to begin with. . . ."), but her husband gave her that bite-your-tongue look and told her to come on, it was time to leave.

"This is *not* the time—out of respect for Gail," Jeanette's husband whispered.

They all thought George was involved in Gail's death on some level, and here he was demanding to spend some quality time with her dead body, as if he had been the most loving husband and partner to her all along.

"He was definitely *playing the part* of the grieving spouse," a friend in town for the mass and funeral later said of George. "No doubt about it."

16

EMILY WORE WATERPROOF mascara as she sat in a front pew inside St. Theresa's Church, listening to a family member sing Bette Midler's "Wind Beneath My Wings." Gail's casket was draped in a traditional Catholic vanilla-colored blanket with a gold band. The coffin stood in front of the altar; the Paschal candle in front of the casket, burning brightly, represented Gail's resurrection in Heaven. The tears had started as soon as Emily sat down, and continued for just about the entire mass. It was standing room only. People were lined up along the sidewalls of the church, looking toward the altar, the Stations of the Cross plaques to their backs. Someone had given Gail's kids several boxes of tissues as they walked in. Good thing. Because those "never-ending tears," as Emily described them later, kept coming. The constant flowing of tears turned much of what was taking place on the altar into a fog, as if the past few days had all been a dream.

Or, rather, a nightmare.

Emily closed her eyes. She folded her hands on her lap. Then the stinking thinking started: *I am so sorry that I could not stop this. . . . I feel so guilty over what happened. I tipped Donna over the edge because I had told her to back off—leave us alone.*

It had been a phone call between Emily and Donna, in which Donna was extremely mad at Emily and hung up on her.

These were the prayers Emily offered to God as she sat, silently whispering, the entire parish around her, full of mourners, blocked out. Her focus centered entirely on these terrible thoughts of what *could* have been, what Emily *could* have done, and how guilt was now penetrating any sense of relief she might have had that her mother—who had the faith of a child—was at rest, being comforted in the arms of Jesus.

Please let me feel what my mom felt when she died, Emily pleaded with God. *Please let me feel her pain so that I may know how she suffered, and this will make me feel better.*

On the way out of the church after mass, Emily was shocked (and horrified) to be greeted by the media snapping photos and taking video of her and her family exiting the church. Emily felt violated. Her privacy stripped from her during this vulnerable moment. She wondered why these people, who did not know her mother, were so interested in the final good-byes of a suffering flock.

"It was such an invasion of privacy to have strangers watch us grieve and [take part in] that personal moment we were having," Emily said later.

"It's news in Texas," Gail's mother explained to her granddaughter. "Your mother, Emily, was the daughter of a federal judge—this is a big story for this area."

After it was all over and Emily settled down later that night with her thoughts, something happened. Something altogether strange. Something prophetic.

Something divine?

Be careful what you wish for. . . .

Emily felt the immensity of the day and previous night. "I got so sick," Emily recalled. "I came down with a migraine, and looking at lights just pierced my brain. My chest hurt so bad, I felt like I had this hole in my chest and my back was so crippled with pain that I was walking around hunched over and couldn't even stand straight. My skin was supersensitive to the touch, and I just started shaking and got feverish and had to lie down in a dark room away from everyone and every sound. . . . This was before that I knew my mom [had been] shot in the places that she was. . . ."

While everyone grieved the loss of Gail Fulton on this day and into the night, George Fulton was receiving e-mails from Donna Trapani, his former boss and lover. One came in just as the family buried Gail. Under the subject "Condolences," Donna claimed she wanted to send George her deepest sympathics for the loss of his wife—a woman Donna had, in many ways, terrorized that previous summer. Here was Donna now saying she was "sorry" for what George and his family were going through. She said she was "worried" about George, his heart and his "BP" (blood pressure—George was on high blood pressure meds then). She considered how "devastated beyond belief" George must have been by Gail's murder.

Gail wasn't even in the ground yet, and here was Donna, as she had once promised, trying to wiggle her way into the lives of her former lover and his family.

What was this woman thinking?

Without explaining exactly what she meant, Donna said she "didn't know much," which seemed to refer to what had happened to Gail and the scant details the media had been reporting. Then she went on to tell George how the police had called her in the middle of the night "asking me when I spoke to you last" and "when I saw you last." She said the cops had not given her any particulars of the murder, but she hoped George would call and fill her in. Donna wanted George to know, also, that "my prayers are with y'all." And then, strangely, she broke into a long explanation of an illness she had been suffering from all that week, telling George she had strep throat, an ear infection, and bronchitis. She told how she had spent most of the week in bed with Vicks on her chest and a heating pad. She claimed to be "aching and hurting all over." She said she had been "having severe chest pains and coughing up green phlegm." She reminded George that she had begun to explain this to him as they talked the other night (the night Gail was murdered), but she didn't think it was all that important then. Apparently, now that Gail was dead and her family in the midst of trying to pull their hearts back together after just burying her, Donna thought this to be the appropriate time to share her ailments.

After trying to draw some sympathy from George, Donna offered a bit of advice, as if she knew George better than anyone else, encouraging him: Whatever you do, don't hold things inside. . . . Let it all out. . . . Take care of yourself. . . . She wished she knew what to say to him to make everything all better, but she could not find those mindful words. She spoke of how "mad" George used to get with her when she talked about the old adage that bad things always happened to good people, and she didn't understand how this could be right in a world God had created. God was supposed to take care of the good people, Donna wrote at one point in her e-mail. It was those "bad people" God should be hurting; as though, Donna suggested, there should be some sort of reward for being a morally decent person.

When she finished with her good/bad people diatribe, Donna Trapani asked George if he could e-mail her about the billing inquiries she had made to him recently. She needed the information so she could gauge how to respond to her employees and vendors, all of whom were looking for money. Donna's company was in the midst of going belly-up. If you never want to do our billing or talk to me again, Donna wrote, she wanted George to know that she was fine with that. But she needed to find out one way or another where George stood. She continued, telling George how much she appreciated what he had done for her company. However, she realized George's family needed him now, not her company. And that was okay, Donna seemed to imply. There was an indication at the end of the e-mail that George had been working for Donna for quite some time without being paid and she wanted him to know that she "felt bad" about his working "so hard" and not receiving proper reimbursement. She wondered why he hadn't quit a long time ago.

In her second e-mail that same night, sent just a few moments after the first, this one much shorter, Donna pleaded with George for his help regarding a job that, apparently, only he and another employee (who had walked out on Donna for not being paid) knew how to do.

George's responses to these e-mails, if he ever wrote back, do not exist.

The OCSD sent several detectives down to Corpus Christi to work with members of the FBI and the Corpus Christi Criminal Intelligence Unit, including the local police and several other officers assigned to the case while George and his children were in town. After setting up and filming all of what went on inside and outside of St. Theresa's Catholic Church and Rose Hill Memorial Park—the Garden of Prayer section, where Gail was interred—there came a time when a photograph of Donna Trapani, which law enforcement had distributed, turned into a discussion among investigators. No one had seen anyone at the church service that looked like Donna, but that changed at Rose Hill. A motorcycle police officer was roaming through the large crowd on his bike when he called in.

"Yeah, we got female here in a beige dress that seemed to want to approach the grave site, but then withdrew."

The cop was told to follow the woman.

"She closely resembles the photograph. . . ."

"Stick with her."

Two detectives set out on foot from a nearby cruiser and ran to track the woman down, but the motorcycle officer lost sight of her.

Could it have been Donna? If so, why in the world would she be roaming around the grave site of a woman she had loathed and wished only bad things upon for so long? Did Donna Trapani *want* to draw attention to herself as a suspect, or was she relishing in victory?

17

PART OF THE trip south for two OCSD investigators, Detectives John E. Meiers and William Dugan, was a planned sit-down with Dora Garza, Gail's articulate and delightful mother. Additionally, the OCSD needed to get a better picture of Gail's life and complete a victimology report.

Dora had some important issues she needed to discuss; she felt she knew exactly who had murdered her daughter and why. This was a strong woman, whose husband had died many years prior. Raising two kids had been one of the most rewarding experiences of Dora's life. To think that a child of hers had been murdered was traumatic and devastating. Dora had brought her children up in a devout Catholic household that emphasized morality, justice, and taking care of one's neighbors. Faith. Hope. Charity. These were everyday expressions that Dora and Noe Garza had spent their lives instilling in their children. Gail was the perfect child in many ways, Dora felt. She had been a passive, compassionate, dedicated wife and mother, with not an enemy in the world.

Or so Dora thought.

Dora met Meiers and Dugan at an undisclosed hotel

outside Corpus Christi. They surely didn't want George to know about the interview. Investigators still weren't sure that George had not masterminded the murder himself and was playing the part of grieving husband, going through the motions of misery and loss, waiting for the appropriate time to pass, so he could run off with Donna Trapani and, as one former friend of Donna's later said, "play house together."

As the two detectives led Dora to an empty conference room inside the hotel, Dora asked if they had a suspect in her daughter's murder, or that quintessential and ever-more-popular term propelled into the mainstream media, person of interest.

"We don't have a suspect right now," one of the detectives explained. It was early in the game. They were still in the information-gathering stage of the case. "We're going to be asking personal questions about Gail and George," the detective added, "but we don't want [you] to *infer* that we are doing this because George is the main focus of our investigation. Our purpose in coming here is to talk to you with the hope of anything you might know assisting us in the investigation to help locate your daughter's killer or killers."

Dora said she understood. She'd do everything she could to help.

As they got settled in the spacious room, Dora presented an audiotape. Emily had given the tape to Dora that morning.

"Your investigators missed this tape when they searched the house in Michigan," Dora said.

"Oh . . ."

"It contains a message left on the answering machine at my daughter's house on July fourth. The message is from Donna Trapani, the woman George was having an affair with."

Meiers and Dugan were curious. What an interesting development.

The tape was of Donna Trapani telling Emily that Gail "really needed her mother right now because [she] was suicidal." Donna went on to say that since she was a nurse, she understood these matters and this was why she felt it her duty to inform Emily of the situation. Donna claimed to be scared for Gail.

Emily, in turn, told her grandmother what was going on. Dora never believed Gail wanted to kill herself; she thought it was something Gail was doing to get George's attention.

Emily felt different: "My mom talked about it enough where it was very real and scary for me and my brother."

As the interview continued with the detectives, Dora appeared relaxed and calm, soft-spoken and eloquent, a report that accompanied the interview noted. She was there to talk about what she knew. Getting the facts as she understood them into the hands of investigators was important to this wife of a former federal judge.

"Our family was very close," Dora explained. "Even though Gail moved to Michigan, I spoke to her on the telephone several times per week."

"What type of person was your daughter, ma'am?" one of the detectives asked. "Tell us about her."

"Gail was wonderful. She was an excellent mother and wife. She became a stay-at-home mom after her first year of marriage to George. She was an excellent housekeeper and always saw to it that a nutritious meal was on the table and that her children were clean and loved."

Harriet Nelson with a few hang-ups—that was Gail Fulton. Yet the man she lived with, Dora found out as Gail and George settled in Michigan, was not the Cliff Huxtable that Dora had thought he was for all those years Gail and George had been together.

Dora was under the impression that George and Gail met at church. But it was a culmination, essentially, of community activities and hanging around with Jeanette Cantu-Bazar, Gail's best friend. Dora mentioned how religious Gail was and "very true to her faith." Gail was a believer. There was no question about her desire to serve God. The indication from just about everyone who truly knew Gail was that she might have stayed in a dead marriage because of her strong Catholic beliefs that marriage was sacred, and she was going to do everything possible to fix what was broken and move on within the bonds of marriage.

Dora explained that because Gail and George had raised the kids in such a traditional Catholic home, "the children never presented [them] with any typical teenage problems." They were all good kids, who had worked hard in school and had great futures ahead of them. "It wasn't," Dora added, "until George started working in Florida that there was trouble in the marriage. Gail was a very private person and never really spoke to me about any of the problems in the marriage. It wasn't until I went up there in June 1998 to visit Gail and the kids that Emily and Andrew approached me and said they had reason to believe their father was having an affair with a woman in Florida."

"What was it they said?"

"They wanted me to speak with George and get him to stop. At that time I didn't believe George was having an affair . . . because Gail had never mentioned it."

During that June 1998 trip, Dora sat with George one day. His attitude, Dora realized soon after seating herself, was more telling than if he had come out and admitted his sins.

"What's wrong with you, George, you don't seem like yourself?" Dora asked her son-in-law. "Is something bothering you?"

George never answered; instead, he stared at his mother-in-law "for the longest time without saying a word." Then he turned and, without speaking, walked out of the house.

"Had George or Gail ever filed for divorce?" Detective Dugan asked.

"As far as I know, they did not. They were separated for a time, but I had assumed that was because George started that job in Florida."

What struck Dora as strange—in the context of George and Gail having marital problems, and the logistics of George's job keeping them apart—was that George insisted that while he was in Florida working, Gail could call him *only* at work. George had never given Gail a contact number for him outside of work (he was living at Donna's house then).

"He told her that the room he was renting didn't have a telephone," Dora explained.

A smart woman, Dora knew better, she said.

"Gail," Dora asked her daughter when they chatted a day after George took off to Florida, "is he having an affair?"

Gail did not hesitate. "Oh, Mother," she responded, "you know George would never do that."

"Wake up, child. Look around. If he won't give you a phone number where he can be reached at night, he's probably living with a girlfriend!"

Gail didn't want to admit it—at least not to her mother.

"Did you know of any marital infidelities that Gail ever had, Mrs. Garza?" Dugan asked.

"No, I was not aware of any. You have to understand something about my daughter. Whatever George did, she was forgiving and wanted to make the marriage work because she was so in love with George. I had asked her on several occasions to leave Michigan and come home, but she always said, 'I cannot do that. I love George.'"

What did this guy have? George certainly wasn't all *that*. It was as if he held Gail under some sort of spell.

"George was a class-A piece of shit," said one investigator. "He treated his wife like trash."

Dora Garza explained that Gail and Donna had had a confrontation back on the Fourth of July inside a hotel room (with George), but she did not go into too much detail about it. This was something that had weighed heavily on Gail and had sent her into a deep, suicidal depression. After being prompted by the detectives, Dora also mentioned that she never knew of George hitting Gail. She said George was unstable and acting odd during her visit to the house in 1998. It was the only time she had ever seen George with a "short fuse." Everything bothered George that weekend, and Dora assumed it was because he had been burning the candle with two women and the pressure was finally getting to him.

"What can you tell us about Donna Trapani?" Dugan asked.

All Dora knew about Donna, she explained, was what Gail and the children had told her: George had met Donna at a bar in Florida as he was getting his own business off the ground. "According to Gail, Donna had traveled to several locations with George as he conducted business around the country and stayed with him. I'm not sure, Gail never told me, whether George had *invited* Donna on the trips or she showed up on her own."

The detectives asked questions about George's weapons. Dora didn't know much, but she explained that since her husband—"an avid hunter"—died, she had given all of his guns ("many handguns and long guns") to George.

After a pause Dora said, "He was like a son to me."

"What about enemies?" Dugan pressed. "Did Gail have *any* enemies that you know of?"

"No one I can think of. . . ."

Then Dora mentioned a conversation she'd had with Gail one afternoon over the phone not too long ago.

"Have you ever seen the movie *Fatal Attraction,* Gail?" Dora asked her daughter.

Gail said she hadn't.

"Well, you should go to see it. This woman, Donna," Dora told her daughter, "is doing just what the character in the movie is doing. If you ever come home and find a rabbit cooking on the stove, you had better watch out!"

As much as the detectives had said they weren't focusing on George, the interview worked its way into pointing directly toward Gail's cheating husband. They asked Dora what George had said about the murder, if anything.

She thought about that for a moment. "I really haven't had that much of an opportunity to speak with him since he arrived and we buried my daughter. I can tell you that after the murder he did not call me. He called my son."

"What did he say?"

"That he had just come from the police station and Gail had been shot. Ultimately a sheriff called me to tell me what happened."

"Did you call the house?"

"Yes. George told me that Gail had been shot in the parking lot where she worked. He also mentioned that a deputy at the scene told him that just before she died, Gail said something, but the deputy would not tell George what she said. He also told me he thought the police were going to arrest him. . . ."

It had been a long interview. Dora was tired and emotionally exhausted. Before they ended, Meiers and

Dugan asked Dora if she had any thoughts about her daughter's murder and who might have killed Gail.

"In my heart I don't think George killed my daughter. I feel the responsible party is that Donna in Florida." She said she didn't know how Donna might have done it, but "I think she paid someone."

18

DEEP IN APALACHICOLA country, Okaloosa County, Florida, Okaloosa County Sheriff's Office (OCSO) investigator Larry Ashley sat at his desk early on the afternoon of October 11, 1999. Ashley had his phone in his hand; OCSD detective sergeant Gary Miller was on the other end of the line. "Detective," Ashley said, "I have something you might be interested in. A couple came into the office down here earlier today with some information."

Miller *was* interested, surely. Ashley mentioned it might have something to do with a case the OCSD was working on back up in Michigan. The two agencies had been in contact ever since Donna Trapani's name had become part of the investigation back in Michigan. Donna lived in the county.

"A husband and wife, April and Roger Craspin (pseudonyms), came in," Ashley explained. "April said she is currently employed by (Donna's company) in Fort Walton. She talked about last July and another employee she knew, Sybil Padgett, who doesn't work there anymore. This Sybil person approached April and told her a few things."

"What'd she say?"

"Well, Sybil said she had a conversation with Donna Trapani, and Donna stated to her that she 'had twenty thousand dollars to have George Fulton's wife, Gail, killed.'"

"She say why she was bringing the info to you now?"

"Yeah . . . apparently, on Monday night, Donna called April to tell her that Gail had been killed in a 'drive-by shooting.' The husband told me that Donna is a loner . . . that she's psychotic. Sybil is Donna's best friend, they both said. April tried contacting Sybil since the murder, but Sybil's phone has been disconnected."

All of this information, as disjointed as it seemed, fit into the matrix of a conspiracy to kill Gail orchestrated by Donna Trapani, and it was certainly a theory that the OCSD had been kicking around over the past week.

"I am doing some background checks on all of them," Ashley said. "I'll get back to you when I'm done."

When Ashley called later that same day, he provided a few stunning details to the OCSD. For one, April and Roger were not married, after all, which could or could not mean something to the investigation. Second, Sybil owned a 1993 Dodge Dynasty, white in color—definitely not the car in the library's grainy videotape. Sybil was what someone in law enforcement later described as a "thirty-six-year-old, unmarried loser . . . failing at most aspects of her life." At five feet eleven inches, 165 pounds, Sybil Padgett was no diminutive woman, by stature—and yet, looking at Sybil's existence, she was often at the painful end of her boyfriend's iron fist and had not been known to be all that smart about the choices she made in life. Sybil's boyfriend became of great interest to the OCSD, at least initially. He was not only violent and a convicted woman beater, but he had a record that, in its totality, lent itself to a guy who would be a good candidate to take on a paid hit. According to what Larry Ashley dug up, Sybil's live-in boyfriend had been convicted of heroin possession and was known to be, at a minimum, a "heroin dealer." Ashley could not locate a vehicle registered in the boyfriend's name. The OCSD was hoping to find a Malibu registered to someone connected to the case, which would fit with the video surveillance from the library on the night Gail was murdered. One school of thought was: Find that Malibu with the cracked taillight and its owner would have some answers to the case.

Meanwhile, back in Michigan, George Fulton finally broke down and decided to give his full cooperation. George had hired a lawyer, David Binkley, who contacted John Pietrofesa, the assistant prosecuting attorney (APA) for the County of Oakland, along with prosecuting attorney David Gorcyca, whose office was going to eventually prosecute this case. The drafted agreement between the two parties stipulated that George would submit to interviews and, essentially, "interrogations" by the OCSD, so the agency could clear his name from the case. Until a person could be entirely eliminated, he or she would remain a person of interest. George was saying, in not so many words, that he had nothing to hide and would help as much as he could. On top of that, George finally had agreed to a polygraph examination if the OCSD thought it necessary to eliminate him in that manner.

No sooner had George signed this agreement with the Oakland County Prosecutor's Office did the results come in from a forensic lab test that the state police had completed on several specimens taken from Gail's body. There had been "no apparent foreign hairs . . . in the head or pubic hair combings" found on Gail. However, chemical tests found that there was blood present on the door frame of Gail's van. Whose blood this was would be a guess at this point.

19

SOME PEOPLE WILL do whatever possible—
regardless of the ramifications or pain it causes
others—to fulfill their unquenchable needs and selfishness. Martha Gail Fulton knew those types of people, but
Gail herself was not a self-centered egotist, driven to stomp
her way through life and take whatever she wanted. Quite
to the contrary, Gail was the one to give up whatever she
had so others could feel content. Before, perhaps, anything else, Gail believed passionately in sacrifice. Gail felt
sacrifice was a gift from God, and all people could choose
to ignore or embrace its full potential. Gail understood that
having a family meant giving up parts of her life (her private self) and freedoms to meet the needs of her children
and husband. Gail wasn't bitter about this. She did it with
a peaceful and loving heart. It wasn't a choice to Gail; it
was part of who she was as a woman, wife, mother, and
Catholic.

During their courtship Gail and George spent a lot of time
apart. George was stationed at bases across the country
and around the world. Gail had no trouble waiting for George.

"They seemed to get along really well," Jeanette Cantu-
Bazar later said. "My [first] husband was in George's
[business] company."

Gail and Jeanette were together whenever their men took off on official army business. Jeanette's first husband was George's best man at his and Gail's wedding. This was a tight group of friends. They knew one another's eccentricities and faults, their loves, hopes, and dreams.

It was 1976 through 1977 when George was called to serve in Germany. He was in his mid-twenties. A year later, Jeanette and her then-husband were sent to the same country. This was the way the movie was supposed to play out: marry a serviceman and be a stay-at-home mother who follows her man wherever the army sends him. Gail and Jeanette had dreamt of this life, and here it was coming to them just as they had envisioned.

"What was difficult for Gail was to be away from her mom. She was very close to her mother. So being away in that sense was tough on her."

Gail was that rare type of person, however, who could make friends anywhere. She was adorable and loveable, and people picked up on her blissful spirit and good nature as soon as they met her. One of the things Gail liked to do more than anything was to bake. She got a kick out of baking something for someone and then seeing their reaction to what she viewed as such a simple, yet warm, gift. If that person liked the recipe, Gail would offer it up. She had all of her recipes in a neat little box, written out on index cards. She'd often bake goods and send them to George's office, wherever he was working at the time. She also took on the role of mother hen to the other army wives struggling with missing their husbands.

"Gail loved being married. She loved George. She loved having children."

The excitement of marrying a military man, having a family, and traveling the world was the image Gail and her friends strove to fulfill—a vision of life they perceived would satisfy their every need and desire as stay-at-home moms and wives.

"But, in all of the excitement, you don't realize what you're giving up," one of those friends perceptively commented later. "You go off, and you think you're going off and seeing what's out there. Corpus was a small town then. You wondered what was beyond."

Gail had come from a home where money was never an issue. Her mother and father had always provided well for the kids. When she and George began living on the salary of a serviceman, though, Gail had to learn how to manage money and budget the household. It was not easy. There was not a lot of money.

"Gail would always do without to make sure George had whatever he needed," said a former military friend. And some later suggested that George, realizing this, took advantage of it. "It might be just music. He would want to buy some music and she would want something different. She would not say anything and make sure that he got whatever he wanted. She was very self-sacrificing. I kind of call it the 'martyr complex' of . . . Catholic girls. Always wanting to do for everyone else. Not to complain. It is what it is. Gail went with it."

Gail was in love with the idea of "forever and ever." She wanted that picket fence so bad that she was willing to do whatever it took to install it in her life, while sacrificing her own needs and wants. Once she dove into being a wife, Gail gave the marriage every part of herself.

For the OCSD, the month of October did not produce any type of substantial evidence leading to an arrest. Everyone had theories and persons of interest; yet the case had not come together as the end of the month approached.

Donna Trapani was a leading suspect, as was George Fulton. The OCSD needed to take a trip south into Florida and see what it could find out; yet there was no reason to head down there when so little was known about Donna Trapani and her potential—if any—involvement in the murder. As hard as it may seem, cops understand that patience is a virtue of police work that must be adhered to in order to solve these types of cases where the trail leads in many different directions. Donna and George had alibis. Sure, they could be covering for each other, but the more likely scenario was that one or both had hired someone to commit the murder. And if that was the case, cops were certain that someone would talk, sooner or later. Two, three, or four people cannot know about a crime so volatile and violent as a murder—grating on the conscience—and keep it secret for long. It goes against all human instinct.

Unless police are dealing with a clinical sociopath.

Then all bets are off.

On October 21, 1999, Donna Trapani sent George an e-mail after he requested that she pay him some of the money she owed him. Donna's business was just about ready to close its doors for good. George wanted what he deserved.

In response, Donna said she had deposited $140 into George's account, apologizing that it was so late. She said she was "doing the best" she could to pay the bills, but it was hard. She told George that there were more bills than there was cash, but she hoped that this small amount will help . . . somehow, Donna wrote. Donna was still depending on George to do the billing for her, because she hadn't yet learned how to do it herself, she related, and could not afford to hire anyone. This was one of Donna's tactics to hang on to a connection to George after he had decided the relationship was over. She'd been manipulating and controlling George for months now. She said she could tell in his voice last night when they spoke on the telephone how "aggravated" George was to still have to do the billing. In a spate of sarcasm, Donna ended the e-mail: I am sorry to inconvenience you.

If George thought he was through with Donna, he was mistaken. This woman was not going to give up. Gail was out of the picture now completely. This was Donna's moment to step into the lives of George and his children and take over—something Donna had wanted to do for a long time.

George received a card from Donna on Halloween. The inscription inside the card referred to Donna being thrilled that George had chosen to "share something so special" and "so meaningful" with her. *I love you,* the card said, and Donna added "still" to the end of that term of endearment. *Happy anniversary,* the card continued.

It had been two years to the day they had met.

The note Donna wrote inside said a lot about where her mind was these days. She was "remembering" that night they met so long ago. Thinking back to all they had done together "put a smile" on her face, as well as in her "heart." She went on to say how meeting and getting involved with George was the most "wonderful time" of her life. She knew he felt the same way. She wanted George to spend just five minutes and think about that night they met. She was certain the memory would warm his heart. She missed not being able to talk to him. She missed his voice. She missed his laughter. She wanted him to know that if he wanted to talk anytime, he could just pick up the telephone and call her. She'd always be there for him to "unload"— an odd choice of words, considering how George's wife had been murdered—should he need someone to lean on.

Along with the card Donna sent George a dozen red roses.

George took the flowers and dropped them off at his

local parish. He wanted no remembrances of Donna Trapani in his house. What she didn't understand was that when George Fulton—at least this time—said he was done with her, it meant forever. There would be no happily ever after, as Donna Trapani apparently still sought.

20

SERGEANT ALAN WHITEFIELD called George Fulton and asked if he could meet him at the OCSD in Pontiac on November 2, 1999. Whitefield said he wanted to go through the case in more detail. Mainly, the OCSD needed to ask George several additional questions and wanted to know if he had been in contact with Donna Trapani since the murder.

George agreed. He said he had a cassette tape of a message Donna had left on his answering machine just a week before Gail's murder that might shed some light on the type of person the OCSD was dealing with in Donna Trapani. Also, George wanted to review a few things about Donna's business and his belief that, after some prudent research and thought, she might be Gail's killer, after all.

It had taken a month for the guy to open up and come around, but George Fulton was apparently ready to open up and help unconditionally.

George was still his old stiff and unapproachable self. His facial and body expressions told detectives that he did not want to be there.

What was on George's mind the most was the money Donna owed him. Sure, she had sent him $140, but that was a drop in a large bucket compared to what she still owed him. He took out an invoice he had sent to Donna just recently and provided the OCSD with a copy. It proved that Donna was behind in her payments to George's company, somewhere in the neighborhood of $13,000. It appeared Donna hadn't paid George in months. He also provided a letter from Florida's Workers Compensation addressed to Donna. The letter indicated that Workers Comp owed Donna's company, Concerned Care Home Health (CCHH), a refund of $6,364 because she had over-paid for a period between August 1998 and August 1999. The letter was dated about three weeks *after* Gail's murder.

"I've been checking her bank for deposits," George told Whitefield. "As of right now, [the check] has not been deposited."

Additionally, George provided some evidence to prove that Donna was due a refund from Medicaid and Medicare in the amount of $5,500.

"This check has not been deposited, *either*," George explained. "Donna owes her CPA about eleven thousand dollars," he added. "The plan was to send him the fifty-five hundred once the check came in" and cleared.

What was George trying to say by handing over this information—that Donna had taken that money and used it to pay off the person who killed his wife?

"Thanks for the information, Mr. Fulton," Whitefield said. The OCSD was skeptical regarding anything George Fulton did. Many of those investigators working the case felt that anything George Fulton did at this point was done for his own benefit. Was he trying to push the scent of the investigation off himself and onto his former mistress?

George said he had more.

"What's that?" Whitefield wondered.

"I feel it's important that you know that Donna's best friend, Sybil, and her better half, Tom (pseudonym), they have very close connections to the local [Florida] DeFuniak

Springs Police Department." George then went on to describe it as being a very "backwoods type of department," the police report detailing this interview said.

"How do you know that, Mr. Fulton?"

"Donna told me."

"Why are you telling us this?"

"Because you should know in case you are ever in contact with the DeFuniak Police Department."

George was wondering when he could pick up all of his stuff that had been taken from the house during the search warrant.

Right now, the detective told him.

"Would you mind hooking up a tape-recording device to your phone to record any calls Donna makes to your residence?" Whitefield asked.

George thought about this. "Yes, I can do that," he said, and he took the device home with him.

A day later, George contacted Donna via e-mail, which seemed to be the best way to speak with her and not have to deal with what could be a very unstable woman. Many would later claim that Donna suffered from bipolar mood swings ranging from laughing and joking and happiness one moment, to pure evil-inspired rants that seemed to be borne from a place in a dark heart the next. George was terse and direct in his e-mail: He said he had processed several Medicare claims he had received that week. He asked Donna to send him any additional claims she had left over.

As much as the guy might have wanted to distance himself from Donna Trapani, he was still working for her.

Donna responded by saying she had more claims, indeed. She came across in the e-mail as upset that he had billed the other claims without first checking with her. She thought they had an agreement that George would bill only twice a month.

George responded without getting into why, noting how he had received a book in the mail, which he had left at Donna's house during his last visit to Florida, and wanted to say thanks to her for sending it.

For the next few days, they spoke of work-related items over several e-mails and faxes. George was careful, as was Donna, not to mix personal issues with work. In one e-mail George asked Donna if she had received his termination letter. He wanted her to acknowledge in writing that she had received and accepted his resignation as of December 18, 1999.

Donna wrote back that she had, and she promised to write him a letter acknowledging such.

George was going back and forth with Donna regarding work-related issues and claims; and with the access he had as the company's chief financial officer (CFO), he was checking into the company's movements behind her back. By early winter, George had written a report of what he had uncovered with his investigation, along with anything else he could recall. Donna had been very close with one of her workers, George noted in that report. Sybil Padgett seemed to be totally under Donna's control. George was under the impression, certainly after studying the documentation he dug up, that Sybil and Donna were running some sort of Medicare and Medicaid scam. There were patients Sybil had made claims for visits that George was certain she had not visited.

That tape of the voice mail message Donna had left on George's answering machine at his home, eight days before Gail was murdered, gave investigators some insight into the type of person they were dealing with in Donna Trapani.

The call came in at 10:34 P.M. It was in response to

Donna hearing that George had planned on bringing Gail down to Florida with him for a final trip to collect some of his things from her house and clean out his desk.

Donna began by saying how his decision to bring his wife to Florida "is one of the lowest-class things you could do."

As the message began, her voice was calm, though flat and prickly. The officers could tell Donna had been angered by what she had heard, but she was—at least opening the call—holding that anxiety back.

"Why would you want to flaunt something like that in front of me," Donna said, referring to bringing Gail into town, "knowing how much I am already hurting?" Donna was still in love with George. And their breakup, about six weeks before the call, was still a fresh wound. "Knowing how much pain and anguish I am going through—how could you *do* something so cruel?" Donna had a very distinctive and obvious Southern accent. She spoke like an educated woman when she wanted. There was a noticeable affect to her voice that spoke to how she was getting herself excited with each word by just talking about the situation. "You know," Donna continued, "I know that she's cold and she's cruel, but [Gail is] turning *you* into being someone just like *her*—one cold and cruel heartless person! I cannot believe you would . . . have the audacity to want to bring her down here and flaunt her in front of me and . . . make my pain worse."

Now there was some excitement creeping into Donna's voice, and that bipolar behavior, which so many had talked about, was beginning to express its angrier half as she continued.

"Don't you know how *difficult* it was going to be to see you, *anyway*," Donna said, finding her rhythm, "and not be able to spend any time with you? But I was willing to do that. And I was willing to give it a try and see if I could stay away from you. . . . But then for you to bring *her* down here—that's just low class. It's evil. It's cruel. It's very low and bastardly of you to do that. And I hope that God *punishes* you for what you're doing. It's bad enough I had to listen to you talk mean and hateful to me this morning. Make up a bunch of damn lies and everything else and all the cruelty. . . ." It was here that Donna began to slip into an honest-to-goodness rant frosted with fury, a virulent rage brewing inside her. "And you want to bring her down here, and you want me to be in my bedroom and know that your ass is out there with this damn bitch, making *love* to her, being in the hot tub with *her,* swimming with *her,* eating with *her,* in my *own* city, in my *own* town!" By now, Donna's voice was cracking as she spoke faster, with venom and wrath spewing from each syllable. "And I'm here and by myself and all alone. That is *so* damn evil and low class of you. . . . You are not even the man I *thought* you were. And I don't know *how* you can be so cruel. . . . That is just like taking a *gun* and sticking it to my brain and my stomach and blowing my brains out."

Donna paused, then started crying. She was talking faster and more authoritatively.

"I was willing for you to come down and you to do your job and us trying to stay apart. I was willing to *try.* I was not going to *touch* you. I was not going to *kiss* you or hold you. . . . I was not going to do *nothing* to you! 'Cause you done just told me you didn't want me, and if you didn't want me, then I didn't want *you.* But you won't even give it a try. You got to go ahead and bring that damn *bitch* down here. Well, that *bitch* is not wanted in this city! She can stay her ass up there in Michigan where she belongs. Because she *damn* sure don't belong here in *my* city. That is her city up there, and this one is mine down here. And that's the way it *needs* to stay."

Donna needed a moment to catch her breath. She had

worked herself up into a frenzy, ranting and raging into a voice mail machine, not even an actual person. The unease and utter contempt for Gail was implicit in every single word she now spoke.

"I cannot believe you cannot come down here and do your job without having to bring your wife on your *damn* arm to make *sure* that you're safe! Low class!"

Click . . . end of message.

After listening, the OCSD knew they were dealing with someone capable of murder—a true live wire. It was there in Donna's voice: the coldness, the sheer hatred she had harbored for Gail, the absolute pure adrenaline she had worked up, just talking to a man who had, in her mind, left her high and dry and was planning on bringing his wife to Florida to rub in her face. Donna was a desperate woman, no doubt about it, eight days before Gail was executed. And yet, save for the spiritual gift of bilocation, how could Donna Trapani be in two places at the same time? If she was talking to George when Gail was murdered, it meant that if Donna had been behind it, she had to have hired someone. This meant one thing to investigators: There was a paper trail somewhere, along with a few witnesses, outlining a plot to murder Martha Gail Fulton. All they had to do was find it.

21

THROUGHOUT THE FIRST few weeks of November, the investigation moved along at a slow and steady pace. There were more pieces of the puzzle to put together than the picture would lead a layperson to believe by studying it. Smart detectives understand, though, that all it takes is a few solid breaks and a case will come together.

That first break came on November 18, when the OCSD got a hit on a rental car. As part of that Oak Force investigative team, OCSD investigator James Lehtola spoke to a rental-car agency in Okaloosa County, Florida, which had obtained information from its Enterprise Rent-A-Car corporate offices in St. Louis, Missouri. This new lead pointed to a master plan for murder clearly coming into focus. Enterprise "had confirmed," Lehtola reported, "that a Donna Trapani" had rented a number of automobiles from the Okaloosa Airport/Fort Walton Beach, Florida, location and had one vehicle out on rental currently. That information in and of itself was not so surprising or significant. However, what Lehtola found out next was enough to raise eyebrows.

Lehtola wrote: *Records indicate that the renter [Donna*

Trapani] prefers Chevrolet Malibu's and rented that type of vehicle on each occasion.

Enterprise gave Lehtola several dates: May 28, 1999, and July 2, 1999. The car Donna picked up on those dates was a four-door white Malibu, with Florida registration plates. An additional date for a black Malibu Donna had rented on August 25, 1999, juxtaposed with a trip she had taken to meet George. Then on September 10, 1999, just about three weeks prior to Gail's murder, Donna rented a 1999 jade-colored Malibu—a car she had yet to return to Enterprise.

Bull's-eye!

"We contacted Miss Trapani," the Enterprise rep told Lehtola, "and let her know that she had overdue payments related to the vehicle, and she needed to pay and return the car. But she said she was in Louisiana because her mother was having open-heart surgery."

The company had been leaving messages on Donna's office voice mail, but she had not returned any of the calls.

"Notify us as soon as she returns that car," Lehtola said.

Lehtola let the team know what he had found. It seemed to fit into place. Yet, the break the OCSD had been looking for all along—that proverbial knife in Donna Trapani's back—came hours later in the form of two telephone calls that would send investigators heading straight out the door on that road trip to Florida.

As most agencies do in this situation, the OCSD referred to the caller as "the informant." His name was Todd Franklin (pseudonym), a Texas native living in Florida, a man who had done some time in a local jail that past summer and had happened to run into Sybil Padgett along the way. As the prisoners were transported and corralled into holding pens, waiting to be sent to various prisons, Todd had a conversation with Sybil, who was also locked up on a drug charge, that sparked a rekindling of an old friendship between them. Todd and Sybil had known each other for ten years, at least.

It was around 8:00 P.M. on November 19 when Todd Franklin called the OCSD. Sergeant James A'Hearn and several investigators were still in the office, talking about the Fulton case. They were commenting on how it was surely a solvable case; it just needed a bit more shoe-leather police work.

Alan Whitefield took the call.

Todd Franklin sounded drunk, slurring his words, unable to articulate things with any consistent sentence structure. Yet, the basis for the call was unmistakably clear.

"He said something to the effect . . . that he and a woman, Sybil Padgett," A'Hearn later said, "had had a conversation about her being involved in a homicide in Michigan."

Apparently, Todd and Sybil had just had sex. They were lying in bed, smoking cigarettes and talking like lovers sometimes do, when Sybil admitted that she had been part of Gail's murder. OCSD investigators called it "pillow talk": Sybil thought she could trust the man with whom she'd just been intimate.

A'Hearn called Franklin the following morning; he was more sober—though not completely—and able to orate his story somewhat clearer.

"Based on that information he gave me the following morning," A'Hearn said, "I arranged to meet him down in Florida."

Detective John Meiers, Detective Sergeant James A'Hearn, and Special Agent William O'Leary, of the FBI, left for Florida a few days later to interview Todd Franklin face-to-face. That break in the case they had all been waiting for—well, it had just occurred.

Todd insisted on being picked up at his apartment for fear of someone seeing him head into the police department (PD) and talk to cops. So they took him to the FBI's local bureau in Fort Walton Beach, Florida. The OCSD was now on Donna Trapani's home turf, in her backyard.

"Tell us how you became involved," one of the investigators asked.

Todd seemed nervous and agitated. He was shaky, maybe more from drinking too much than being scared to talk about what he knew. He gave no reason why he was coming forward, other than he wanted to help.

"I—I . . . while I was incarcerated in Franklin County Jail this past summer," he explained, "Sybil, a longtime friend of mine, asked me if I knew anybody that killed people."

That was the beginning of it, Todd went on to explain; the first time he had heard anything about Sybil being involved in murdering someone. It shocked him. Sybil was a bad girl, sure. She was a little trashy and definitely easy, but she didn't strike him as the type to be involved in a murder-for-hire plot. So Todd wrote it off as Sybil playing around, trying to be someone she was not: a tough girl trying to play the part.

Todd explained to Sybil over the phone at one point that he had done some time with a dude who had, in fact, killed people. The conversation with Sybil ended there. However, after Todd was released from jail some days later, he ran into Sybil again and the conversation picked up. They even rekindled an intimate relationship and started sleeping together on a regular basis. Todd still wasn't certain whether Sybil was serious about wanting to hire someone for a hit.

"She said she had someone who wanted it done," Franklin explained.

Sybil ended up introducing Todd Franklin to Donna
Trapani. During that first meeting Donna and Sybil made
it clear to Todd that they were looking to get "this woman
in Michigan killed," as Todd explained to A'Hearn and
the FBI.

"Put me in touch with someone who can make the hit,"
Sybil pleaded with him. Donna stood by, but she didn't say
anything. She certainly knew what was being said and, in
many respects, Donna was the "boss lady" behind the
scenes who was calling the shots.

"I also had several conversations with Donna about
her troubles with this woman in Michigan, but Donna
never directly asked me for assistance" at that time, Todd
stated.

"Well, what *did* she say?" A'Hearn wanted to know.

"From what Donna told me, her boyfriend's wife
wouldn't give him a divorce, so she said that she wasn't
going to worry about that, but that she would find somebody to have her killed and the problem would be solved
forever, and it wouldn't cost nearly as much money [as a
divorce]."

It sounded an awful lot like a murder plan. This im-
promptu meeting among Sybil, Donna, and Todd, whether
any of them realized it, was a capital felony, punishable—
if convicted—by the death penalty in most instances.

"I didn't take it seriously," Todd said. "They talked
about it a lot. But then it was about a week or two before
the woman was killed when Sybil called me."

"What'd she want?"

"I asked her where she was, because I had not seen her
in a while."

"I can't tell you where I am," Sybil told Todd over the
phone that night. It was about ten days before Gail's
murder.

"Come on . . . ," he pleaded. "Why not?"

"Nope. Can't do it."

A little later into the conversation, Sybil gave in, saying, "I'm at a pay phone in Michigan."

"She told me she was with some guy, Patrick something . . . and they had gone to Michigan to check on Donna's boyfriend's wife. She said she had been following her [Gail] and knew where she lived. Sybil thought it was funny that she (Sybil) had put a wig on and even followed the woman into her bank one day."

Sybil and this Patrick person had been stalking Gail, doing Donna's dirty work, following Donna's lead all the way.

While they were in the bank, Sybil bumped into Gail, saying, "Oh, excuse me. . . ." It was all a joke to Sybil. She was having fun following around Donna's archenemy, tracking Gail's every move, searching for that perfect opportunity to kill her.

"Did Sybil ever say why she was in Michigan?" A'Hearn asked.

"I don't remember what she said, but *I* knew why she was there. When Sybil returned to Florida, she contacted me again and told me that she was unable to kill the woman because [Gail] always had friends around her and she was going to [different places] . . . where there were always people around."

Investigators asked Todd to talk about his personal relationship with Donna. A'Hearn wanted to know if he had ever spoken to Donna alone—just the two of them—and what she might have said.

"Numerous occasions," Todd admitted.

"Who contacted whom?"

"She normally called me. Donna would often talk about how much trouble her boyfriend's wife was causing her . . . and how much easier it would be if she was out of the picture. She was very casual about having this woman killed and spoke of it often."

They asked Todd if Donna ever talked about her boyfriend, George Fulton. The thought was that George was maybe the mastermind behind it all; he was there behind the curtain, telling Donna what to do, having Donna go out and find the right people who could give them the freedom Donna had told Todd that she and George had been yearning for since they met.

"I asked her once, 'This guy, your boyfriend, *he* knows you want to do this?' Donna's response was 'Heavens no!' She used to ask me all the time if my friend could do 'the hit' for *her*."

"Have you spoken to Donna since the murder?"

"Yeah . . . yeah . . . but every time I mention the murder, she changes the subject and says she has to go, and immediately gets off the phone."

"When was the last time you spoke to Miss Trapani?"

"Oh, it's been about a month or so."

A'Hearn asked Todd Franklin if he knew what happened. Had Sybil told him how it all finally went down, by whom, and how long it took to plan? Was Donna actually there when Gail was murdered? Phone records indicated that George's telephone and Donna's telephone were in touch on the night Gail was murdered. But that did not mean Donna and George were on each end of the line. Perhaps George Fulton was covering for his lover?

Todd took a breath. "She did. She told me everything."

From there, Todd Franklin proceeded to explain to three investigators what had actually happened on the night and preceding days leading up to the murder of Gail Fulton— and yet that deadly narrative, the beginning of the end of Gail Fulton's life, began on a wintry day in 1996, when George Fulton and his family moved from Texas to Michigan.

II

THE BLACK
CLOUD

22

IT WAS SNOWING that afternoon when the Fulton family pulled up to their new home on Talon Circle in Lake Orion, Michigan. This was the next chapter in George and Gail Fulton's lives after leaving the warmth of Corpus Christi, Texas. Everyone was tagging along to live out George's dream. It was his decision to pack it all up and move. They had arrived in Lake Orion that summer and stayed in an apartment until the house on Talon Circle was finished.

"I would say my mom liked the house because she got to help customize certain features," Emily Fulton said.

The new house was a fresh start for George and Gail: They had two kids still in high school (their oldest child had stayed in Texas), a devotion to their Catholic faith, and George was beginning a new job. Gail had been reluctant to move, but maybe it could all work?

Gail wasn't all that thrilled about moving so far away from her mother, but she knew that unfamiliar surroundings and new friends could be a new beginning for her life, wherever it was heading. The house was lovely. It had all the essentials any homemaker could ask for. The neighborhood was a suburban dream: clean yards, plush landscaping, people who waved and said hello while washing cars and shoveling snow.

No sooner had the Fultons settled down, however, when Gail experienced a loneliness—one that would be harder and harder to contend with as each day passed.

Gail didn't get to know any of her neighbors. There were block parties, but Gail and George—private to begin with—never attended.

"Living [there] was fine," Emily recalled. "I lived in the house from the time I was sixteen . . . until I was married [at twenty-four]. I think my mom liked the house enough and I know she liked working at the library, but I also know she missed her family and would probably have been happier being closer to her mom and other extended family. . . ."

Gail was friendly at work and while she was out and about in town, but she was not one to hang out afterward or attend social events. Gail was more of the subordinate wife; she enjoyed the role she played in her family's everyday lives. Home wasn't a prison to Gail. She didn't feel confined by her duties as wife and mother. She understood that raising well-adjusted and kind kids took sacrifice.

On the other hand, when Gail's children look back on her life inside that new house, they see how much Gail had changed and withdrawn from not only society, but also the things she loved.

"When I think back on this," Emily remembered, "I think how lonely this must have been [for her] to not have anyone to confide in [or] to be able to talk girlfriend stuff with. Everyone needs friends, and females especially need female time. I know me and my brother spent some quality times with my mom taking her out to eat and to the movies, but I can't help but regret that I did not do more. You never really know how short your time is with someone. Maybe it was good to have my friends come over to eat dinner with us when I was in college. At least this gave my mom other conversation besides me and my brother."

Emily soon saw a dramatic change in the atmosphere around the house as her mother's attitude in general deteriorated.

"I must admit that I preferred to not be at home because it was such a sad and lonely place, and it was hard for me to bear it. I mean, I was there for my mom . . . but I still often think I could have done more [household chores]. When I was growing up, I was always helping my mom around the house and I would always help my mom make dinner. I would ask her, 'What can I help with?' And she would give me a job. That is how I learned to cook—from watching my mom. I think when I got to high school, I stopped helping as much, since I didn't get home from after-school activities until dinnertime and was so busy with school stuff. . . . I was my mom's helper out of the three of us, as my siblings were often off playing with friends or doing something else. Maybe I could sense my mom's loneliness and that is why I usually [offered] to help her versus playing outside. . . . I have always needed a purpose, and my purpose was to spend time with my mom to make her job easier. . . . I miss my mom."

Back in Texas before the move north, according to several of Gail's friends, George and Gail were unhappy. Their marriage was going through a rough period that literally showed on Gail's face. There were family photos of Gail taken during this period that captured the suffering she endured. In these pictures her face was emaciated and hollow; her cheekbones were defined. There were definitive bags under her eyes, and her posture spoke of a woman suffering from a depression so encompassing it literally manifested itself into weight and hair loss.

George wore a mustache during these times—a common

change, someone close to him later noted, that would become a signature of certain behaviors.

It was during the mid-1990s that George was unable to find a job that, a neighbor said, "he thought was *good* enough for him." George had been out of work; yet, under his military training and army "mentality," added that same source, "George believed he should start at the top."

A friend was trying to help George get a job. They sat together in the friend's office one day. "What type of job do you want here, George?" His friend figured he might be able to get George into the company at an entry-level position or slighter higher up and George could show his stuff.

"I want *your* job," George said.

"He didn't feel he should have to work his way up the corporate ladder," said the friend.

George thought he deserved it—that he did not have to prove himself.

Out of work George started selling insurance and offering financial planning for couples and families. The first policy he sold was to Gail.

Life insurance.

Gail was extremely upset by his new career path, considering that George had the skills and education to do so many different things that could earn the family more money. As it happened, that previous Christmas before they left Texas, Gail had sacrificed so much and made do on a shoestring budget, getting the kids the bare minimum for holiday gifts. Gail was not happy about it, but she accepted the changes as a bump in the road. During this time, as they struggled to pay bills, George went out and "bought a one-hundred-dollar tie," Gail told a friend. Thinking back on it, Gail was in tears. She couldn't believe how selfish George had been. The argument for George was that since he was going to be selling insurance and offering financial planning, he needed to look the part.

"It showed," said a neighbor, "another little thing about him that was *me, me, me*. It was always what was best for George, *not* the family."

And then this job in Michigan came along and George jumped on it.

"It was heart-wrenching to see Gail," said one of her friends, "when the decision was made to move up north, away from her church and family and friends."

Gail had built her life in that Corpus Christi community. At a time when things in the marriage and the household itself were not going well, it was the only true lifeline she had to cling to. Everything else could fall apart around her, but Gail knew she had her church, her friends, and, especially, her mother there—and now George took all of that away.

Gail's first thought was with her mother, who was a widow by then and needed Gail around to help her through those latter years. This move halfway across the country came out of left field. There was no discussion; there was no family meeting. No "Honey, what do *you* think? Is it something *you'd* like to do?"

George made up his mind, and that was it.

"But, Gail," asked a friend when Gail confided they were moving, "what do *you* feel about it all?"

"This is what George wants," Gail said. "For our family it is right." One of Gail's concerns was sending the kids to college and making sure they had enough money for the kids to attend good schools. If she had to move north to accomplish that goal, Gail was ready and willing to—again—to sacrifice.

In that respect, a neighbor said, "George likely dangled the kids' educational futures in front of Gail. . . ."

(According to Emily, however, her father would later

refuse to pay for the girls' college educations when it came time to apply.)

"She was the most loving and kind mother and wife," said another friend. "She just wanted her family. She wanted to be close to the church. It was all about being a good Catholic—and George took *total* advantage of that! He blindsided her with her loyalty and with 'you're married till death do us part.'"

Gail forgave her husband and accepted the move because that's who she was. She did not know, of course, it was a decision that would ultimately kill her.

23

DONNA TRAPANI OWNED and operated a home health care business in Florida that catered to elderly clients in need of daily care. They are sometimes called "visiting nurses." The job George had taken in Michigan wasn't what he had expected. As the winter of 1996 became the spring of 1997, George found himself looking for work, itching to start his own business. This work history of her father's seemed to fall into a pattern, Emily later suggested. George dreamt of sitting behind the desk of his own company, calling the shots, controlling every aspect of his financial future—which was where Donna Trapani fit in.

"Donna helped one of my dad's dreams come true," Emily observed. "He always wanted to start his own business."

When they lived in Corpus Christi, George started an electronic medical-claims business. It turned out to be some sort of scam and ended up costing him thousands of dollars, Emily said. She added, "I was too young to understand at the time, but I just remember that my dad got duped."

Part of the connection George and Donna had stemmed from each coming from similar economic backgrounds.

"Not sure how much of this was lies from Donna," Emily said, "as I assume that some of it was . . . so that my dad would feel closer to her and to make it seem that only *she* really understood him. I think my dad wanted to marry my mom because she came from a well-to-do family and would make a good officer's wife to help him with his career. . . . I know for a fact that he resented my mom due to her upbringing because she did not struggle like he did. I firmly believe this because he even resented us kids for having it 'so easy' when we were growing up. My dad was too selfish to understand the full impact of how he treated us . . . and even how he handled the affair we knew about, and our mother's death, as anything bad for us, as it was always about *him.* So when Donna offered him this job in Florida, *along* with the sex, this was all too much for my dad to pass up—as this sort of gave him some of his redemption, I imagine, and made him feel smart again, as he was finally able to have his own business and put his claims idea to good use."

It was 1997 when George and Donna first met. She was a flirtatious, foul-mouthed, married floozy who liked to go out after work and party at the neighborhood bars and meet men. On October 14, 1997, George was in Florida on business. He happened to be staying at a hotel near the Seagull Bar. Locals called it the "Dirty Bird," because "it's a dive," one regular later said. Donna fit right in with the bar's clientele. She dressed flashy and trashy. Her clothes were new, but always too tight, too loud, too glittery.

"Trailer trash with some money," said a former coworker. "That was Donna."

George was working for a Troy, Michigan–based automotive safety company as its senior operations research analyst. He went out for a drink one night to the Seagull, said one police report, and saw Donna at the bar.

"You wanna dance?" George asked.

Donna looked him over. "I don't like the song," she said, playing hard to get.

George asked her two more times that night.

Donna didn't like any of the songs, she repeated.

"When you hear a song you like," George finally said, "you come and get me." He pointed to his seat at the bar.

No sooner had George gotten comfortable did the song "Caribbean Queen" by 1980s icon Billy Ocean come on. Donna loved that song ("It became *our* song," she said later), and she motioned for George to meet her on the dance floor.

No one needed to twist his arm.

After the dance they sat down.

"We mostly talked about his mother's death and how he wished he would have known about home health care because that may have made a difference in how long his mother may have lived," Donna told police.

Throughout that night George "never told [Donna] anything personal about himself," she claimed, "other than he was working at Eglin [Air Force Base] as an engineer. . . ."

What's more, George never mentioned that he was married and had a family in Michigan.

"And I never asked," Donna said.

The lights flickered inside the bar. It was time to go.

"We parted without exchanging phone numbers," Donna said. "As a matter of fact, I did not even know his last name."

George went back to his hotel and—metaphorically speaking—started growing a mustache.

Two weeks later, on Halloween night, Donna went to the same bar to meet friends, but they never showed up. As she walked around the bar, looking for her friends, Donna spotted George, and, as she put it, "our eyes met. . . ."

This time George introduced himself, sharing his full name. They danced. Laughed. Drank. George had found someone, it seemed, who understood him—a woman who felt the same as he did about life in general. Still, within all the hours they talked on this second night, George never told Donna he was married with children.

"Come on," Donna said. "Come out to the parking lot. I want to show you something." She was a little tipsy, smiling out of the corner of her mouth.

George grinned.

"What do you think?" Donna asked. "Since the last time I saw you a few weeks ago, I bought a new car."

George stood and stared at what was a brand-new Lincoln Town Car. The thing was sharp. It definitely impressed George. Donna had money. Power. She owned her own company. He envied Donna. She was brassy and spoke up for herself. Gail was passive. Donna was aggressive and boisterous. What Donna had, George wanted—at least a piece of it.

"Get in," Donna said.

"Okay."

They sat. Donna locked the doors and turned on some music, low and slow.

They talked.

"You want to take the car for a spin?" Donna asked.

"No thanks," George said, "but maybe I can drive it tomorrow or the next day."

They embraced. Like a pair of twentysomethings meeting at a club, they kissed inside Donna's car. As she later described what happened next, "one thing led to another. . . ." Soon they started "touching."

"You want to go home with me?" George asked.

"Yes, I do," Donna whispered.

"I'm married," George admitted, tossing it out there at what was a no-turning-back-now moment. "But I have

been extremely unhappy for years and years and years
and years."

Donna asked George where he was staying.

Right around the corner.

"Take me back there," Donna demanded.

They left.

After sex, they talked. Then had more sex, and talked
some more. George opened up, as Donna later explained,
saying, "I talked to my mother before she died about my
marriage and she told me that because I am an officer in
the military, my wife will take everything. She told me to
stay in the marriage until the kids were grown and gone.
You're the only one that I have been able to open up to."

One night with this woman and the guy was spilling his
life story.

"You're not over the death of your mother," Donna
asked, "are you?"

"No."

Donna spends the night, said a police report, *and leaves
in the morning.*

That next afternoon George met Donna for lunch—and
a "relationship" began.

According to one source, "Donna told me [she and
George] had a 'very sexually charged relationship,' so I am
sure that they are very sexual in nature. She also told me
[George] shared so many things with her about his life and
dreams that [Gail] never really knew or understood."

The bond between them, for whatever reason, was in-
stantaneous.

In a way George figured he was stepping into one
more good time. At home in Michigan he was having
"problems" with Gail. "Guys need sex," said someone
close to George and Gail then. "[Gail] wasn't into it"—as
if this was some sort of reason for the guy to jump from

bed to bed. He was going to be spending a lot of time in Florida. This could be the ideal situation: to have someone there who could appease his sexual fantasies and do those things in the bedroom that his supposed oppressed Catholic wife never even thought of.

George had no idea who he had just slept with, or the psychopath he was now attached to. Donna Trapani was unlike any other woman George had encountered.

24

CONCERNED CARE HOME Health, the first name Donna gave her company, was probably not the most appropriate, considering what a consensus of her former employees later revealed. For one, Donna was not the most compassionate person or employer, often calling her employees—even on off days—in the middle of the night to ask basic questions that could have waited until the following morning, if not the next person's shift. But that was only half of it. At best, Donna was incompetent; at worst, she was negligent and criminal.

One woman, Christine Stokes (pseudonym), took a job with Donna shortly before Donna and George met. She took the position solely, Christine admitted, "because the money was so good. Donna paid her employees well."

For that money, however, Donna expected loyalty and obedience. Nothing less would suffice.

When she met George in 1997, Donna was a forty-four-year-old, five-foot-seven woman, with beady, penetrating, and glossy green eyes. She weighed about 120 pounds (yet there was a reason, Christine Stokes learned, behind what was Donna's obsessive weight control), and had long brown locks, routinely unkempt, and a problem with split ends and dried-out, thin strands of hair. Donna had an issue with facial hair, too, and spent lots of money to keep it under control with expensive trips to the spa. Donna was about keeping Donna happy.

The business was located in Fort Walton Beach, Florida, on the Gulf Coast—north of all the "sun and fun" action down in, say, Tampa or Miami—in between Pensacola and DeFuniak Springs, on the edge of Eglin Air Force Base. This is backcountry territory. Donna's husband, Chuck, was born and raised in Louisiana, same as Donna, who had lived in New Orleans most of her youth.

Donna had one of those textbook stories of being abandoned, later adding to it: "I was raised by Momma since Daddy left us when I was six weeks old." According to Donna, the impetus for her daddy's departure was a "last straw" violent episode inside the house that she experienced. "He threw me against a wall," Donna explained, "and my momma told him to get out."

Not long after Donna turned seven, she and her mother moved from New Orleans to Mississippi. A few years after that, they hightailed it back to Louisiana, this time outside Baton Rouge, in Denham Springs. Donna eventually graduated from Denham Springs High School with a 4.0 GPA, in the top 10 percent of her class. She had beaten the odds of growing up fatherless, with a single mother, to be an outstanding student. From high school she went on to a junior college to work on an associate degree in data processing, which led to attending the nursing program and the University of New Orleans. In 1981, she graduated with a registered nurse's degree. The future for Donna was about hard work and dedication to study. Donna wanted to help people and serve the community. She worked at a local hospital for a time and performed field duties for a home health care firm, which planted the seed of an idea to break out on her own and start a company she could manage the way she believed home health care should be.

It was several years later that she met Charles "Chuck" Trapani (1989) and got hitched. Seven years into the union, Donna and Chuck moved to Florida to start Home Health Care Systems (HHCS). It was February 1996 when Donna opened the doors to her office, but it was August that same year before she was able to secure the necessary licenses to send her nurses out into the field. It was September before they could start serving patients' needs.

"We had a staff of RNs, LPNs, VNAs," Christine Stokes recalled. "We were a Medicare and Medicaid agency." (RNs were registered nurses; LPNs were licensed practical nurses, and VNAs were visiting nurse aides.)

Donna came across as "scattered and weird" as Christine got to know her better while working directly with her every day, but again, "she paid very well. She paid more than any other agency in the area, and we can be, sometimes, motivated by pay. . . . You put up with a lot of things in the medical professional world—there are a lot of weirdos, and it's just something you have to do."

Almost immediately Donna exposed herself as aggressive and controlling in what was a hostile work environment. Heading through the door in the morning, employees never knew what type of day it was going to be, or the type of person they were going to get in Donna. It all depended on her mood.

"She was absolutely the worst micromanager I have ever encountered."

Donna had to have her hands in every piece of the business; and most of the time, she made things worse, simply because of control and self-esteem issues of having her workers submit to her every whim.

Power hungry, envious, and jealous that others knew more—that was how Donna came across most of the time. Smart people intimidated Donna. She hired an extremely intelligent nurse, for example, a woman who had her master's in nursing. The gal knew her stuff. Donna, however, badgered the woman about her work ethic, letting her know how incompetent she was. Donna left her nasty written messages on some of the orders the woman placed, telling her she was *the worst nurse [she] had even run into. . . . How the hell could you even work for the [government]—you're illiterate!* And yet Donna never fired or reprimanded her. Instead, she found it a power trip to degrade and ridicule her every chance she got. This made Donna feel superior. It gave her that emotional high she got from simply bossing people around.

It all came from a fear of being inadequate; Donna never felt "good enough," and often used her manipulative skills to make people understand that she was the boss, that *she* made the decisions, and no one was *ever* to question her authority. She ran the show.

There was one time when a major corporation wanted to buy Donna out. It would have meant a tremendous amount of money—likely enough to ride off into the sunset with her husband (or whichever man she was bedding down with at the time) and retire.

When the white shirts came to the office to discuss the transaction and have a look around, Donna was "absolutely horrid to these people," a former employee said. "Every other word Donna used was the 'F' word." It was bizarre, erratic behavior, as if Donna wanted somehow to sabotage the sale (which she ultimately did).

When asked a day later about her behavior, Donna responded, "Look, when you're in a man's world, you have to act like a man. You have to *talk* like a man."

"What the hell is she talking about?" that same former employee had said.

But here was a glimpse of Donna's skewed vision of the world.

"Donna was a white-trash woman all dressed up! She had a mouth worse than any sailor's!"

Donna was obsessed with her weight and focused on her figure. There was even some indication—although Donna never came out and admitted to it right away—that she'd been obese at one time and had had gastric bypass surgery.

"Yes," Donna's husband said in the healthcare office one afternoon, "she had a gastric bypass."

Donna had lost a lot of weight. She was proud of it, but she did not want to discuss how she did it. When she sat down to eat, many noticed, Donna could not eat more than a handful of food without being full. And she would spend nearly a half hour in the toilet after eating.

"She had [once] said that she had abdominal surgery and had lost a lot of weight because of that," said a former employee. "She was very skinny at that point."

"Donna was nasty, nasty," said another employee. "She'd take all of her paperwork into the toilet with her and then start handing it out to us after walking out of the bathroom. It was disgusting. One of the girls in the office used to spray the paperwork with Lysol after Donna gave it to her."

The other point Donna made clear to everyone was that she "absolutely hated and despised her husband." Chuck worked at the office. "Chuck was, bless his heart, a Cajun. He presented himself in the way that he was Donna's whipped puppy. He adored her. [He] would do anything for her."

And Donna took advantage of it.

25

THE AFFAIR GEORGE and Donna initiated in October 1997 took on a life of its own after that night they spent together. During the Thanksgiving holiday George returned to Michigan to spend the long weekend with his family. He did not seem any different. The same old George: stoic, reserved, content, a bit on the angry side. As Donna and George spent their first extended period of time away from each other—after nearly every day together while George was in Florida—they communicated via e-mail, fax, and phone.

George wasn't gone but a day when Donna sent him a fax indicating how much she missed him. He needed to be "alone," she wrote, when he read the fax. She explained how "lonely" it was in Florida without him. She noted: *a body here that sure does need your services.* Then she said her two legs were *longing to be wrapped securely around your body, feeling your powerful urges. . . .* Her breasts were in need of his "gentle, warm" lips and his touch made them *come alive, erect, and [excited].* From there the fax went into a long, tedious, eighth-grade fantasy, talking about what Donna dreamt of. She sounded desperate and foolish, talking about bodies being "close together" and "powerful urges." She confided how her *warm, dark tunnel [was] awaiting to be deeply explored by your/my wonderful joystick,* along with *the hardness of you.*

Not a month since they met and Donna was "addicted" to [George's] "passionate lovemaking."

Many of George's responses to the plethora of letters, faxes, and e-mails from Donna do not exist (probably not by chance). And yet some do. In one short letter George wrote to his new lover, he said Donna inspired him. In another, during this same period (dare one call it a "courtship"), George told Donna that life was full of "the element of chance." He explained how he wanted (and needed) to be overly cautious. Donna said George's trepidation where it pertained to falling in love was "due to Gail." George's wife was the cause of his unhappiness. George's wife was stopping him from totally giving himself to Donna. And George's wife was standing in the way of the two of them riding off into the Florida sunset, working, and living together.

For Donna, she claimed to have never found joy until she entered into the "true calling" of being a nurse. Since George had entered her life, however, Donna said she was happier and more mentally stable. She had a new enthusiasm for life. She had energy. She wasn't getting frustrated as easily. George had calmed her. She could accomplish more. She felt as if she had an "inner strength," which she had never known. George had given her reason and purpose to get up every morning and go to bed at night.

On December 19, 1997, George told Donna, "I love you."

Donna wasn't sure about her "faith," a part of himself George had instilled in Donna many times. She needed to be a believer, like him, George had told her. God *could* move mountains, if only you let Him into your heart. Donna talked about how, with George, she had mastered "love, desire, sex, hope, romance, and enthusiasm" (whatever the latter meant). The only negative emotion she could truly admit to still struggling with was fear, which derived from the constant thought of her business failing.

In an *Oprah* moment, George told Donna she must know what she wanted in order to obtain it—or it wasn't possible.

In her e-mails and letters and faxes heading toward the Christmas holiday, Donna asked George about coming to work for her on a day-to-day, full-time basis. In January 1998, Donna sent George a "classified ad." It was a gesture on her part to show George how serious she was about him working for her company. By now, George had agreed to work for Donna, although in what capacity they had not yet discussed. In a fax sent on January 8, 1998, Donna said she was going to be placing an "ad in the local paper," but she wanted to send it along for "review and approval."

In the "wanted" section, Donna wrote what she was searching for: *one sexy male by the name of "George of the Jungle." [This man must be willing] to swing down from cold Michigan [and end up in the] warmth of sunny Florida.* George of the Jungle's "mission," the mock ad continued, was to use "every inch" of his body to satisfy his "most precious" lover. The reason Donna gave for her search was simple: *There is one hot and horny female in desperate need of delightful pleasures. . . .*

In the ad Donna talked about their "previous encounters," without going into great detail. She mentioned the "skills" George of the Jungle needed in order to fulfill his job requirements: *Slow moving hands that titillate . . . Warm, moist, soft lips . . . A soft, moist tongue and wonderful mouth . . . [to] send hot sensations thru [my] breasts. . . . A tight well-shaped butt . . . [and] slow, deep pelvic thrusts . . .* After a long and tired description of how those thrusts had the potential to make her pelvic area

"explode" in astonishing ecstasy, Donna talked about the
most important job requirement of all was to be able to
"penetrate" her "warm, moist dark tunnel of love," but
only with his "most prized possession." She likened it to
the "firmest, hardest, hottest erectile" she had ever felt.
She said it created the highest levels of ecstasy and "elated
orgasmic explosions."

The pay, the ad concluded, was "negotiable."

Donna hired an old friend to work with her: Sybil Padgett. Sybil was a thirty-four-year-old "redneck" woman,
so said a former coworker. Sybil lived in DeFuniak
Springs, not far, as the crow flies, from Donna's house.
Part of Walton County, DeFuniak Springs is sometimes
called the "Gateway to the Gulf." It is a small, remote community, somewhere in the neighborhood of five thousand
residents.

"It's very, um . . . *country,*" one former local said. "It's
very redneck out there. Sybil was, well, incompetent."

And, in many ways, she was Donna's puppet.

Sybil was making good money, and she would do just
about anything that the older woman asked. Even George,
when pressed to comment on what investigators called
"Donna's potential hold on Sybil," did not have many
pleasant things to say about her. He accused Sybil of
taking drugs. He talked about her "strange behavior during
the time I was employed. . . ." Part of her conduct at work
included Sybil not calling in, an "argumentative and uncooperative" [attitude toward] "her supervisor." She would
not answer her beeper, [and] "not comply . . . with company policy."

Strangely, George said, although they believed Sybil
was a drug user, Donna never tested her.

What does this comment say about Donna and her

business? Can any rational person imagine sending a
known drug-using nurse into the homes of elderly patients
to care for them? It sent a message to her employees that
Donna was not interested in running a business centered on patient care and proper medical ethics.

[Donna] had a deep-seated need for control and power,
said one law enforcement document. *She had grown . . .
accustomed to being a manipulator of people and life
circumstances. . . . Nobody crossed Donna without suffering consequences; she was driven by revenge.*

The fact that Donna let Sybil get away with such bad
behavior was Donna's way of controlling Sybil and, fun-
damentally, having things to dangle over Sybil's head when
the right time came.

Speaking about Sybil's possible drug use, George said,
"If so, Sybil could lose her Florida nursing license, since
Donna could report her to the state board."

Is this what Donna had in mind: to hold Sybil by the
collar and threaten to have her license revoked?

More than protecting her on the job, Donna loaned
Sybil money from her personal accounts and gave Sybil
cash advances on her paychecks.

"Sybil and Donna go back a long time [about four
years]," George later said, "and have been together since
the start of the agency. So Sybil 'owes' Donna for all the
breaks and favors of the past."

One of those "favors" Donna routinely did for Sybil
was rent cars.

There were days when Sybil worked under Christine
Stokes, who thought Sybil was one of the most useless and
inept nurses she had ever worked with. Christine had been
promoted several times. She had a lot of responsibility
within CCHH.

There came a point when Christine made phone calls under a quality control program she initiated. In the home health care business, you are as good as your reputation. A few bad nurses working out in the field can take down a company. Christine had been in the business a long time.

As she called several of Sybil's patients, Christine found out Sybil had not been there. Not once or twice—but never.

First thing she did was go to the charts Sybil had kept on each patient. Lo and behold, there were notes, indicating Sybil had been to the home and had made reports of each visit.

Christine went to see Donna. "Sybil's got to go! She's going to ruin your business." Christine showed Donna the reports.

Christine and Donna went to see Sybil. As it happened, George was there.

"You know," Christine said, Donna and George looking on, "you cannot be doing this. We're going to have to get rid of you."

Crying, Sybil was devastated.

Two weeks later, Donna called Christine into her office. "Listen," she said, "Sybil is really having a hard time. I think we need to give her a second chance."

"I disagree with you, Donna. I'll tell you what: My license will be on the line. You want her back? *You* supervise her."

The indication was that Sybil, who had a few kids, could not help herself because she was being beaten by her significant other, but she refused to report the dude. She'd come to work with black eyes and bruises. Donna felt sorry for Sybil, Christine contended.

At the expense of the business, Christine thought.

Sybil was a solid woman: nearly six feet tall, 160 pounds. Average-looking, she wore her hair long, maintained a charming smile against arresting blue eyes. Men used Sybil—that much was clear by the way she "presented herself." Sybil was weak in that respect, afraid to stand up for herself, in fear, perhaps, of being beaten harder. Yet there was more to it. Donna's and Sybil's relationship was something no one at work knew the inner workings of. There were reasons why Donna put up with Sybil's drug use, poor work attendance, and unacceptable work actions.

[Sybil's] only perceived salvation, law enforcement reported, *was to maintain her employment as a health care professional with Donna's health care operation. Donna . . . took advantage of Sybil's weaknesses and convinced her, that if she did not help Donna . . . then Donna would ensure that Sybil would lose her job and eventually [lose] her children.*

Sybil was motivated, primarily, by a "sense of despair." She had no one else to turn to.

The way in which Donna took advantage of Sybil— slowly and deliberately—over a period of time, grooming her and allowing her to stumble, picking her up and brushing her off (playing the good mother), was what made George and Donna a pair to be reckoned with: Donna and George were alike in many ways, especially the way in which they treated people.

26

DONNA WAS BLISSFUL, walking on air around the office, bursting with smiles and fleeting adolescent emotion. By the middle of January 1998, Donna had kicked Chuck out of the house and sent him back to Louisiana, promising to see him in divorce court. That was Donna. She berated the guy for years, took him for a fool, used his muscle in the office where she needed it, and then kicked him to the curb after meeting George, whom she was referring to around the office as "this wonderful engineer" she had met and was soon going to be bringing into the company as a full-time employee. But not only was Donna bringing George into the fold to take care of the claims for CCHH and oversee its finances, George had agreed to rent a space from Donna inside her home to use as an office for a new company he had started. George would be doing work for Donna as a private contractor. The agreement was that George reported twice a month to Florida for business and, of course, Donna's personal pleasure. A lot of the work he could take back to Michigan and do from a home office.

Donna was getting exactly what she wanted.

Same as the situation with George, Donna's life and business were about to take on enormous change. She soon received a letter from George, and Donna knew from the context that she had perhaps reeled George in completely by this point. George had typed out the lyrics to the popular song "My Heart Will Go On: Love Theme from *Titanic*," by Celine Dion, and sent them along with a few closing remarks, calling his new flame "Dear Love," "Dear Friend," "Confidant," and "so Much More." He signed the note: *George, the One who Loves and Adores you so much!*

As her father spent more time in Florida, Emily sensed he was stepping out. It wasn't just the mustache George had grown; it was his attitude, too.

"He seemed upset with my mom."

All the time.

Whatever Gail did.

Nothing was good enough.

According to Emily's recollections, whenever George was mad at Gail, or snappy with the kids, or especially when he retreated off by himself, something beyond the household was taking up space in his heart and in his mind. It was almost, Emily noted, as if her father was punishing the family for his lack of control when it came to his sins, especially lust.

Gail would never visit George in Florida—likely because George told her not to go there. Gail also was not interested in seeing in person what she undoubtedly knew in her gut. The other factor was that the kids were still in high school when George started dividing his time between Michigan and Florida. Gail felt her place was at home, caring for the kids.

"We had no family in the area," Emily remembered.

Everyone was in Texas or Virginia. "My mom was paranoid that something might happen to us."

Gail was devoted to—and loved—her children. She was never going to leave them alone and chase her husband around Florida. This was another aspect of this woman, one could argue, that George took great advantage of with his conduct.

George changed, Emily noticed. One telltale sign to Emily beyond her father growing facial hair was that he got angry with the kids and Gail for no apparent reason. He might get excited and gesture, *I'm going into my cave—leave me alone!* It was George's way of responding to shutting out everyone around him. He wouldn't talk. He wouldn't answer questions. The mustache, Emily was convinced, was her father's way of disguising who he was, or becoming, effectively, someone else.

It didn't take much to get George upset, Emily explained. "And the mustache? Oh, my . . . it's a sign that my dad is trying to change who he is. Trying to mask who [he] is by growing facial hair."

During Emily's senior year (1998), as George and Donna's affair became hot, George moved to Florida in a more permanent fashion. Not completely. But he was going down and staying for a while to get his new business—that dream he'd always had—up and running smoothly. He told the family it was "because of the job working with Donna."

Emily felt blindsided. She had not been getting enough sleep because of schoolwork, sports, and being a member of the student council. She depended on her father to drop her off at school early every morning so she could get in extra calculus study. But there was one morning as they drove to school when George, looking down at the floorboard, then up into his daughter's eyes, said, "Shorty"—

his pet name for Emily—"your mom is really going to need you while I'm gone."

George had always supported the family financially. If he wasn't there, he sent money.

"But he had checked out emotionally by then," Emily recalled, "and probably before that."

That day of the car ride, "I knew," Emily said, "my dad was essentially leaving us for someone else." George couched it as "the job" taking him away. But Emily felt the weight of what he had said and, particularly, *how* he had said it. What a blow. In not as many words, George said he was leaving and not coming back.

Emily felt her father was saying good-bye.

George was never honest with Gail, as far as admitting the affair, Emily thought. But that choke hold he had just put on her heart—that he was leaving the family (a wife of over two decades and two kids still in school) for another woman—was devastating. Everything this guy did, the decisions he made that would affect his family—be it moving north, quitting a job, starting a business, buying a $100 necktie—came like a shot in the dark, sucker punching everyone. And now, after all they had been through, after moving everyone north, away from family, here he was saying *he* was leaving.

Emily thought: *Who is this person? What does* she *have that Mom doesn't?*

"She's really gonna need you, Shorty. You understand me?"

Emily looked at him. *What is this—good-bye?*

"You need to step up," George continued. "Be there for your mother."

It was times like these when Emily felt an overwhelming black cloud hovering (even smothering) her father.

"I could see auras at the time," Emily recalled, "and I

would literally see black around my dad. I can always feel when people aren't right, but sometimes I can *see* it, too."

As Emily closed the car door and watched her father drive away, it was almost as if he had disappeared, like he had been swallowed up by that black cloud.

27

EMILY FULTON NEEDED answers. She had a feeling what her father was up to. In retrospect, she said, it was no secret what her dad was doing, nor whom he was doing it with. At times Emily played the arbitrator between her mother and father, trying to be the bond that held the marriage together.

"My mom told me stuff. My dad told me stuff," Emily said. "I was right in the middle." This was happening at a time when she was finishing high school and thinking about college. Gail protected Andrew, Emily said. And, as Emily thought about it later, being the person that her mom and dad could go to was "a role I took on myself."

Gail had an interesting upbringing. She was the first grandchild born on both the Garza and Salinas side of her extended families.

"I remember my grandma telling me that Grandma Garza (my grandmother's mother-in-law or my mom's grandma on her dad's side) was a very stern woman who did not smile much, but when she saw her first grandchild (my mom), she became a totally different person. She took my mom and unwrapped her from the blanket she was swaddled in . . . and proceeded to kiss each of my mom's little fingers and each of her little toes. My grandma said it was such a loving and tender gesture, and this made her view her mother-in-law in a whole new light. She said Grandma Garza was so grateful she gave her a grandchild and that my mom was treasured. . . ."

Gail's mother described her as the "perfect" child. What she meant was that Gail never gave her parents any problems; Gail learned to do things on her own from an early age, which made her self-sufficient—a trait, albeit good or bad, she had passed on to her youngest daughter.

Donna called the house when George wasn't in Florida. She knew when there were problems in the Fulton household. How? "Because," Emily said, "my dad told Donna *everything*." So, being the consummate control freak and manipulator she was, Donna did her best to take advantage of the situation.

Gail was always on Emily, but it came from a place of love and concern, Emily felt. Gail wanted to make certain Emily wasn't overextending herself with school, work, and all the extracurricular activities Emily was involved in. Emily grew up with a drive to be the best at whatever she put her mind toward. She knew that in order to get into a decent college under a scholarship, she'd have to work harder than her peers. Emily felt George was not going to help her. She embraced this work ethic, however, knowing that, in life, you worked hard for what you wanted and earning it built character and nobility.

One of the criticisms Emily commonly heard from her mother was about her weight. "You weigh too much, Emily," Gail would say. However, it wasn't said in a derogatory fashion, or with an air of a stage mom sizing up her daughter in a negative manner. Gail didn't understand that Emily was an athlete who had developed muscle and bulk in order to compete. "My mom was obsessed with weight and being in shape." She didn't want her daughter to be unhealthy and develop bad habits she'd carry into adulthood, so Gail spoke up.

"Mom, it's not about weight," Emily said. "It's about how you look!"

They agreed to disagree.

George was on the periphery of these conversations, but he would relate them to Donna—likely, Emily was certain, with a negative connotation toward Gail. Emily was a smart girl. When Donna called the house and tried to influence the situation to her advantage (as she squirmed her way into the lives of not only George, but his children), Emily wasn't going for it.

"Hi, Emily," Donna said once, calling the house out of the blue.

"Yeah? . . ."

"How are things going?" Donna was always trying to get in "good" with Emily. She knew a large part of George was tied to his kids. If she could win them over (especially Emily), she'd be that much closer to taking Gail's place.

"My dad's not here, Donna."

"How are things going between you and your mother?"

Emily rolled her eyes. "Is there anything I can do to help you?"

Emily understood Donna was her father's boss and signed his paychecks. So there was always a bit of putting up with whatever nonsense Donna instigated. For example, during spring break one year, Emily wanted to go somewhere hot and sandy—take a bona fide vacation and forget about her studies for a week. She told her mother she deserved the trip.

"It's too dangerous," Gail responded. "It's not a good idea."

George must have overheard and had told Donna that Gail had denied Emily. The next time Donna called the house, she said to Emily: "Look, why don't you come down here to Florida for spring break. I have a house on the beach. . . . You can stay with me."

Emily was appalled by the invitation.

"I won't judge you," Donna continued, "like your mother does."

Why is my dad's boss doing this?

The conversations Emily had with Donna during 1998 added up: Emily realized there was more to her father's relationship with Donna than employee and employer. She observed the mustache, the acting out on her father's part, the snide remarks at home, and the *anger.*

Why is this woman *trying to be my friend?*

"Listen, Donna," Emily said, "you cannot try to manipulate *me.* This is what you're doing. Yes, my mom and I are having some issues. Every daughter and mother go through that. But don't you try and use that. . . ."

Emily lived in a constant state of optimism. She knew her mother was the perfect sense of balance in her life. Gail had a way of keeping Emily grounded. People need guides in their lives, not to mention stability. Some saw Gail's parenting as harsh and negative, brought on by her years of living with George. Others viewed Gail as overbearing. But Emily learned to embrace this aspect of her mother as the right amount of stability she needed in order to fulfill all her dreams. Her mother was her guide. Her biggest supporter. Her friend.

Emily spent many nights not long after the Fultons arrived in Michigan (during her junior year) crying for reasons she didn't understand. But as Donna tried to manipulate her, and Emily put things together between her father and Donna—along with her mother being so deeply troubled and walking around in a state of depression—the way of their lives began to make perfect sense.

Friends at school would ask Emily if she was okay. She'd

brush it off. "Sure, I'm fine." She needed to maintain a façade among her peers, she said. Emily didn't want any interference in her studies or sports/extracurricular activities. She needed to focus.

Emily put up a great disguise, emotionally. Her pain came out, however, when she got home and it was just Emily and her best friend, Jamie: tears, worry, panic. And this is where the selfishness of adultery (when children are involved) comes into play—the price the kids pay for the extramarital behavior that those involved often don't think about. Children are often—if not always—the forgotten component of adultery. Sure, you can argue that George and Gail's children were grown; but they were not yet adults, or emotionally adjusted enough to deal with the stressors of a marriage falling apart, an absent father (in more ways than one), and a mother trying to cope with a marriage falling apart before her eyes and no one there with whom to share the pain. The hurt Gail experienced was something she was forced, in a sense, to internalize.

"What if one day my mom wasn't around to keep my balance," Emily told Jamie one night after Emily felt she had figured out her dad. It was one of Emily's biggest fears—that her mother would be gone. Not necessarily murdered, but taken away. "What happens if my mom is not here?"

"I recognized the role my mother played in my life," Emily said.

As the affair became more obvious around the house—however unspoken—and Emily drifted through her final years of high school, she wondered what type of end was near. There was a period for Emily when she believed she was going to die, or be killed herself. That feeling likely stemmed from the quiet chaos building in the house; that subtle hint of everyone walking on glass, not speaking, that a storm was gathering. George and Gail were no more than roommates. Gail was losing weight. For a kid this sort of subtle dysfunction can be devastating—and Emily was feeling the effects of it burdening her.

"I don't know what it is," Emily told her mentor one night, a school counselor Emily looked up to and met with regularly, "but I feel that it's coming." She was referring to something dark, something final, something lethal. Emily had a sense of an end. "Something is going to happen," she continued, "and I'll be dead by the time I'm nineteen."

That dark cloud had now consumed George's daughter.

Emily said she witnessed "how my father was always more domineering and controlling over my mother—it's part of the Latino culture. It's very common in a lot of Latino families." Emily talked about it with her mentor/counselor, a Latina, who explained that she had counseled a lot of Latina women who had been abused—verbally and physically—and felt controlled by their husbands.

"Sometimes," Emily observed, "they [Latina women] don't realize there are other options for them. Most don't have an education, financial independence, and many don't have anywhere else to go. My mother gave up her career [as a speech therapist] to be a stay-at-home mom."

Emily learned from the situation; she was not going to be dependent on any man for her future. She was determined to take care of herself. She might have felt death knocking on the Fulton door, but she was not going to allow that feeling to saddle her ambitions.

"It's one of those hidden secrets," she said, "that in the U.S. we are so concerned about the rights of other women and people around the world . . . what people fail to understand is that it's a *domestic* issue, too, and we *all* need to be aware of it."

28

H IS MARRIAGE to Gail, Donna wrote to George, was "not real anymore." In two years, Donna explained, your kids will be grown and starting their own lives. What would George have left in Michigan after that? Donna wondered.

Gail?

It's clear from this letter that George sent Donna mixed messages of devotion, giving strong indications that he was willing to walk out on his family, but under certain conditions only. It wasn't going to be as easy as Donna had made it sound.

Truthfully, George was on the fence. Sure, running around Florida with Donna while he was in town was fun. Having sex and pillow talk about the future was exciting and daring and mysterious. But was it real? Was this what George Fulton wanted for his future? Was the guy actually in love?

Donna pleaded with her lover, once she got a sense he was playing both sides against each other. She laid everything out: Gail had not worked in a long time. The library, yes. But not at a full-time job where she could take care of herself. Donna warned George that he had better "position" himself in the right company—hers, of course—*now,* so he could provide for Gail *after* he left and "until she's remarried." Apparently, Donna had thought this thing through all the way to Gail's future husband.

It was clear to Donna that George had not expressed what he wanted from her or her company. She promised George he could easily make 50K per year and that it would likely be enough money for him to take care of Gail until she could find another man. Donna said she "wished" George all the success he deserved, wanted to be a part of it, but she didn't know exactly if he thought she ever would be. She wished they had met sooner in life so they "could have more time together."

The tone of the letter focused on Donna "missing" George when he went back home. Donna told George— something she never considered would give him a considerable amount of power and control over *her*—that while he was back home and missing her, as she would him, all he had to do was pick up the phone and call. She would fly into Lake Orion for a day or two. *You could tell me where,* she wrote, meaning another city, *so we could be "safe."* She would not expect George to spend the night with her at the hotel. He was free to leave after sex.

George could have both women in the same day if he wanted. This must have done tremendous amounts for his ego. Yet, George must have become worried about losing Donna, because he turned around not long after receiving this letter and sent Donna a card she referenced in a second long, tedious letter, full of schoolgirl grandeur she had been spewing on her married lover for the past few months.

29

DONNA WAS NOT a stupid woman. Some later said she could have turned CCHH into a multimillion-dollar corporation if she just allowed others to help her run it and, most important, kept her damn mouth shut. But Donna was about control, manipulation, revenge, and selfish pride. People didn't cross Donna; she would get them back—maybe when they least expected. What many around the office realized after George came into the picture was that Donna had changed: her attitude, the way she acted, dressed, spoke. Everything was different—except her bipolar mood swings and angry approach to running her business.

"She started confiding in George about her business," said a former employee. Donna leaned on George, asking him to help her make major decisions. At the time, the work colleague said, "I liked George a lot. We knew he was married, but we thought that he and his wife were separated."

When George wasn't around, Donna talked about him as though he was the "be all and end all," not only for the business, but for life. In a short time she had become infatuated (obsessed!) with George. She had developed a dangerous and soon-to-be-lethal concoction of possessive love, a fanatical sexual desire, and a skewed outlet on life in general—all of this was based around what this man said and did.

"She loved him . . . said he was so wonderful and this perfect man," said a coworker. "But she . . . became *obsessed* with him. We could never, ever understand, for example, what he saw in *her*. She wasn't all that!"

This preoccupation Donna had with George became apparent as the 1997 holiday season wound down and she wondered where she and George stood. Near the end of the year, Donna wrote to George, explaining how she needed him to consider several of her ideas as "food for thought." She mentioned how she had been "considering lots of options" because she was a firm believer in the notion that things happened for a reason. She thought their relationship was a "positive thing." When they were together, she felt it was "very magical" and "right." George could do no wrong in Donna's eyes. Whatever he did (and she compulsively analyzed the guy's behavior) was something she weighed considerably against the grain of his love for her.

The way he ate, walked, looked at her.

All perfect.

As the letter continued, Donna said she needed to be honest. She felt he was not "very happy" in his life. Of course, this was a slap to Gail. She said Gail wasn't treating George in the manner that he should be. She called George a "very gentle, wonderful man," who deserved someone who could make him feel "important, needed, loved, wanted, respected." The woman he had stayed married to for twenty-three years wasn't giving him that.

It was the beginning of Donna pointing at Gail and saying two things: First, you do not deserve this man. Second, stay out of my way—he's mine.

This letter was Donna's innermost thoughts. She wanted George to think about their relationship in a different way while he was back at home. Figure what he had with her, what he had with Gail, and weigh the two.

Maybe make a damn choice.

During that break George had a lot of time to consider all that Donna offered: a home, job, bed partner, good money, a business maybe to acquire and co-own someday.

George sent Donna a card on January 6, 1998, addressing it to "my love." He wished Donna a "happy belated New Year." It was nice, he said, to hear her voice the other day. It had "seemed so long ago" that he was in Florida. (The last time George had been with Donna was a week prior.) He talked about a tape Donna had sent him. He had listened to it that morning as he took his daily walk around the neighborhood. There were lyrics that had moved him to tears. It had even made him think about those times with Donna and the "passion" he felt for her and their "lovemaking."

He signed the brief letter: *The One Who Loves You Very Much.*

This short letter brought Donna to tears, she wrote in return. It was the first time Donna felt as though she had roped herself a bull. George wasn't all hers—yet—but Donna knew this was the beginning. The more time they spent together, the deeper they felt about each other. She said she read his words "over and over." She held the letter in her hands "so often and close to [her] chest." She cried and cried "like a baby sometimes." She went on about how she had not felt the feelings George was bringing up in so long that she had wondered if they existed anymore. She had been crying so much because she'd had no idea before then how George "really" felt about her. She suspected George was falling, but he had never articulated those feelings into words on a page—until now.

Then, near the end of the letter, Donna mentioned Gail, who was becoming the focal point of her anger. She was the one person standing in the way of her happiness. Donna said it "hurt" her to think George was "spoken for." When she sat and thought about George "touching [Gail], kissing her," having his arms around her, "making love to her, caressing her, smiling with her," and "having fun" with Gail, it was enough to make Donna's suffering the worst she had ever experienced. She said every time George reminded her of the fact that Gail and the kids had "claims" to him first, she felt nothing but "pain" and "fear." She wrote: *[There is a] heaviness in my chest, a lump in my throat. . . . I am just second.*

Donna closed the letter saying she had "hope" that someday she would become first in George's life: *[That thought alone] has made me to feel a little more secure.*

30

"HE TOOK HER away from all of us," said a good friend of Gail's from Texas. As Gail Fulton experienced real problems within her marriage (not the first time), she had no one—save for phone calls—to stand behind her and say, "You can get through this. We'll help you. You do not need to put up with it."

It did not surprise any of Gail's friends that once she got settled in Michigan, Gail fell into a job at the local library. One of Gail's outlets to get away from life's problems was reading.

"I was jealous," said a childhood friend, "that Gail had all of the—I mean *every* single one of them—Nancy Drew books. She adored those cozy mysteries. She read voraciously. She loved romances. Gothic-type stories. History. It more surprised me that she went to school for speech pathology. . . . She should have gone into library science."

Gail was private to a point where she'd only unload real pain on her priest. When her friend from Texas called, it always went: "Gail, how are you?"

"Fine. . . ."

"Really, *how* are things going?"

"Fine. . . . Fine."

Gail's favorite topic was her children. Her friend didn't

mind, but she could always tell when something was eating Gail up inside.

"It was a strange thing," said that same childhood friend. "When I was going through problems with my first husband and he asked me for a divorce, it was Gail's father who got on the phone and told me exactly, step by step, how to *not* lose custody of my children, to keep myself safe. . . . They (Gail and her parents) took care of me. They called me every fifteen minutes at times to make sure I was okay."

Now here it was, an opportunity for that friend to return the favor. Gail's father was passed on, and she didn't want to talk about divorce or child custody issues. She wanted to think—wanted to *believe*—that her marriage was salvageable. By 1998, she and George had been married for nearly twenty-five years. She didn't want to give up.

According to a close friend, George had always been "dedicated to his mother. He was the star child. He was always the responsible one. He would always send his mother money. You look at him then and you think, 'Wow, this guy's good to his mom . . . brothers and sisters.'"

What a catch!

There was one time, shortly after being married, when George and Gail were stationed in Germany. An incident occurred there. Gail called a friend to explain, but again, Gail was mysterious about what was going on, whitewashing the situation.

"There was an inventory and it didn't match up," Gail said. George was responsible for the military building. "We have to pay it all back."

Afterward, according to what Gail told her friend, the military took money out of George's paycheck to recoup the loss. This saddled an already-struggling young family even further. Gail could stretch a dollar, but not as far as this situation seemed to be headed for.

"Yeah, George was so naïve," Gail said. "He didn't know that he should have gotten an inventory before he took over command of the building. Now all these things are missing. It wasn't him, no way. But now we have to pay it all back."

Soon after this, George was stationed in Panama. Gail went down to live with him, but then she returned home, without warning, not long after.

When her friend saw Gail that first day back in town, she could not believe her eyes. "She was so painfully thin and she had these incredible headaches."

Gail's friend wondered what was going on.

"Oh, nothing," Gail said, brushing it off. "It's just this and that. . . ."

Gail's hair was falling out. She had black circles under her eyes, on top of bags. Her cheekbones were drawn in and pointed. She looked skeletal and depressed, curling into herself.

"She knew what was going on with George . . . ," said that same friend, "and she internalized it."

And eventually just let it go.

Forgive, forget, pray.

31

ON **JANUARY 21, 1998,** George sent Donna a card that had to make her year, even though it was only twenty-one days old. She must have known she had indeed roped herself a cowboy and had him now tied to the stable, there to do what she wanted with him.

Dearest Donna, he began. On the inside cover was the drawing of a caveman holding a club, a bubble caption reading, *Who, me?* The card inscription read: *Now, there are still men, not a lot has changed.* George had written a cute little message in parentheses by the bubble caption, *George (OTJ??).* This was a recurring joke: George of the Jungle. The idea was that George had been so manly, so aggressive and savage in bed, keen on doing "wild" things underneath the sheets, Donna referred to him as "G.O.T.J."

George sent the card to say how thoughtful it was Donna had sent him all the "recent heartfelt e-mails." He appreciated it. On the way over to a client's office, George explained, he listened to the Celine Dion tape and thought how great it was that Donna had gone to the trouble of sending it to Michigan: *You are going to spoil me!*

Donna responded by sending George a card, pointing out, *You have made my life complete,* and other wishy-washy things new lovers say while, blinded by lust, in a euphoric state of courtship.

George's response: *I'm just waiting for my chance to snuggle up close to you. . . .* Inside, a male mouse was pictured with open arms, heading at a female mouse. George said how "fortunate and blessed" he felt to have Donna. His writing was scribbled and hard to read at times, but the gist of it all explained how "trapped" he felt at home without being able to hold his true love in his arms and make love to her at will: *It feels like we have lived a lifetime. . . . I will always be there for you, Donna. . . .*

This sort of horny, "Dearest Donna," you rock my world, I cannot live without you, you're the greatest thing since sliced bread, went on all month; Donna and George were exchanging card after card, letter after letter, e-mail after e-mail, fax after fax. Little of it had to do with work.

George wrote the same sentiments—almost word for word—in each card, and Donna lapped it up as if Shakespeare was the man's muse. At times George would e-mail Donna sexually charged jokes he had heard.

Part of the fascination and obsession between them was augmented by their distance. The fact that they couldn't be together all the time seemed to inspire the desire they shared for the next scheduled rendezvous. There was always a buildup to the next tryst—always a boiling period where they anticipated it, and allowed time to be a catalyst to what they presumed to be genuine love.

As February came, George said he enjoyed "opening up" and being able "for the first time" to share his "innermost thoughts and feelings" with someone he loved.

They celebrated ninety days together with a spate of e-mails, recalling in each how much they missed each other, ending or beginning the e-mails with juvenile sentimentalities of a haughty, embarrassing tone: I get so scared that I am going to wake up and find it was a dream,

Donna wrote once. To her, it was a "fairy tale" she never wanted to end.

Within her letters and e-mails, Donna dropped subtle hints about Gail and how she viewed Gail as a third wheel in all of this. Donna herself was in the process of divorcing her husband. She couldn't understand if George had felt the way he said, why he could not do the same. Though she rarely—if ever—challenged George on this point, she said she knew it was a "very difficult" decision for him to make. She was clear George had shared with her how much he "did not want to hurt" Gail, but, on the other hand, it was becoming "very hard" to deal with it for Donna. She said how easier things were, once she had officially separated from her husband. Donna knew it would be the same for George. The fear was in doing it, not the aftermath.

George answered that e-mail by sending Donna a link to an article referencing how important it was for males of his age to have sex, which spoke to how this man dealt with serious issues. To George, his mind was on his needs, both sexual and emotional. He did not care to discuss separating from Gail. He made it clear that Donna needed to focus on their relationship and forget about the decisions he needed to make.

Donna responded with a rant about how the body responds to good sex, both female and male, and how, as a nurse, she had been trained in this sort of behavioral science. She said it was a good thing she never grew "tired" of "making love" in the "morning, midday, evening, night, or whatever." She wrote back in her e-mail: I just can't get enough of you.

George sent Donna a card full of sexual references, letting her know once more that she was all he ever thought about and couldn't wait to get back to Florida and do all the things he had talked about with her over the phone.

[George] Clooney has absolutely nothing *on you,* Donna wrote. She continued, saying how much more "sexy, exciting, and good-looking," and how much of a "better butt" George had than the Hollywood actor.

The cards George sent hit Donna hard and heavy; she fell deeply for the man behind those funny and "cute" sayings. The cards told Donna, she admitted later, just how much George cared about her and how their relationship was now much more than an affair.

What's strange about this correspondence—and maybe it offers some insight into the fate of Donna's business— was how very little actual business was discussed. Donna went on and on for pages about how great it was to be in love, how wonderful a man George was, how "fine" and "sexy" parts of his anatomy were. Then, at the end, maybe a sentence or two, she'd casually mention work: *Oh yeah, and what about those accounts? Have you gotten to them yet?*

CCHH became an afterthought.

By the end of February, George was planning a Florida trip. They were anticipating this visit with as much energy as a soldier returning home from a tour of duty.

On February 25, 1998, George said some rather interesting things to Donna after she e-mailed and asked if something was wrong. She had sensed coldness on his part in a few recent exchanges. George wasn't being his old self.

When one looks at the relationship over its course, one can see that, whenever George was back home and knew there would be a considerable amount of time between his visits to Donna, he poured on the sincerity, romance and charm. As the time grew closer to his visiting her, he began to pull back, becoming taciturn and withdrawn. This was, one can assume, a tactic, done subliminally or consciously. George had always wanted to keep Donna at bay, never making any promises he couldn't deliver. After all, George was getting the best of both worlds: Gail and his family in one state, a mistress in another. In this letter where Donna felt a cold chill, George had told her when his flight would arrive that Thursday. He warned Donna not to think that what he had to say was "bad news." It isn't, he wrote. He said he felt "the same about you and us." He didn't want Donna to "jump to any conclusions," adding how she and Gail were both "very perceptive and feeling women. What a pair!"

Then, with nerve, he concluded that he had the "utmost respect" for the both of them.

Here was a guy cheating on his ultra-conservative Catholic wife of a quarter century, playing his mistress for as much good times as he could get, then turning around and telling Donna how much he respected his wife!

The visit went off as expected: They frolicked and worked and had sex and went out to expensive dinners and acted like a couple. Afterward, George returned home and Donna went back to sending him e-mails, faxes, letters, and cards. In one letter she talked about a woman she knew who, she thought, had made a pass at her. This same woman had once "mooned" the Mayor of DeFuniak, Donna wrote. Donna had been doing some work for the woman, but she had since lost the job. She was trying to "win" her back, but she wasn't getting anywhere. Since the woman had made the pass, Donna explained, she stopped going to see her. *Sybil does say she is both ways,* Donna wrote about the supposedly bisexual woman. There was also some question whether the woman was defrauding the hospital she worked for.

Two days later, George sent Donna several love quotes. As quick as George talked about how much he missed

Donna and enjoyed the time they'd had together, he said how he and Gail and Andrew had gone out to run some errands.

After answering several questions that Donna had posed, George said he in no way wanted Donna to "go under" for "cosmetic reasons." (Donna was planning on getting plastic surgery.)

He ended the letter by saying he was thinking about a lot of things and couldn't wait to hear Donna's voice when they spoke next, concluding, *See you before you know it.*

This banter between them, with short visits here and there, went on throughout the spring. George had not fully committed to working for Donna on a full-time basis. He had been subcontracting certain jobs. Furthermore, Donna began to put more pressure on George regarding his having it both ways. George wrote that he was pissed off because Donna had broken down and called his home number, not the business line downstairs. She said she was sorry, but she could not handle it anymore. The fact that she had to "share" George, as she put it, was too much. She pleaded with him, saying he had no idea how it felt because he did not have to share her with another man: *You belong to someone else. . . . It hurts so much. . . .* Donna said she went through periods where she was forced to walk around feeling like a "knife cutting my heart." She would talk herself out of a rage by repeating, "Perhaps it won't be long and you will be . . . mine."

What upset Donna most was when George talked about Gail. He had a way of bringing up Gail as though she was part of their relationship. Donna despised Gail because of this. It was clear to Donna that Gail was the one who stood in their way of being together forever. George framed it to sound as if it was difficult for him to leave Gail. He could not just walk away.

Donna acknowledged that Gail had a "great hold" on George. She added that he was "having doubts" and really did not "want it to be over" with his wife.

The guy was sending mixed messages, according to Donna: *You said you "guess" you could stay with her. . . .*

According to Donna, George said that he did not want to "make her mad or hurt her."

Donna was getting "mixed signals" and felt very confused. She reprimanded George, telling him that he could not love two women equally. It was impossible. She added, *I guess I really don't know where I fit into your life. . . .*

George told Donna that divorce was going to be tough because he would not know how to explain it to his brothers and sisters. He would be letting them down, as well as his kids, and he could never be with another woman in front of his family.

"Even though I take off my ring," George once told Donna, "I still feel married."

In no uncertain terms Donna was telling George that she was tired of being the "other" woman. Even when in Florida, George was forever looking over his shoulder, wondering if they'd run into someone he and Gail knew. They hardly ever went out together any longer.

Donna demanded a time frame. She needed to know where they stood as a couple, and what George saw for the future. She was sick of crying all the time and wondering. Her stomach was in knots. She could never call George when she wanted. She could never see him when she wanted. She could never plan on anything because she didn't know what the future held. One night she'd be "crying tears of joy" at something he had said and the next she'd be "crying tears of sadness."

Now George needed to make a decision.

32

THAT LAST LETTER stirred George up. He realized he could no longer play both sides. He tried pacifying Donna by writing her another one of his "my love" letters. A little ditty ladled with love quotes he had copied and pasted from the Internet. He tried calming Donna with saccharine thoughts of "relax, my love," it will all work out, just give him more time. "Yes, it is difficult" and how he felt he had lost her.

Donna wasn't falling for it. She didn't want anything to do with the spin George put on their lives. She didn't want that pep talk he was so good at giving. She didn't want broken promises, which he had parlayed in the past into another round with her in bed.

Firing back, she asked George if he had even read his previous e-mail. She said he had not come close to answering *any* of her questions. He had ignored her, saying he would talk to her about it all in person someday.

Donna begged for some "kind of answer." She was not eating, not sleeping, and could not concentrate at work. She demanded to know where she "fit" into the plan. She asked George how he felt about Gail and if he was "being honest with her." Had she been right in saying George decided not to "end things" with Gail?

She wanted to know if he "still loved" Gail and if he still wanted to "be with" Donna.

A day later, Donna was again asking hard questions after not receiving any type of answer from her lover, telling George he had better get his "shit together." She wasn't about to play second fiddle any longer.

The plan was for them to get together in two weeks. But after those disparaging e-mails that Donna had sent, with little or no response from George, she wondered if he was ever coming back. After not hearing from George for a few days, Donna sent George a letter on April 6, 1998, opening it with that typical crass chat-room type of cheesy dialogue that is standard in these situations. She called him "lover boy." She said he needed to be in Florida "tending to business" and that his "sugar mama needs some tending to." She said she was "extremely horny," and she was in need of "caressing, loving, and kissing" all over her body. She wanted "great pleasure," which only George could deliver. She asked how his "sex life" had been while back home, warning that even if he "had it once," it was "one more" than she had. Then she took a guess, saying George had had sex with Gail three to four times, demanding to know how close she was—all those "hand jobs" in between aside.

Donna then said she could not wait until he moved to Florida—so George must have promised what she wanted to hear. Then she "hoped" he was "excited about it," concluding how "sorry" she was for the tiff they had gotten into the week before.

The next day George sent Donna a long, single-spaced letter—awkwardly and oddly written out like a business plan—detailing those "answers" she had been seeking. In numbered paragraphs George outlined where the relationship was headed, from his point of view, further telling Donna what she wanted to hear. The future had not changed. The "mixed signals" he had been sending were just emotions churning inside him. George was confused about some things, but it had nothing to do with loving Donna and being with her forever. The confusion was in dealing with the demise of the marriage and how to proceed with its dissolution.

He asked Donna if she could bear with him for an additional few months, because he needed to find the "right time to set" the end "in motion." He warned that he did not have everything planned out. If he were able to see into a crystal ball, he would include hitting the lottery. He asked Donna to "calm down" and try to understand the predicament he was in with Gail. It wasn't easy walking away from all those years—and kids. Such drastic change couldn't happen overnight. But he wrote, *I want out of the marriage. . . .*

Donna was bowled over by the letter. She was ecstatic. He was clear about his feelings: They had a future. Together.

They were scheduled to meet in a week, and Donna's e-mails and letters heading toward that period were full of schoolgirl lust and teenage nonsense, with which she had spoiled George.

George had Donna back where he wanted. Yet he knew that unless he made some sort of a move, Donna would go back to her old self.

By the time George returned from his most recent trip, he had decided to accept a full-time position within CCHH as its CFO. The first e-mail George sent to Donna after arriving home said it all—not so much in what George included, but rather in what he had not. First he applauded Donna for being a "good person." He said he was "very fortunate" to know her and have her in his "life at the moment." He said he "looked forward" to "working" with everyone at CCHH. At the end of the e-mail, George said he would "beep" Donna after he got things "settled down at home" with Andrew and Emily. Gail was out of the picture now, completely. He was not going to mention her anymore. When George spoke of being home, he meant with his kids.

It was near the middle of May. From his Michigan home George wrote: **Be with you before you know it.** Then he asked Donna where she was staying: **The Comfort Inn, right?** He wanted an address to make sure he went to the right one.

They had a plan.

Donna came up from Florida to meet George and pick up his things. He was finally moving to Florida and into Donna's home.

33

EMILY FULTON KNEW her parents were having problems. She also knew that they were centered on Donna and the affair her father was having. The talk Emily and her father had on that morning George dropped Emily off at school ("Take care of your mother") told Emily he was leaving. She was sure of it. Why would he say such a thing otherwise?

By now, Donna was calling the upstairs home line when she couldn't reach George downstairs.

"Is work *so* important that your *boss* has to call up here all the time?" Gail would ask.

George would shrug it off.

Emily was a senior in high school, just about to graduate. There was no love in the house. At least not the way there used to be. It was always so cold, lonely, and hollow.

"My dad," Emily remarked, "had trouble showing love. A lot of people that are angry like that do not feel worthy. If you don't know how to show love to other people, it means you do not love yourself. . . .I think my dad had self-esteem issues. He came across as cocky and arrogant, but I think it was a front because deep down my dad had feelings of not being worthy."

It brought tears to Emily's eyes; her voice would get

choked up to talk about her father and relate this deeply personal part of her history.

"I know my dad loved me," she said, "but he was not very expressive. . . ."

The situation inside the house became caustic as the month of May closed. Emily and her dad were at odds; Gail and George were not talking; and Andrew had withdrawn into himself, spending time with friends and his girlfriend. They were a family, but they were living separate lives. They passed one another inside the house, but little was ever said beyond the normal stuff that gets a family through their days. According to Emily, the root cause of it all was Donna.

"Donna would call and tell me that she had a hard childhood," Emily remembered. "She told me her father had beat her. I don't know that it's true. But I know that this is one of the ways that she and my dad identified with each other—that they both had these hard childhoods. . . ."

Justifiable adultery—the point of the relationship at which Donna and George could pivot the sneakiness and pain they were causing others. They made a connection through childhood trauma, Emily said. And as she further pointed out, her father's dad had passed when he was young. This had caused a great hurt to grow inside George. Whether Donna was beaten as a kid, who knew? But the fact that the two of them felt this became some sort of bond.

After Gail was murdered, there was one day when George went to the kids, according to Emily's recollection, and said, "You do not know what suffering is—I am the one who knows true suffering."

Emily and Andrew looked at each other: *Is he crazy? What the heck is he talking about?*

With that one statement, Emily felt, her father had invalidated everything Emily and Andrew were going through as they mourned the loss of their mother.

By May 23, 1998, George was living in Florida with Donna. She had made the drive to Michigan in a U-Haul on May 20 to help George pick up his things. George drove the U-Haul trailer over to the house himself that day. Emily and her mother watched him pack.

"What is that? You're packing and leaving us?" Emily asked.

"You have to stay," Gail said.

"No . . . I don't."

George closed the back of the U-Haul. Andrew came out. Gail went back inside, crying. Emily and Andrew stood in the driveway.

"What are you doing?" Emily pleaded. She was bawling.

"Dad, come on," Andrew said. "Let's talk it over."

"Please, please stay," Emily said again and again and again. Then she begged. "Don't leave us, Dad. What can we do? We'll be *better* kids. What can we do to make you stay? What do you need us to do? Whatever it is, we'll do it. Just please, *please* stay here."

As Andrew and Emily looked on, their dad drove off into the Michigan sunset, heading toward Donna, who was waiting for him up the road.

George finally left Gail and the kids. Yet, during this entire time George said he was going south to rent a room in Donna's house so he could get his business started. Some time and distance between him and Gail might help the marriage. It wasn't yet over.

When George arrived in DeFuniak Springs, escorted by

Donna, there was a surprise party waiting for him, staged around Donna welcoming George officially into the company. Most of the guests were Donna's employees.

Emily Fulton gave a graduation speech to her class that spring, just a short while after George moved away. During the ceremony she felt that her father "just didn't want to be there." George had already let go; Emily knew that his heart was somewhere else. "He resented being there. He was so very angry. He had that dark cloud over his head. . . ." It was suspended above, following him around. Emily could not only feel it, but she could once again *see* it.

Emily could not believe that her dad had come all the way up from Florida, and yet he held on to such hatred and anger for being there, as if his daughter's graduation was keeping him from something else. Emily graduated at the top of her class with honors. She won awards. She had an incredible future ahead of her.

"And here is my father, and he's there, and he cannot even *look* at me," she said, "or acknowledge my existence. . . ."

Here I am doing all this, Emily thought. *I want so bad for my dad to be proud of me. I want him to acknowledge that I am a* good *person, that I am worthy, and he couldn't even do* that.

More tears.

"All he could do was slip nasty remarks in here and there."

Gail beamed. Nothing was going to take away from her daughter's special day. She was so proud of Emily. It was a remarkable moment for her to see Emily realize her dreams and begin her adult life. Emily had gone through a terrible time at birth. Doctors didn't really know if she was going to make it. When she had first started to talk, Emily had a speech impediment and teachers wanted to put her in special classes. While George and Gail were in Germany, German doctors wanted to classify Emily as "mentally retarded." They conducted all sorts of bizarre tests on her. Gail was certain there was nothing significantly wrong with her child. Emily was just slow to develop motor skills. It didn't mean she had something medically (or genetically) wrong.

"I remember my mom saying they wanted to put a wheelchair-handicap stamp designation on my school record to show that I was disabled in some way," Emily recalled. "Now, I am not sure if it was my speech alone or maybe it was combined with how I tested on certain standardized tests that drove the school to this conclusion. I have never done well on standardized tests. My sister and brother score in the highest percentiles. . . . My mom was afraid if they labeled me as 'learning disabled' early on, then I would never have a chance, as people would always judge me and try to classify me. So my mom fought to keep me in regular classes and said that since she had a speech therapy background, she would personally work with me if they put me into regular classes. . . . My mom . . . wanted to help me and make me as 'normal' as possible, I imagine."

But here was this same child graduating with honors, heading off to, truthfully, the college of her choice, and Gail could not have been more excited. What's more, it was happening at a time in Gail's life when the walls around her were crumbling.

After a terrible day with George at the graduation, they all went out to dinner.

"And he tries to make it all better by handing me fifty dollars," Emily said.

Despite how she acted and felt, Gail looked horrible.

She had lost a lot of weight, which her petite frame could not afford. She wasn't sleeping. Definitely not eating, as she should have been. And she was not drinking enough water. Like during that period after she and the kids returned from Panama unexpectedly, her eyes were once more sunken and dark and punctuated with sadness, anxiety, and emotional exhaustion. She suffered terrible migraines. It was all, Emily concluded, her father's fault. He could have stopped all of it. Gail was willing to forgive and move on.

"Why is he so angry?" Dora Garza asked Emily the night after graduation. "What is going on? Why would he ruin this day?"

"He's having an affair," Emily said.

It's funny how self-esteem works within a child's developing mind. "It didn't matter what anyone else thought on that day," Emily later said. Everyone was congratulating her, patting her on the back, telling her how great she was and what a wonderful future she had. "But none of it mattered. It did not matter how good I was, because I felt I could not prove to my dad that I was *good enough*."

Emily told Andrew and her grandmother she believed her father was having an affair with Donna, his boss. George was out running errands.

Dora Garza said, "No way. . . . He was an officer in the army. He has too much integrity. He would *never* do that."

"Nope," Andrew said. "Not a chance. Not Dad."

34

NEITHER GEORGE NOR Gail Fulton sat down and told the family, "Look, George is leaving and moving to Florida to go be with Donna." It was one of those slow progressions whereby George allowed everyone to figure it out by themselves, couching his leaving around needing to be closer to his work as the CFO of CCHH. He had always wanted to start his own company. This was going to be George's big chance to branch out. He and Gail were "having problems." Some time away from each other might be just what the marriage needed.

But Emily was not one to take no for an answer. Emily convinced her grandmother "with facts," she said, after laying it all out: the phone calls, the trips to Florida, Donna saying bizarre things to her over the phone, the anger and bitterness between Gail and George, Gail not eating or sleeping. Then there was the fact that George had packed some things and left with Donna! Plus, George had told Emily to take care of her mother. There was a certain finality to that.

Dora still did not want to believe it, so she confronted George.

He denied it.

Dora, however, knew right away he was lying.

Emily said that "a lot of people want to live in denial." It helps them cope with the situation. Not facing the truth is easier. Humans are nonconfrontational beings. People do not like conflict. This alone was one reason the situation got so out of hand inside the Fulton household, Emily felt.

Still, Emily wasn't going to stand for it.

George was gone, living in Florida. He was calling the house to talk to the kids. He was also calling his other daughter in Virginia. The house in Michigan did not have caller ID then. So Emily and Andrew never knew from where he was calling. George had phoned down to Virginia and told his daughter he was calling from home. But Emily's older sister had caller ID and saw the name *Donna Trapani* on the liquid crystal display (LCD) screen.

"Why, if Dad is at home, is his *boss's* name showing up on the caller ID?"

Emily knew, of course, but here was some tangible proof.

Things blew up, Emily explained, after that. No one could deny George was living with Donna.

George was flying back home less and less as June, July, and August came and went. He and Donna, meanwhile, went down to Panama City for a weekend. Then to Orlando for a three-day Medicare seminar—two days of which they spent on the beach and enjoying fine dining. Then it was Mobile, Alabama, for yet another tryst. Back from there, they traveled to Gulfport, Mississippi, and rented a beach condo.

As they grew closer, George noticed things about Donna that he did not like.

"She talked down to employees of restaurants," George later told police, ". . . and did not care how she treated people."

That was Donna all right: Servers were below her, and parking-lot attendants were scummy, uneducated nitwits.

Anyone who did not live up to Donna's standards was no better than the dirt underneath her fingernails.

Throughout that summer George became bored with Donna. Gail's forty-seventh birthday was coming up on September 6, 1998. So he flew back to Michigan and spent some time with the family to celebrate Gail's special day.

Donna was livid. She couldn't let go of Gail. (And neither could George, for that matter.) Donna had her man, but she still wanted—and perhaps by now needed—to take revenge on her rival. On CCHH stationery Donna scribbled some notes for her next conversation (be it a letter or a phone call) with Gail. This short hodgepodge of Donna's thoughts—scratched out as if having a fit of rage, and having no other way to get it out of her mind—was a prelude to something much more sinister and manipulative Donna would soon put into play.

Hate festered inside Donna like a cancer spreading. Anything Gail said or did now ate at Donna. Her notes were numbered, beginning with *1.) prisoner in his own home.* Donna pointed out how Gail "expected" George to call her at all times of the day and night. *This is selfish . . .* , she wrote, *mean + hateful. . .* Donna wanted Gail to know she would never stop George from calling home. She accused Gail of being "very unfair, unfeeling, and cold." She wanted Gail to know that because of this, George felt guilty. *He pays all the bills for the house . . .* , she continued, but George felt that *he could not be his own person in his* own *house!* It was "shameful" and "embarrassing" to George; the guy felt like a "stranger in his own home."

Was George giving Donna the impression he had told his family he had left them and moved in with her? Or was George still playing both sides?

Donna's notes continued. She started underlining words, writing certain phrases out in all CAPS, and using additional exclamation points to make various points. She claimed George didn't want to talk to Gail anymore. She accused Gail of calling her house and spewing "hateful remarks" at the both of them: *He's not the person that did anything wrong. . . .* She wrote, *[George] ran away from you because he was sick of you and your horrible ways!* She wanted Gail to know she had been "killing" George slowly, over a long period of time, and she had never been there for him "like a man needs." She said all Gail wanted was for George to be the "breadwinner," the man who brought home the bacon so she could lounge around and take care of kids all day. Donna insisted Gail's entire focus was to strip away any "happiness" and "peace of mind" George had managed to find with her.

If Donna did say these things to Gail over the phone, or in a long letter, as she had planned, she never recorded Gail's responses. Donna and Gail talked several times on the telephone and it generally ended with Donna and her truck driver's foul mouth spitting venom at Gail.

On October 31, 1998, Donna and George celebrated their one-year anniversary by spending the day and night at Bluewater Bay, a gorgeous marina resort along an inlet of Choctawhatchee Bay. They walked hand in hand along the beach, had cute and colorful drinks with little umbrellas at a seaside bar, and spent the night having some of that nasty sex, which former friends said Donna often bragged about.

A month later, George was in Michigan, carving the turkey, playing the Norman Rockwell role of dad at the Thanksgiving table. As much as Donna wanted to think she had George all to herself, he was still invested in his marriage, making promises to Gail and the kids.

A week later, George was back in Florida, and he and Donna were on a plane to Las Vegas to spend a week partying, gambling, having sex, and acting out that fantasy of being the couple they were telling each other they were.

Arriving back in Florida from the Las Vegas trip, George went to work for a week and then explained to Donna he was heading home for Christmas.

On December 22, 1998, George boarded a plane for Detroit. His return home, however, would be cut short after Donna, stewing back in Florida, came up with a plan to get him back into her bed.

"Donna tried every conceivable method to keep control of George," law enforcement said. "When George denied Donna this control, she resorted to the classic method of guilt."

35

DONNA COULD NOT allow George to spend the holidays with his family. It just wasn't in her to step back and allow the due course of time to dictate how her relationship with George ebbed and flowed. If Donna didn't know by now that George made decisions like a scientific researcher working for the government—slowly and meticulously—she was fooling herself. Bottom line: If the man had been that head over heels, he would have dropped everything, divorced Gail, and married Donna. That whole "he's just not into you" was playing out in front of Donna, but she wasn't getting it. Sure, George could charm his way into convincing Donna that going home for the holidays was his way of letting the family down slowly, and it had to be done in order for him to proceed with a divorce. However, George was at home, documentation later proved, playing Gail, too, trying to do whatever he could to get her to fulfill his voracious sexual appetite.

"You are needed back here in Florida," Donna said one night near the end of December.

George asked what was happening.

"Cut it short, George, the company needs you!" Donna insisted.

George was able to book a flight the following day.

Donna took meticulous notes in a journal, detailing the next few weeks. George's lover was waiting for him at the airport. Anticipating his arrival, Donna was gratified to see the expression on his face when he spotted her: *joy and love when he looked at me.*

When they got back to her place, Donna helped him unpack. At one point George stopped, hugged her tightly, and said, "Everything is going to be okay. I missed you so much."

Donna smiled. "I need to go back to the office for a few hours."

"I'll meet you there around five-thirty."

George sat down. Donna started walking out of the room.

"Hey?" George said.

"Yeah," Donna answered, stopping.

"You are the reason I look forward to coming back."

Donna embraced George and they ended up on the floor, *and he held and cuddled me, rubbed my hair. . . .*

Touching her face lightly, George said, "I missed you *so* much. . . . I thought of you all the time, every day, and longed to see you and hold you."

"I know, honey," Donna responded.

George cried, according to Donna's journal. Then said: *"According to Gail, I am not supposed to feel this way. . . . [She] says I am not supposed to love you, want you, or need you—but I do, Donna. I do."*

Donna tried to speak, but George kissed her. It was at that moment, she wrote, when she *knew where his heart was* and they *laid on the floor holding each other, telling each other how much we loved and missed each other. . . .*

"Gail just doesn't understand how much we mean to each other, Donna," George said. "She doesn't want me to be 'me' anymore."

"What's your biggest reason for not divorcing Gail?" Donna asked.

George thought it through. "You know, I am afraid she'd hurt herself. She'd go off the deep end. On top of that, I don't want the kids to hate me, Donna. Gail tells me they will."

Donna thought: *It's really sad and unfair that he is being blackmailed to stay with that bitch!*

As they sat talking, a fury built inside Donna. Blackmail was the "worst kind of crime," she concluded while listening to George bellyache about the hold Gail had on him.

To me, she wrote, *it's worse than being a prostitute or murderer.*

A blackmailer is a lowly person . . . [with] *no better thoughts than their own wants. . . . Nobody else matters.*

She was mortified and made angrier by the fact that Gail was "forcing" George to stay at home. Donna put the entire onus on Gail. And this was where it became clear how good at playing one against the other George had become. Donna pressured him to make a choice, and George came back to Florida with this sob story of Gail chaining his hands and feet together, using the kids as a means to make him feel guilty. Donna was certain Gail was threatening to commit suicide if he left. This riled her. She felt Gail was lying about the suicide, solely because of the kids. She never thought that maybe George was making it up, even as she observed in her writings that Gail could never justify suicide as a Catholic. Moreover, Donna believed that Gail would "never give him" to her "so easily."

She called Gail "selfish" and a "prison warden" for keeping George contained.

George was able to turn the tears on and off in front of Donna, gaining tremendous amounts of sympathy. Donna bantered on and on, blaming Gail for every personal defect George expressed, on top of depriving him of any "excitement, passion, fulfillment, and enjoyment."

As she wrote through her feelings, Donna turned the rant into a letter addressed to Andrew. She claimed that at the time George married Andrew's mother, George was depressed and a young West Point grad who just "wanted to get married." It could have been anyone, Donna implied. Gail was just, well, there.

He thought she would get better, Donna wrote, *after [you] kids came.*

Poor George. According to what he was telling Donna, he had lived a life of hell with Gail. All twenty-four years of it.

She went on to say that right before Melissa (Andrew and Emily's sister) was born, George wanted to divorce Gail, but he couldn't because of the pregnancy.

(He was so unhappy that he and Gail had two more kids after that! A fact Donna chose to ignore.)

Donna wrote that after Emily came along, *The marriage even became <u>worse</u>.* Gail turned into "only a mother." She had never been a wife, Donna maintained. The only part of Gail's life she "ever cared about" was the kids. Gail was "never, never, never" a wife. George was treated as though "he didn't matter." No one in the household—Donna was certain about this because George had explained it many times—knew "how much pain and hurt" George had had to "endure" for all these years. Gail "deserved every bit" of what she was "now feeling" for the torturous years she had put him through.

She blamed Gail for George's "failure to progress" in the military.

She blamed Gail for "never trying to help" George "succeed" at anything he ever did.

For any "discouragement" George felt in his entire life.

For "harass[ing] him to death," to "give up and do nothing."

For not being able to "better himself."

For never meeting "his needs."

For never being able to talk about certain things he had become "ashamed of" and not been "able to tell anyone" except Donna.

For never allowing George to "have things" his way.

For "trapping" him into having children.

For giving him "no other choice" but to stay with her.

For keeping quiet and accepting "years of heartache."

For stifling "all his dreams."

Donna said Gail had not even had 10 percent near "the pain and hurt" George had endured living under the same roof, calling Gail a "poor, pitiful, selfish mother."

Then Donna said when George needed his children most, *they all turned their backs on him.* It made her wonder, listening to George talk about how bad the kids were and how spiteful they had become (like their mother), how "uncaring and ungrateful" they actually were. She asked Andrew—as she was still focused on him as someone who could talk some sense into the other two kids—if by knowing all of the facts now, George's kids could stand behind him for once and support him through this tough time.

After this, Donna fell into a discussion about God and how Gail had been lying to God, and that "God knows it." She said Gail was "so dependent" and "weak" that it drove George "crazy." This was always the impetus for his "going back" home. She said George had told her he "wished he could die now" so he didn't have to live in all the pain Gail had been putting him through. It was Donna who brought George the "most happiness" he'd ever had, and here was Gail trying to destroy *that.*

She always wins, Donna wrote of Gail, calling her "selfish and self-centered." She pointed out how Gail used her children as pawns against her rival to make all of their lives hell. The "only reason" Gail wanted George was because, when the kids were grown, Gail wouldn't be alone. Gail didn't "care about what" anybody else wanted. It was about *her* needs. In fact, Gail's goal in life at the current time, Donna was convinced, was to make George suffer more than any other human being. If she persisted, Donna warned, all she was going to do was put so much pressure on George that he was going to have a heart attack and die. Why not just let him go?

She wrote to Andrew: *Do you hate your dad so much to want him dead?*

The entire Fulton family, Donna said, "fail to realize" how deep George's love was for her. Something George "never had." She explained how passionate their love was, how emotionally connected they were, how exciting it all was to George. She wrote to Andrew, putting it into a familiar context: *The same way you feel about* your *girlfriend.*

Whenever Donna dropped George off at the airport to send him on his way back to Gail, she said he'd turn before walking through the catwalk "and have tears in his eyes."

One of the most hurtful moments, Donna concluded, was when George took Gail to see the movie *Titanic.* She said George cried through the entire film—not because he was taken in by James Cameron's characters, but because all he thought about was Donna and the love they shared.

Donna ran out of paper while writing, and she finished what was an incredibly disparaging document—written to a kid not yet finished with high school—on several Post-it scraps of paper. The ending to this maddening outburst gave her a certain emotional footing to stand on. Donna warned Andrew that his father loved her, and there was nothing his mother could do to stop it.

Your mom will never be me . . . , Donna wrote.

Finally she observed that Gail could "never give" George what she had, saying how marriage was "built on trust, love, and commitment." She called Gail "insecure" and "hopeless." Donna encouraged Andrew to talk to his mother so that she might "seek professional help" and "move on with her life."

36

GAIL FULTON SHOWED UP for work in tears one day. It was close to the end of December.

"What's wrong, Gail?" one of her colleagues asked. No one could stand to see Gail like this. "Sit down." Gail was about to lose it. She couldn't work anymore.

"Well," Gail said, "I just found out that George is having an affair with his boss in Florida."

Hearing herself say it out loud brought on another round of tears for Gail.

"I'm so sorry, honey."

It was tragic to see such a nice woman suffer so deeply. Gail had been honest with everyone in saying that her marriage was going through a rocky time over the past several months. Many people had suspected George was cheating. Still, something had happened to make Gail announce this affair to her coworkers. George had moved down to Florida, after all, six months prior to Gail having this breakdown at work.

"Her name is Donna," Gail continued. "I truly feel this is it—we're heading for a divorce."

Gail had been optimistic and hopeful there was a chance to salvage the marriage, but she felt different now. Here it was days after Christmas and Gail was staring at the end of a two-decades-plus marriage. The New Year celebration was a week away. What was she going to do?

Gail went about her days as her husband stayed with Donna. She tried to figure out the best way to handle and accept that the marriage was over. Change was not something Gail had experience with. She knew a lot about modifying her life to suit her husband's needs. Moving to Michigan wasn't something Gail had been all that shocked by when it happened. Since they married on June 6, 1975, in Corpus Christi, Gail and George had moved nearly a dozen times. That first year after they were married, George was restationed in Georgia. Then it was on to Boulder, Colorado, Mannheim, Germany, and Kettering, Ohio. Each of their three children was born in a different state or country. They spent time in El Paso, Texas, and Fort Amador, Panama (at an army base), the White Sands Missile Range in New Mexico, and, finally, back to Corpus Christi in 1992. It was shortly after that, with twenty years in the military, when George retired.

Gail had nothing to do with George leaving the army, as Donna had been so certain of in her letter to Andrew (a letter Andrew later said he never received). It's highly unlikely George Fulton, a man who made all the decisions in the Fulton household, would allow Gail to convince him to leave the military.

"Served twenty years on active duty as an infantry officer, an analyst," George later testified. "Retired in 1993. . . ."

"My parents were supposed to stay here for good," Emily said, referring to Corpus Christi. "My dad promised my mom that they would *always* return to their hometown after he retired." That was why the move to Lake Orion when Emily was a junior came as such a shock to everyone back home. They were settled in Corpus Christi, set on living out the remaining years of their lives. Family and friends were all around them there.

"I think my sister mentioned once how she felt abandoned by our family, since we moved [to Michigan] without her and she stayed behind."

Life was not easy for Gail and the kids during those years. That much Donna never really quite grasped. As a child growing up, Emily said, "we did not realize we were Hispanic until my dad retired and we started going to public schools in Corpus."

It was there, Emily recalled, when some students, "wanted to label me as 'Mexican' and put me into a box. We grew up with so many other different people that I just viewed us all as American, despite our various backgrounds. My parents didn't speak Spanish to us, so maybe that is why, but even if they had, I would not have noticed. Many of my friends spoke other languages. And if they were American, I still simply viewed them as that, as I was too innocent, or naïve, and did not understand what ethnicity was."

George grew up speaking Spanish (as a second language), but Gail did not.

"When my mom was raised," Emily said, "it was not good to have an accent as Hispanics. Along with blacks and any minority, they were discriminated against. My grandmother told me that it would make my grandfather so mad how people treated him as stupid or less of a person because he was Hispanic and had an accent. My grandfather was brilliant, my grandmother says, as he could do math in his head. [He] predicted so many things that would happen in the future, and just had a good sense for business and working with people. He started out as a lawyer and then was appointed as the second Hispanic federal judge position in the United States. Because of the discrimination that my grandparents faced, they decided to raise their kids—my mom and her brother—*without* speaking Spanish."

* * *

Gail Fulton pulled herself together. She decided to deal with a husband who had run off on her and the kids. She'd spoken of killing herself. She'd said things weak and submissive, making her attitude about life in general appear worthless. She'd nearly begged her husband to stay—and perhaps that's what he had wanted—to work things out, to go to their priest, ask for forgiveness, and take refuge in the sacraments. Gail believed with the Church in their corner, Jesus directing them, the Fulton family *could* move mountains.

Donna would not give up, however. What made matters worse for Gail was Donna calling the house to harass Gail and make her feel miserable and worthless for forgiving George.

There was some light here for Gail, however, when, after the first of the year, Gail told a friend, "We're trying to work through our problems, and George is trying to get out of the relationship with Donna, but the woman is *obsessed* with him."

Whatever George was telling Gail, she perceived it as though they could move on and repair the marriage. Gail would not have said this if she understood completely, without question (as she had just weeks prior), that the marriage was doomed. She had hope now.

As Donna grew more insecure, sensing Gail wasn't going to roll over and give up George, she amped up her rhetoric and proceeded to degrade Gail anytime she spoke to her on the telephone. Donna didn't care about anyone but herself and her own needs. She was in an entirely different place. The cards and letters she sent George throughout that winter and spring were loaded with the same sort of he's the "love of my life" bombast she had been mind-vomiting all along.

Strangely, reading these sentimentalities, there was no indication George and Donna were having any problems—at least not from Donna's point of view.

Donna's divorce came through and was finalized in February 1999; her piece of the puzzle now in place. As each day passed, she felt more secure about her relationship with George and their future—which could only mean George was telling Donna they were on.

If one looks into George's life back home, a vastly different picture of the relationship emerges. On March 4, for some unknown reason, George and Gail wrote to a Boston, Massachusetts, bank under the subject "Partial Withdrawal Option," demanding $5,000 of their retirement/investment money.

Had George and Gail decided to rekindle the marriage and make amends? Asking for this money appeared to be a step in that direction. And then, a few weeks later, on March 23, 1999, George put in his letter of resignation as CFO of CCHH.

He was quitting.

Reacting to that, Donna Trapani had some big news. Although she did not share it with George immediately, Donna was telling people she was pregnant with his child.

37

GEORGE FULTON LATER said that even before he met Donna, he and Gail were having problems. Yet he framed those problems with a bit of sugary glaze, saying, "Well, we just had—my wife and I had disagreements, but it wasn't anything that I would call 'major,' just an accumulation of things, small things that became. . . . There were things that needed talking about and sorted out."

As George started his own business in 1997—before he met Donna—and traveled to Florida "once a month," he added, for "three or four days" at a clip, he and Gail got used to the idea that their marriage would involve time away from each other. Gail was cool with the three-day and four-day trips, according to George. After he met Donna, George spent more and more time in Florida, extending four-day trips into weeks. Gail assumed it was business keeping him away. When asked later if he had effectively lied to Gail by not telling her the extended trips were because he had met and bedded down another woman, George said: "I didn't tell her. I didn't lie to her. I didn't have to lie because there wasn't anything to lie *about*. It was just not told. There was deception, if you want to classify it as that, but *not* a lie."

He noted that his behavior as an "untruth" wasn't right. "It was incomplete, yes," George corrected.

George's last day with CCHH was April 16, 1999. He agreed to continue processing claims for CCHH, but only from his Michigan home. When he spoke to Donna about this, George said the relationship wasn't over in his mind. Yes, he had made a decision to work things out with Gail. However, he was still struggling to cope with having made the right choice. In fact, there was still a chance for them, he said.

For a while Donna didn't react one way or another—besides, that is, the standard "Why, why, why?" She didn't—at least not then—call the house and threaten Gail and call George and spew every foul-mouthed name in the book. (She was doing this behind his back in Florida to coworkers.) Donna seemed to accept defeat.

But then George went out to his post office box (POB) one afternoon in late April—and everything changed.

Donna Trapani is pregnant . . . , the letter said.

George's eyes bulged. His jaw dropped to the ground, one could assume.

No way . . . how could this be?

Then another surprise: *Donna has terminal cancer,* the missive continued.

It wasn't written by Donna, but rather by a doctor. Donna must have known that a simple letter from her might have sounded desperate and contrived, but this important information coming from her own doctor—a man George knew—was an entirely different matter.

Walking away from his POB, George looked at the envelope, which was definitely Donna's handwriting.

George had a trip coming up to Las Cruces, New Mexico, something connected to a defense contract he was trying to nail down. Donna knew about it, but George did not in any way want her to go with him. He needed some time to think through the situation and figure out what to do. The stakes had changed. Now that Donna was carrying his child, it was no mere simple decision of choosing marriage over mistress.

"It was a moral dilemma, what to do," George later said. ". . . not emotional. Moral . . . what was right by my wife and children and by [Miss] Trapani, who said she was dying and with child?"

At his hotel one night in New Mexico, George was startled by a knock on the door.

Donna.

"I'm here. . . ," Donna said after George opened the door. She had a bag with her; there was a smile on her face that effectively communicated, *You didn't think you could get rid of me that easy now, did you?*

"What are you *doing* here?" George asked, letting Donna in.

"Change your plans," she said. "Stay with me. . . . Let's have a vacation."

Donna suggested four days. Dinner. Sex. Long walks. Time to think.

"No," George said. "I have work to do. I have to be home . . . in two days."

Not long after Donna walked in, they had sex. Donna ended up staying.

"I could have [kicked her out]," George said later in court. "But knowing Miss Trapani, [I felt] she would have created a scene and started cussing and kicking the door in, and it would have been embarrassing. Plus, I was weak for her."

On the way to the airport after the weekend, Donna said, "I have cancer."

"I know. . . . I got the letter from your doctor."

"So you know about the baby, too?"

"Donna," George said, "I will try to be there for you and the baby."

In Donna's view the relationship was back on. George was home with his wife and children, but Donna felt his days in Michigan were numbered. Now that she was having his child and dying, George had no choice.

Falling in love with you was one of my life's most perfect moments, said the inscription on a card Donna sent George on May 31. It was a poem, describing how she felt about the rekindling of the bond they once had shared.

Sometime later, Donna wrote a desperate plea (in the third person), which she had planned on sending to George (although there is no indication she ever sent it). Through a series of questions, she was begging him to stay with her. Sentences along the lines of: *Is your wife as pretty as Donna?* The questions asked if Gail was as "smart" as Donna? As "unselfish"? What had Gail done to prove her "unselfishness" to George? Was Gail as "vibrant" and "energetic" and "passionate" and "sexy" as Donna? Did Gail please him in the way Donna could? Would she "sacrifice" or make as much "money" as Donna? What was it that George "learned" from his wife? When was it that he last "had a stimulating conversation" with his wife?

Pathetic didn't even approach how desperate Donna sounded.

In that same letter Donna wrote of a divine threat, showing how fast she could turn on someone she supposedly had loved. She wrote that if Gail was George's ultimate choice: *May God bring you all the pain and hell you deserve.* She said no man on "the face of the earth" would ever dream of "giving up what you have with Donna" to return to the dark hole in Michigan.

Concluding this bizarre rant, Donna stated that since she was dying, she had many things "to regret." But none of those regrets compared to what George would feel if he abandoned her and returned to Gail. She could not figure out why this decision was so tough. The only answer to Donna was his wife was "holding something over your head." Donna speculated that maybe it was something in George's past that would all at once "ruin you" and "send you to prison."

As they worked through their relationship difficulties, despite what George later said about juggling that "moral dilemma," a letter he wrote to Donna on June 13, 1999, spoke of a man who had not withdrawn—or claimed not to have withdrawn—any of the feelings he once had. George was indeed coming back around. Perhaps all the begging and threatening and constant badgering on Donna's part had paid off.

Opening the letter, George apologized for the way he had talked to her yesterday. . . . They had fought. George had sent Donna another round of what he called "mixed messages" and "inconsistent words." He said he "felt so bad" and wanted to know what he could say to "make up" for his behavior. Saying he loved and admired and adored Donna "sounds so empty and inconsequential." He begged Donna to believe him.

George talked about the "life growing inside" her and how much he loved the idea of Donna having his child. He called the baby a "product of our . . . love." He suggested that if the child turned out to be a girl, they name her after Donna, so that Donna "will continue to live on." He was going to do everything in his power to spend Donna's "last days" with her.

He mentioned he was at home praying for her and the "Little Kahuna." He knew there was a God and that God was "watching over" Donna and his child when he wasn't in Florida to take care of them himself. He warned Donna that she had ruined his future with women because after having her, he could never be with another woman.

Concluding, George reconciled how he hoped Donna would "return" his page that night so they could talk: *I will love you forever, My Donna!!*

38

EMILY FULTON WAS preparing for college enroll-
ment. As summer approached, she could not ignore
that her mother was once again suffering from bouts of depression and anxiety brought on by a father who had been
taking the entire family on an emotional roller-coaster ride.

"She was losing weight again and also losing her hair,"
Emily said. "She was getting these headaches . . . terrible
migraines."

From Emily's position she never believed her father and
Donna broke up.

"He said that," Emily observed, speaking of her father
quitting CCHH and ending the affair, "but he was still
doing claims for her."

To Emily's way of thinking, if the guy was still working
for his mistress, he was still interested in keeping a connection open between them.

Emily would come home and there was her mother:
sitting in the kitchen or alone in her room, absolutely destroyed.

"Crying all the time."

Emily and Andrew got together and took Gail out for what
Emily later called "dates." The movies. Dinner. Shopping.

Anything to keep Gail's mind off herself and the utter life-sucking situation at home.

"You kids shouldn't have to do this," Gail said one night. "You kids should be out with your friends. You shouldn't be hanging out with your mother because her husband *left* her."

Gail was once again talking about killing herself. This obviously upset Andrew and Emily, who would turn to her school mentor and vent.

"Generally," Emily's mentor said, "people who talk about committing suicide don't ever do it." Still, Emily and Andrew routinely told their mother that they loved her, she was desperately needed in their lives, and suicide could *never* be an option. They depended on their mother to be around for their entire lives, and they let her know this any chance they got.

"How could we *not* spend time with her?" Emily said later. "She needed us. My mom couldn't hide it anymore, like she had in the past."

The kids were older. They could tell when their mother suffered. Plus, it was all out in the open: Gail's coworkers knew; her mother knew; even some of the neighbors knew.

Donna played off this. On June 20, 1999, she sent George a card, imbuing it with the idea that there was a strong "probability" that she wouldn't be around next Father's Day. She wanted George to receive something special from "'us.'"

The card went on about how Donna had become so comfortable in her role as the soon-to-be mother of George's child and couldn't wait to give this gift from God to her lover and then depart from the world herself. Her life was complete.

She signed the card, *your Little Kahuna,* soon *to be your princess one day.*

* * *

A week later, as the first of July came, George made a calculated decision that the best thing for him to do was have Donna and Gail meet. Why not have them get together and talk this thing through? If Donna was going to die, George and Gail would have to raise his child. Thus, Gail needed to get to know the mother of her husband's child.

"[I wanted them to talk] about what to do and what needed to happen," George later said. "What was going to happen with the baby and see if we could get along, because I didn't know what to do at that time. I felt responsible for my wife and kids and also for Miss Trapani and her condition."

George suggested Donna come up to Michigan for the Fourth of July weekend and stay at a nearby hotel. For some bizarre reason George thought it seemed like a good idea to drive Gail over to meet Donna, leaving the two women to chat for as long as they needed to hammer out any difficulties.

First he asked Gail.

According to Donna, it was George who invited her not only to visit him and Gail in Michigan, but to live there, too.

"Well, the main reason I came was because George had changed his mind *again* and had wanted us . . . to move . . . so he could be with me and the baby. . . . He had always wanted Gail and I to meet," Donna stated, "and he also thought that maybe I could try to talk to Gail and she would be able to meet me. We would become friends, maybe, and that because of her emotional trauma that she was going through . . . maybe I could try to talk to her, because she had had some attempted suicide threats, verbally, that she had talked about."

After George confided in Donna about Gail, Donna thought about it. Maybe she could convince Gail to go and "talk to someone."

"I had a friend that owned [a health care company] in Troy, Michigan . . . and I had already talked to him. He had psychiatric nurses, and he had social workers, and he was willing to provide it for free for me."

Donna called Dora Garza and explained to Gail's mother that she should go up to Michigan immediately to be with her daughter, relating this gem of compassion: "George is leaving her to come back to me and be with me and the baby."

Inside her hotel room, waiting for George and Gail, Donna made notes on hotel stationery. This was, obviously, her "argument" to win Gail over and make her understand that Donna deserved George. Of course, the entire four-teen-page document was directed at Gail, and each page grew in anger as Donna worked herself up into a whirl-wind of hate.

She accused Gail of "limiting" George's "dreams, ambitions, desires, wants." She noted how Gail was turning their children against George, how selfish Gail had been through-out all of this, and how she wasn't giving George the oppor-tunity to be a real person or lover. She ranted about how George kept most of his anger and resentment and hate for Gail "inside," and it would eventually kill him. How he "hurt for so long now" and how Donna had to help George through all that pain. How George felt his entire life was dedicated to "pleasing Gail." Donna blamed Gail for George leaving a company that Donna considered "him part owner," mention-ing how it would ultimately "kill him" because he had left. She planned to tell Gail how George had given her "his entire adult life." George was an "honorable, strong" man who had "never put his needs first." She accused Gail of questioning him "to death" about "every little thing." Any anger George had displayed in Donna's presence, Donna claimed, was brought on by Gail. And on and on, it went. . . .

So, in Donna's twisted view of the relationship, she wanted Gail to understand that any difficulties she and George had were because of Gail. She ended by telling Gail that although George wanted to be with his lover, not his wife, it did not mean he didn't care about Gail or her "welfare." She wrote: *He does care, just not how you want him to.*

Donna was ready for the showdown.

39

"YOU READY?"

Gail did not want to go. How could she do this? It might have sounded like a favorable plan a few days ago, but now Gail did not want to be in the same room with the woman who had caused her so much pain.

"I insist," George said (according to what Gail later said).

Gail thought about it. "Okay."

Little did Gail know then that the plan Donna and George had concocted was to sit Gail down and ask her if it was okay if George moved back down to Florida to stay with Donna until she had the baby and then died. After that, George could move back to Michigan to be with Gail and either raise the child, or give it up for adoption.

"I felt responsible for both women," George later told police, "and did not know what to do at that point. I was unable to make a choice between Gail and Donna."

They drove to the ConCorde Inn in Rochester Hills, a twenty-five-minute ride south of Lake Orion. Gail likely stared out into the open spaces passing by, tears in her eyes, wondering how the hell her life of praying nightly rosaries and helping people and going to mass had come down to this.

Donna was waiting inside her hotel room.

George knocked. Gail stood in back of him.

According to George, Donna had a slightly noticeable bump, indicating that she was pregnant. If a person didn't know Donna was carrying a child, however, that individual would have had no idea by looking at her. George had even asked Donna why she wasn't showing more. After all, he had seen her naked. She was supposedly six months pregnant by then.

"Since I had that stomach surgery," Donna told him, "I am not able to eat much—*you* know that! I'm not really able to gain much weight, so the baby is undersize."

George responded later: "She looked a little bit thicker, but I don't know if that was from fluid or tension, or what it was. But, no, I—I thought . . . [she was pregnant], but don't know if I was one hundred percent on that. [She] looked like [she] might have been. . . ."

The three of them stood and stared at one another for a moment: the wife, the husband, and the mistress.

One of the reasons why George told Gail that Donna was carrying his child, he later explained, was that "I learned in the army that bad news doesn't get better with age. I told my wife because she would find out one way or the other. . . . I had cheated on her. I had deceived her. I had lied to her. Now this woman says she's pregnant and dying. It just gets more and more complicated. . . ."

"I want to talk to him alone first," Donna said, looking at Gail.

"No," Gail sassed back, walking into the room behind George. "You will *not* be alone with *my* husband." Gail was on the verge of tears. ("Very, *very* upset," George explained.)

"This is Gail, Donna," George said, making the introductions.

The two women locked eyes.

They stood for a time and talked. Not about much. Then George suggested lunch. "Olive Garden?" It was nearby.

"Sure," Donna said.

Gail agreed.

So they piled into George's car and went to the local Olive Garden for endless breadsticks and salad.

After lunch George drove them back to the hotel.

"George, you wait outside the room while Gail and I speak for a moment," Donna suggested.

George looked at Gail to make sure she was okay with this.

"George . . . go," Donna ordered.

George stepped out of the room and went down to the lobby as Donna closed the door behind him. Then she walked toward the bed. Gail had tears in her eyes.

"You see this," Donna said, rubbing her belly, "this is your husband's love child! I love George, Gail! You *cannot* stop this."

Gail was bawling.

"You cannot stop us! Why won't you *let* this man go?"

According to Donna (and yet this would be extremely out of character for Gail), Gail snapped, "I hope you *lose* your baby!"

"Why is it that you have to always get what *you* want?" Donna said. "You've had George for twenty-five years, bitch. Now it's *my* turn! You got that?"

Gail didn't respond. Donna wasn't allowing her a word in edgewise.

Gail Fulton with her husband George during one of the couple's happier moments. *(Courtesy of Emily Fulton)*

Gail felt secluded and alone after George moved the family from Corpus Christi, Texas to this new house in Lake Orion, Michigan. *(Courtesy of Emily Fulton)*

Gail had always confided in friends. *(Courtesy of Emily Fulton)*

After moving to Lake Orion, Gail found a job at the local public library. *(Author's photograph)*

The employee entrance where Gail walked out— and into a killer's sights— on the night she was murdered. *(Author's photograph)*

These stills from the library's security video tape show Gail's killers. *(Courtesy of Oakland County Sheriff's Office)*

The killers drove into the parking lot and approached Gail's van. *(Courtesy of Oakland County Sheriff's Office)*

This grainy close-up shows Gail Fulton (the white figure facing the driver's door) approaching her killers.
(Courtesy of Oakland County Sheriff's Office)

These stills show Gail standing next to the car with her killers looking on from inside. *(Courtesy of Oakland County Sheriff's Office)*

7

8

Here, Gail's killers leave the scene after shooting three rounds
into Gail's upper torso and head. *(Courtesy of Oakland County
Sheriff's Office)*

With her killers speeding toward the exit, Gail Fulton lies barely breathing, fighting for her life in the parking lot of the Orion Township Public Library. *(Courtesy of Oakland County Sheriff's Office)*

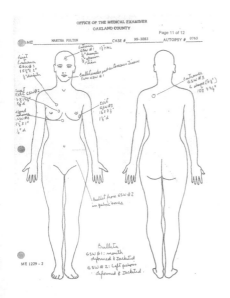

This document from Gail's autopsy shows how the three rounds fired into Gail's body ricocheted off bones and organs and reentered and exited her body. *(Courtesy of Oakland County Sheriff's Office)*

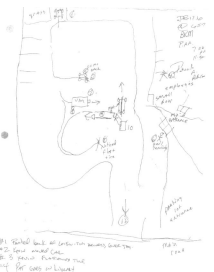

These documents—one of which was drafted by Gail's killers—show how the murderers pulled into the library parking lot, quickly mowed her down in a hail of gunfire, and left.

(Courtesy of Oakland County Sheriff's Office)

red roof inns (SM)

207 Reg. # 93432

Thank you for choosing Red Roof Inns!

| Room # | Last Name | First | Rate |
| 307 | OUeLLeTe | KeviN | |

In Date: 10/3
Out Date: 10/4
Adults

I agree to pay for all charges incurred with respect to my room, including any damages to the premises, by the method listed below:

Children

Cash ☐ Visa ☐ M.C. ☐ Amex/Optima ☐
DC/CB ☐ Discover/Bravo ☐ DB ☐ Other ☐

Rollaway/Crib Signature
X

GSR License Plate # State
077

I.D./C.C./Red Card #

Company Name Account #

Company - City State Zip Code

Other

Continuation # From: _____ To: _____

300-205 (6/97)

A murder plot began to come together for police after these two motel receipts (one dated the night of Gail's murder, the other dated weeks before), came to light. *(Courtesy of Oakland County Sheriff's Office)*

PALACE INN 2755 Lapeer Road • Lake Orion, MI 48360 REGISTRATION CARD

NAME PATRICK AlexANdeeR
STREET
CITY STATE ZIP
REPRESENTING N/A

MY ACCOUNT WILL BE HANDLED BY:
TYPE

☒ CASH ☐ CREDIT CARD: NO.
CAR LICENSE NO. STATE
MAKE OF CAR Malibu NO. IN PARTY 2
  EXP. 1-4-03
DRIVERS LICENSE #
REMARKS

ROOM NO. 10
RATE $ 10/76
DATE IN 9-14 AM/PM
DATE OUT 9-16 AM/PM

DAYS OCCUPIED
SUN.
MON.
TUE. X
WED. X
THU.
FRI.
SAT.

TOTAL DAYS 2
TOTAL $ 96.00
TAX $ 5.76
AMOUNT PAID 101.76

NOTICE TO GUESTS - This property is privately owned and reserves the right to refuse service to anyone and will not be responsible for accidents or injury to guests or for loss of money, jewelry or valuables of any kind.

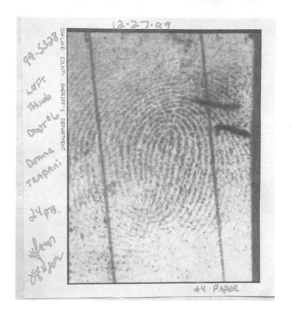

Investigators discovered a map with Donna Trapani's fingerprints all over it, which detailed Gail Fulton's every move.

(Courtesy of Oakland County Sheriff's Office)

Sybil Padgett, 36, Donna Trapani's employee and friend, was the first domino to fall as the plot to murder Gail Fulton unfolded for cops. *(Courtesy of Oakland County Sheriff's Office)*

Sybil's 19-year-old boyfriend, Patrick Alexander, did not need much convincing to give up his girlfriend and their co-conspirators, Kevin Ouellette and Donna Trapani. *(Courtesy of Oakland County Sheriff's Office)*

Kevin Ouellette was the muscle and—arguably—the brains behind the murder.
(Courtesy of Oakland County Sheriff's Office)

Donna Trapani, George Fulton's mistress, was the mastermind behind Gail's murder. *(Courtesy of Oakland County Sheriff's Office)*

Investigators uncovered the car used in Gail's murder, matching its broken taillight up to the grainy video taken the night of the crime. *(Courtesy of Oakland County Sheriff's Office)*

Much of the evidence against Gail's four murderers was in this house Sybil Padgett rented in Defuniak Springs, Florida. *(Courtesy of Oakland County Sheriff's Office)*

Today, Sybil Padgett and Donna Trapani are still good friends. Both are housed in the same Michigan state prison.
(Courtesy of Oakland County Sheriff's Office)

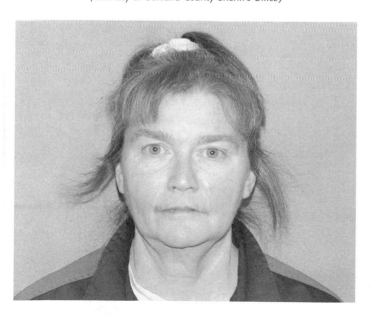

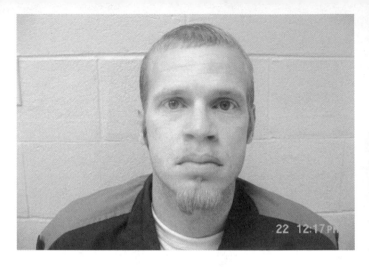

Patrick Alexander was a young man when he entered prison.
He'll be an elderly man when—and if—he is released.
(Courtesy of Oakland County Sheriff's Office)

Today Kevin Ouellette is not the same man he was when he
murdered Gail Fulton. *(Courtesy of Oakland County Sheriff's Office)*

"After I'm dead, you can feel free to have him back," Donna said.

From where George sat in the lobby downstairs, he could see the door into Donna's room. He looked up about ten minutes after sitting down and saw Gail barge out of the room. Donna was running behind her, trying to stop her, tugging at Gail's blouse. ("Physically stop her," George remembered later. "By holding her. Grabbing her.")

Gail found George. "I want to go home! I'm very upset."

The torment Gail had been through.

Unimaginable.

Unbelievable.

Unforgivable.

Donna ran down the stairs while holding her stomach. "I need to talk to you, George."

George said, "You know I love her, Donna." Then he turned to Gail, "Can you wait a few minutes? She wants to talk to me for five minutes." George's demeanor changed. He sounded sincere when addressing Gail, angry when speaking to Donna.

"What!" Donna shouted. Things were getting out of hand.

"Gail, please wait here," George said kindly. "I need to talk to Donna alone."

Donna and George went into the pool area of the hotel. Donna slid her key card to open the door.

Gail waited for what she later told her mother was "over an hour." (George claimed "five minutes turned into forty-five minutes." He and Donna "talked about everything.")

When Donna and George emerged from the pool area, Gail was gone.

40

U P UNTIL THE moment she received the call, it had been a beautiful summer day on the water for Emily and a few close friends. They were enjoying the long holiday weekend aboard a boat on the lake.

Sun and fun.

"Come home, come home!" Gail shouted over the phone to her daughter. Gail was hysterical. George and Donna had left her there alone at the hotel. The day had been a mistake. She went to meet Donna and talk things through, but it all went terribly wrong.

Emily was startled by the call. "Mom . . . where *are* you?"

"Your dad is going to leave us again. . . . She's pregnant. . . ."

Emily couldn't understand what her mother was saying because Gail was so frantic, crying and talking in quick breaths. Before she left to go out with friends earlier that morning, Emily had heard Donna was in town and that her mother and father were going to meet Donna. But Emily was under the impression "that my father was going there to tell Donna it was over." Emily had even suggested that her father take *her* with him instead of her mother. "Mom's been through enough, Dad. *I* will tell Donna to leave us alone," Emily had suggested.

"Mom, what's going on? Slow down," Emily said, trying to calm Gail. It sounded like Gail was outside somewhere.

Gail mentioned the hotel. She said she was walking home. Emily realized then that they had gone through with the meeting and something terrible had happened.

"I'll be right there, Mom."

Emily got her things together and took off.

"But I decided," Emily said later, "right then and there, I was going to go to the hotel and have a confrontation in person with Donna."

Emily was tired of this. Now her father and Donna were involving her mother. It was time, Emily figured, to get in Donna's face and tell her to back the hell off.

From a pay phone near the hotel, Gail called her mother next. She was walking home, she explained. She had heard and seen enough. They left her in the lobby and took off together. How low. How pathetic. How mean. It appeared George and Donna had brought Gail to the hotel to humiliate her.

"I looked around the hotel grounds," Gail explained, "but couldn't find them. I'm walking home."

"Honey . . . don't. . . ." Dora was upset, unable to understand how George could do such a thing to a woman with whom he had spent his entire life.

Gail said she'd call later.

As she walked down the street away from the hotel, Gail heard a car pull up behind her.

And then another.

It was George in one; Donna was behind him.

"Gail . . . get in," George said. He had driven all the way

home, searched the house, and then backtracked. Donna followed in her car the entire way, not letting George out of her sight.

"Why?" Gail asked. She was visibly upset. She was hugging herself, a balled-up tissue in her hand, tears streaming down her face. "*Why,* George?"

"Just get in. Let's talk."

George convinced Gail to get in the car.

Gail sat. "I'll be right back. Don't leave." George walked over to Donna, who was parked in back of his car, waiting.

He returned a moment later: "We have to follow Donna back so she gets there safely," George explained to his wife.

Donna drove away. George followed. Gail didn't say much during the ride. At one point George looked into the rearview mirror and noticed Donna's car veering off the side of the road, stopping sharply as though she had crashed.

George pulled up alongside Donna's car. He stopped and quickly got out.

Donna was slumped over.

"Hey," George said, "you okay?"

"I must have passed out," Donna said.

"Come with us," George said. He helped Donna into his car and drove Gail home.

"What are you doing?" Gail asked as George packed an overnight bag inside the house. Donna waited outside in the car.

"I have to go stay with Donna tonight," George said.

41

WHILE EMILY WAS home earlier that day, before this fiasco started, Donna called. Emily made note of the hotel name on the caller ID. Now back from what was supposed to be a quiet day with friends, upset that her mother sounded so in despair, Emily walked in and was met with a "crying and very upset" mother. Her father was "just sitting on the couch in 'his own world,'" Emily said.

"Your father is leaving to go take care of Donna," Gail explained. "Because," obviously repeating what George had just told her, "'she has no one else.'"

"What?" Emily asked.

"Yes. Donna's going to have your father's child! Oh, and she's dying, too, Emily. She'll be dead in a matter of months."

Emily couldn't believe it. George did not interrupt or butt in. So it must be true, Emily considered.

"Look, I cannot have Donna commit suicide and have that on my hands," George finally said. "I won't let it happen."

Emily's friend Andrea was with her. "I'm taking Andrea home," Emily told her mother. "I'll be back soon."

By now, it was late evening. George had dropped Donna off at the hotel and had come back home for more clothes.

Emily walked out the door with her friend and drove straight to Donna's hotel. She parked and got out; together they approached the front-desk clerk.

"No, I can't tell you which room she's in," the clerk explained.

"Call her and tell her I'm here," Emily said.

The clerk handed Emily the phone.

"Emily?" Donna said, startled, but also cheery and elated, sounding as if they were old friends.

"Yes. I thought maybe you would want to meet me in person, so I came."

"Oh, yes, yes," Donna said. "But I just threw up all over the bathroom. I'm sick. I need some time to clean it up. Give me five minutes, then come up." Donna never said where George was, but he was not there then.

Emily hung up. She and Andrea walked up to Donna's room.

"Emily, do you want me to come in there with you?" Andrea asked. Andrea was not a woman to mess with: She was five feet ten inches, husky, all business. "Come on, you shouldn't be alone with that woman. She's crazy." Emily had confided in Andrea since it all began. Andrea knew the history here and how it could easily manifest into violence, once these two got together in the same room.

"You wait outside the door here," Emily explained, "and if I scream, you come in." Emily was going against her own advice here. She knew that anyone close to a situation, as she was in this particular case, could not be rational. ("Your instincts are down," Emily said later. "You're too entrenched. You're not paying attention to the signals. I could not, at that point, sense the danger I was in, or the danger my family was in.") They were dealing with a crazy, obsessive woman, capable of anything. Donna was desperate.

"Well," Andrea said, "you're in danger going in there."

"No, I'm not."

"Look, I am giving you fifteen minutes—then I'm coming in."

Part of the visit for Emily was to find out if Donna was, in fact, pregnant. Emily believed in her ability to read people and the auras she sometimes saw hovering over and around a person—that dark cloud she had seen so many times over her father. If she could get in the same room with Donna, Emily convinced herself, she could read Donna. Emily had just finished reading a book about auras. According to the book, pregnant women "would have these stars around them," Emily said. Emily wanted to see if Donna had those "stars" shrouding her. ("I did not believe Donna was pregnant," Emily recalled. "I thought she was full of it and just, again, trying to manipulate my dad.")

Donna opened the door.

("It was really weird," Emily said through tears, recalling this moment of her life. "She wanted to hug me. Donna, this woman who had destroyed our lives, she wanted to *hug* me.") Emily was crying as she walked in. ("And here she is . . . the woman who has caused so much pain in your mother's life, in *your* life, your *family's* life. Here she is. And she's so *ugly*. How is *this* the woman responsible for all of this pain and anguish?")

Emily thought: *She's not in as good a shape as my mother. Why did my dad throw us away for her? Why is she so much better than all of us?*

As Emily looked around the room, she was immediately freaked out to see what could only be described as a "shrine Donna had built to my father" on the nightstand.

Cards.

Letters.

Photographs.

Candles.

All were arranged in some sort of homage to George, as if Donna were praying to it. It was strangely spiritual and yet oddly psychotic. One letter she had out on the table was more of a journal entry. It talked about how George had "cried several times" before he last left Florida. According to Donna's written account, George said, *"I wish I was staying . . . I feel like I am deserting you."* He placed his hand on Donna's stomach and rubbed it gently: *"I love you both—always."* He called Florida his "real home." That night, before George took off for Michigan, he paged Donna and said: *"I would rather be with you than anyone else in the world. I have been crying all day long missing you. You are so good to me. I don't deserve you."*

Wow, my dad threw everything away for this *woman?* Emily later pondered when she heard this statement.

Emily stared at Donna and looked at the shrine. To Emily, Donna was dumpy; she was the polar opposite to the woman Emily had envisioned. A man generally cheats with some hot young chick, living out a twisted sexual fantasy he would never dream of with his wife. But Donna was plain and unpleasant.

"Oh, you're so pretty," Donna said, trying to make it sound as if she meant it. "Sit down on the bed. . . . Sit down." She patted the spot.

Emily didn't know what to think.

"You must have heard by now," Donna said, rubbing her stomach, "we're pregnant."

"We're . . ."

Ouch.

It was hard for Emily to tell if there were stars hovering around her father's mistress, because Emily was so upset and taken aback. Emotion got in the way of Emily's "gift," for lack of a better way to explain what was going on.

"Me and your father are going to have a baby," Donna

said, beaming. Then she dropped her voice down a pitch, almost to a whisper: "I'm dying, too."

Donna must have realized she wasn't getting through to Emily. Emily wasn't saying much. She wasn't running into Donna's arms, throwing herself at the woman, looking to work things out. Emily came across as a daughter there to defend her mother. After all, when it came down to it, Gail had done *nothing* wrong. This entire affair—the entire dynamic now playing out in this hotel room—was George's doing. Emily was there to protect her mother's soul, to tell the woman who had destroyed their lives—not taking any of the blame away from her father—to stay the hell away from all of them. Baby or no baby . . . back off!

"Look," Donna said, resurrecting that earlier argument she laid on Gail, "your mother has had your father long enough! It's my turn now. You and your brother and mother never truly appreciated your father, anyway. But I—I . . . damn it, *I*"—Donna pointed at herself in a spate of fury—"*I* know him better than *any* of you!"

Donna paced, breathing heavily.

Emily sat, listening to what was turning into one of Donna's infamous rants.

"Your father loves me more than *any* of you—get that through your heads. Look!" Donna pointed toward the shrine. "Read those cards. Read those letters he wrote to me. Look," Donna screamed, "*read* them!" She picked up a card and shoved it in Emily's face. "You can see that he loves me more than *any* of you! Not your mother. He loves *me,* Emily. He doesn't love you, Emily. He loves *me.*"

Emily was crying. She picked up the card. It was her father's handwriting, all right.

Heavens no . . . Dad?

("And I had *never,*" Emily recalled later, giving into an onslaught of tears while reliving the memory for me, "seen my father write those types of words to my mother." That was what hurt the most. "He never told us *any* of those things. Why is he giving these expressions of love to *her*? Why is she more worthy than the rest of us?")

What has my mother gone through? Emily thought as Donna forced more cards and letters on her. *What had my mom gone through—not only in this same room, with this same woman—hours ago, but all this time?*

The thought of how much pain her mother had endured at the hands of this woman consumed Emily. She was ready to confront Donna.

"You cannot keep *doing* this," Emily said, standing. "We want to have a family. It cannot keep going on as this, back and forth. Can you *please* just stay out of our lives!"

"Don't worry," Donna said. "I'm going to be dead soon. You can have your father back after I'm dead."

There was a knock on the door. Andrea's muffled voice interrupted from behind it. "What's going on? Come on, Emily, you need to get home. Open this door!"

"Please stay here with me tonight," Donna asked.

"What?"

"Please. We can talk some more. I'll give you a ride home in the morning. Let your girlfriend take your car home. Please, please stay."

Strange, Emily thought, *she claimed to be throwing up earlier and sick to her stomach, but she wants me to stay here?*

"Uh . . . *no*, Donna. I don't think so."

Emily walked toward the door. ("[The meeting] didn't really help," Emily later remarked. "There are never really good enough answers to what I went through. I could not believe that I had finally met this person. . . .") She was drained.

George and Gail had been waiting for Emily back home. George had packed more of his belongings and was ready to leave, but he didn't want to go anywhere until he knew Emily was home, maybe more for Gail's sake. By now, it was late into the night. Emily walked in. George was sitting on the couch, with his head in his hands.

"Where were you?" Gail asked. "We were worried."

"I went to see Donna."

"You *what*?" both Gail and George said, almost together.

Emily looked at her dad. "And there was that black cloud over his head. It was back."

42

GAIL FULTON HAD TRIED slashing her wrists the night before George left, but George grabbed the knife out of her hands and scolded her, "What are you doing?"

Emily couldn't believe it had come to this.

Gail said she took a bottle of Tylenol, but the pills hadn't done anything.

"So these acts could have been to get my dad's attention that night," Emily explained, "but my mom talked about [suicide] a lot when my dad was *not* there."

Perhaps after that run-in with Donna and a husband who wanted her, essentially, to take care of his lover's baby after his lover croaked, Gail decided it was too much.

Emily confronted her mother. "What are you doing?"

George had left to be with Donna by then. They were alone.

Gail laughed it off, saying, "You can't kill yourself with Tylenol and a paring knife."

"She was trying to make fun of herself, I think," Emily recalled. "We almost stopped being mother/child and almost reversed roles. In fact, because I knew that Andrew was her favorite, I made sure that *Andrew* knew how she talked about suicide so that he and I could both tell her that we loved her and needed her, and she could not commit suicide and leave us by ourselves. Of course, we listened to her, but then we would say 'committing suicide is the easy way out and it is selfish' and 'we know you love us so much that you would not do this.'"

Emily said, "Please, please don't do this, Mom. We love you and we need you, please."

She and Gail cried together.

If they could just get through the next few months, Emily thought. If Emily could have some time with her mother alone, she could convince Gail to move on and forget about her father. Gail could find a better-paying job. Take care of herself. Emily could help. In time Gail would see things differently.

Emily reflected on one night in particular after the Fourth of July weekend fiasco. She was sitting on the floor next to her mother's bed. Andrew walked into the room. Gail was lying in bed, and Emily and Andrew soon sat on the bed around their mother and cried because neither had seen Gail in so much pain before. Gail had tossed in the towel at that point. She had internalized the entire marriage and its failures. She had taken it all on.

"But at least we had each other through this, and [I had my mentor] to listen to me and to tell me how to respond to it all," Emily said. "I didn't know you had to tell the suicidal person to not commit suicide and reiterate how much you love them and need them with you alive."

A day after the hotel incident, Gail asked Emily if she thought Donna was pregnant. It was the first time Gail had questioned whether Donna was making it all up. Gail knew how her daughter could read people.

"I don't know," Emily said. "I cannot think straight. I don't know."

George came back the following day, July 5. Apparently, he'd had a rough night, too, with Donna. It wasn't champagne and caviar out on the hotel terrace; Donna had been hostile and bitter. George had that look in his eye. He wasn't just coming back to grab things and take off. He was finished with Donna. It was finally over. For good this time.

"I told her," George explained to his family. "She's gone back to Florida."

According to Emily, when Gail sat down with George and told him about the rotten things Donna had said to her inside the hotel room, "my father did not believe my mom."

"You owe us an apology," Emily said.

George wouldn't give it. After all, he had run back to Donna at that hotel and then returned home. What more did they want? Whatever the reason, George was home. He would take care of the baby financially, he explained, but that was it. Gail had won. She had gotten her husband back.

"I stayed with her one night that weekend," George said later, referring to Donna, "and then I had a change of heart and realized that's not what I wanted to do, to leave my wife, and I said I had to leave and it had to be over. And that's when I said [to Donna] that's when the physical relationship [between us] was over."

"My dad never apologized," Emily explained. "He was dictating everything we had to do. There was a lot of tension between us. In my view he needed to get down and beg for forgiveness, but he didn't. He never once apologized for his actions. He never showed us or had remorse. He simply wanted us to take him back and act like nothing happened. I was irate."

Gail was more than willing to forgive and forget.

"How can you do that?" Emily asked her mother. "He has to *earn* your love! He has to earn all of our love. We cannot just take his crap."

Her mother didn't have much to say. Gail was ready to bring George to church, have him confess his sins, speak to the priest, and then move on.

"You deserve better than this," Emily said.

To Emily, her mother had turned into "this frail . . . childlike creature that was begging for love, begging for my dad's love. It was so pathetic."

The idea that George did not believe the kids or Gail about the things Donna had been saying to them—even after he moved back in—became a recurring issue for Emily, Andrew, and even Melissa, Gail and George's oldest child, who was living in Virginia. Melissa wrote her father a letter on July 6, 1999. She wanted to let him know that all of them—including Gail—were saying the same things about Donna. He needed to step up and admit Donna had been an awful person who had tried to destroy the family. Take, for example, the "nature," Melissa wrote, of Donna's phone calls to Grandma on July 4.

Dora had stopped answering her phone after that first nasty call came from Donna. Instead, the answering machine picked up and recorded Donna in rare form. Donna warned Dora that she was "entitled" to her "own feelings," but she wanted Dora to understand she "was calling to tell you that you needed to speak with your daughter. She has tried to commit suicide for the past six months. Only Gail, George, and I know about it. . . . You don't know what's been going on for the past sixteen years in that marriage. She is sick and has been sick for the past ten years mentally. She needs help. . . . If you care, reach out for your daughter. You gave birth to her. You raised her. So

if you love her, you need to reach out to her. . . . You need
to be there for your daughter!"

After detailing the nature of the phone call, Melissa
wrote how she hoped: *You will see things and believe us
once and for all—your family.*

43

GAIL STOPPED CRYING—at least as a daily occurrence. She was falling back into her role as library clerk, wife, and mother. Things weren't back to normal, and likely never would be, but life moved on. Gail and George weathered what was a hurricane within their marriage; they had come out the other end with a few bumps and bruises.

"They had been working things out," Emily told police, "and for the first time my mother was very happy. . . . My father started going back to church and was saying prayer before dinner."

Donna continued calling the house, spewing spiteful and vengeful things to Gail and Emily. Most of Donna's calls were centered on George still working for her, but she seemed to always have an earful for whoever answered the phone.

On July 14, 1999, a mutual friend of George and Donna's, a woman George introduced to Donna, e-mailed to say something was wrong with Donna. The e-mail began with a sincere wish: I hope . . . things are improving in your marriage. This was an indication Donna had gone back home and explained—at least to this woman—that she and George were finished, but there was also an underlying message in the e-mail explaining how Donna had rushed back to Florida and told everyone there was still hope for her and George.

The e-mail explained how Donna had called and left her a message, sounding "very distressed." The woman asked George pointblank if he had "broken it off" with her "completely"? The e-mail writer hoped George had, but she would respect any decision George made.

Then there was an interesting query in the correspondence: She wanted to know if George had called Donna's doctor to find out if Donna "was terminally ill."

George tapped out a response, saying, all was "sort of fine" with Gail, adding that it was a "long story," one that he would rather not discuss via e-mail. He was "trying to make things work" with Gail, but he admitted it had been hard for them. George said he had phoned Donna's doctor, but he hadn't received a return call. He wasn't sure what was "truth and fiction." He admitted he was probably "too close" to the problem to be "objective."

George said he was trying to work things out with Gail *and* Donna, but felt he was "failing miserably." He was going away on a business trip and would think about what he needed "to do with" his life. He had one request of his e-mail pen pal: Don't return Donna's calls. If everyone stuck together and left Donna alone, she would, "hopefully, go away."

To Donna, things had changed between her and George. However, an e-mail she wrote on July 27, addressing him in it as My Sexy Butt George, gave no indication that the relationship had been the least bit soured. It was written in a way that led one to believe Donna was certain Gail was reading George's e-mails. Knowing that, Donna twisted the knife as deeply as she could, writing how much she missed holding on to George's butt and kissing it. She also stressed how she loved "those thrusts it makes inside of me." George's lovemaking skills were "pleasurable," and she spelled out how she missed spending time with him in bed.

The next paragraph talked about how Donna wanted to take Friday night—she was writing the e-mail on Tuesday—to relive their "first night together." It was as if George had made plans to visit that coming weekend. Clearly, the e-mail was written to make Gail jealous. Donna said she wanted George to meet her at the Sea Gull and reenact that entire first night. They could dance together and sit and talk, and Donna wrote, I could play with your legs again. She wanted to take one car home, so she could "play" with him and get George "hot and hard" and "ready" for her.

By the third paragraph of what was a six-page, single-spaced e-mail, reality finally struck. Donna described how much "pain" she'd endured while they were riding this rough patch. She played up the cancer, saying how none of the surgeries she'd had compared to the pain George had caused. She couldn't even enjoy the wonders of being pregnant, she complained: Each day is worse. . . .

Then Donna spoke of how much George had said he wanted to be a part of the child's life, from womb to crib, going with her to her doctor's appointments and buying baby furniture and clothes. Then came a sad soliloquy regarding how Donna would not be around to see the child grow, talk, and walk. Donna said how she wished to share those moments with George. Then a request: Could George visit Florida and take one photo with her and the child after it was born? I would like very much to be buried with some pictures of us as a family. She complained about never having "been part of a family" and how she thought George was going to give her that one wish to help her "die happy."

Only you could give me this dream come true.

She was taken aback by the notion that he had "thrown" her away and was "giving" himself to "another woman"— a comment that unleashed a tirade directed at Gail.

Donna accused George of the biggest sin a man could commit in abandoning her and their child, saying Gail had a family already. She warned that "thou shall not kill" was a terrible sin, and George was not only killing her "but also your little baby." George's decision to stay with Gail would "kill the baby" because Donna was now more at risk of miscarrying. And if that happened, she warned, George would have blood on his hands.

She said the more she thought about it: **Maybe that's what you want?** Donna knew it was what Gail wanted, and perhaps Gail was poisoning George to think the same. If she lost the baby, she challenged: **It would be yours and Gail's fault.** She asked George, was he prepared to "live with this"?

It was almost as if every bad thought and disparaging remark Donna could think of was packed into one tedious, hateful, rage-filled e-mail. Donna said, without giving an explanation, that her own mother hated her now because of what George was doing to her.

She attacked George and Gail's faith, claiming that it wasn't God or Jesus calling the shots in the Fulton household anymore. Instead, it was the Devil himself "telling Gail what to do."

Donna even brought her doctor into the act: **Dr. [Bevins, pseudonym] . . . thinks what you are doing is wrong. [He] does not ever want to see you again.** The doctor, according to Donna, had questioned George's worth as a man. He supposedly told Donna that George "should divorce" Gail and "marry" her. Anything less was an "unforgivable" sin.

Donna called George a "coward," a "snob," "selfish" and "childlike." She accused Andrew of being the true motivation behind the breakup, *not* Gail. She added that if George was a real man, he would give Andrew a "swift kick in the butt." What was George teaching his boy? How to run out on a woman and her child.

Donna would likely have to give birth by C-section. She was not eating. She was not sleeping. She was throwing up all the time. She had chest pains, heart palpitations, and fainting spells. She had started to "spot." God was "going to take" her soon. She blamed it all on George.

The e-mail concluded as Donna came down from her soapbox and tried a different approach. She begged George for his love and asked him to reconsider raising their child. She backtracked at the end of the e-mail, noting how everyone at CCHH wanted them to be together and for George to raise the child after Donna died.

To say that the e-mail was pathetic would be to praise it.

44

DONNA TRAPANI WROTE AGAIN a day later, responding to an e-mail from George. She was close to a breakdown. She was swaying at the end of a long, fraying rope, hanging on every word George spoke. Part of the torture Donna was now putting herself through involved—once again—mixed messages from George Fulton.

In another over-the-top e-mail, Donna did nothing more than attack George for the ups and downs of their relationship, asking him repeatedly what he was going to be doing about his child. She said George should be on his "knees asking for forgiveness" for not being there for her and the unborn child. She asked him why he was mad at "us." She asked why he would say he cared, if he really did not. She mentioned something about George stopping to visit her while on one of his most recent business trips. George might have been telling Gail he was through with Donna, but this e-mail and a second e-mail he would send Donna in the days ahead told a different story.

Donna blasted George, saying: When you were here, you saw me starting to get sick. She mentioned how George had "massaged" her breast and underarms; how he had helped her back to bed after she vomited all night; how he had fed her soup and put her to bed, kissed her, and told her how much he loved her. Donna said she was sicker now than ever. She was mad because he had promised to spend the Fourth of July (even though they had that confrontation with Gail) with her "doing something nice." She claimed she didn't have "many holidays left." How dare George spend twenty-four July Fourths with Gail and "ruin the only one" Donna had left.

Oddly, Donna demanded to know "how many times" George had given flowers to Gail since he officially moved back home.

She talked about a new buyer for CCHH and was hoping George could help with the sale, before carrying on about Gail and how everything George did was now with Gail. Donna felt she and the baby were playing second fiddle. Clearly, this was beginning to provoke Donna, placing Gail at the center of her deep hatred.

"If you care about us" (George had apparently said he did), she wondered why he had such a hard time showing it. She had—at best—three months to live; she wanted to know George was going to be there, not just by phone, but in person.

A few days later, George wrote Donna a succinct e-mail, letting her know that he had spoken to Dr. Bevins "about an hour ago." The doctor finally called him back. George warned Donna about a call from the doctor regarding that "April letter," the one George had received via his post office box, written supposedly from the doctor on his practice's letterhead, telling George that Donna was pregnant and dying.

George said he was sorry for following through with the doctor, but he "had to know for sure."

Donna was not pregnant.

Yet, in spite of the truth (not pregnant and possibly healthy), George signed off: I still love you. . . .

Donna was livid at the prospect of having to "explain" herself once again. This was the second time George had questioned the authenticity of her pregnancy. She was tired of it: You keep doing this.... She spoke of a time the previous year when George had made her "have a test" in order to "prove to Gail" that she "did not have any venereal diseases." She accused him of not wanting to face up to the fact that he fathered a child, making a point to say he was looking for any way out.

Further, Donna explained that it wasn't gastric bypass surgery she'd had years ago. No, it was stomach cancer, and told George that he was the only one who knew the truth. How dare he question her?

From that point on, Donna listed a host of ailments she had. Many of these were brought on by her pregnancy: dizziness to malabsorption, cramps, her feet turning purple. The woman was a wreck. She even went so far as to say how George had watched her "passing blood in [her] stools." That ailment alone should have convinced him she was sick. She had colon and back problems, chronic anemia, and a laundry list of health issues. Before ending the e-mail, she carried on for another two pages, laying into George for just about everything under the sun, including how much of a man he had turned out *not* to be. Dr. Bevins was right, Donna raged, when he had said George was not fulfilling his obligations as a man.

Home alone one night, near this time, Donna made a call to a young man she had met only once.

"Hi, how are you?"

The man had no idea who was calling.

"We met at a Christmas party last year," Donna said.

He vaguely remembered.

After a bit of catch-up, Donna said, "I need you to come by and change a few lightbulbs for me." The guy was a handyman whom two friends of Donna's had introduced her to. As she spoke, he later said, he thought the request—to change her lightbulbs—was odd, considering he had met her only that one time. How in the hell did she even know how to contact him?

Nonetheless, he knew she wanted to have sex and took a ride over.

"I changed the lightbulbs," he later explained. Yet Donna, he figured out rather quickly, wanted something else.

He "went back there two or three times [after that] and had an intimate relationship with her." The handyman explained, "She became obsessed with me. She offered to buy me a fishing boat. She would stop by my apartment in the early-morning hours and knock on the windows. She even walked into my home once uninvited and left a rose on the table, and never announced her presence" while he was home.

Donna waited a few days after writing that last e-mail to George. When she didn't hear from him, she lashed out with another series of e-mails focused on what she viewed as the genuine root cause of all their problems: Gail.

It was *Gail* behind George's attitude.

Gail was forcing George to question *everything*.

And *Gail* who should pay the price for their breakup.

After what . . . Gail did to me . . . it is unforgivable, Donna wrote.

She explained (as if George had forgotten) how Gail had told her (that day in the hotel room) that she wished the baby and Donna would die—and here it was going to happen. Donna felt betrayed by Gail, as if Gail had sabotaged the entire past few weeks and had a hand in everything that George had been doing.

I thought she was supposed to be Miss High and Mighty, [who] never does anything wrong, Donna wrote. During the past month, as she got to understand Gail's true desires, Donna suddenly realized that she didn't want Gail to raise her child: Hell no. She could "never, ever forgive" Gail for what she had done to keep George away from her and their unborn child. The adjectives she used to describe Gail: evil, cold, and a disgrace to womanhood. Donna claimed never to have met someone in her entire life as "mean and hateful." Gail made her "sick" to her stomach. Living with her and being married to her all those years must have been akin to George "living in hell." She mentioned how sorry she felt for George. However, since he had dug this hole with Gail, *he* was to blame, too. Gail was "useless" and "insane" for knowing how they (George and Donna) had slept together so many times and been in love, and yet she *still* wanted to be with him. It told Donna how weak and desperate Gail was for a man.

There was a complete change in tone. Donna had turned a corner. She was no longer begging George for his love. Instead, she had turned her rage and hate toward the woman she believed stood in the way of her and George sharing a life together.

It was Gail this, Gail that. Gail was the rival. The stumbling block to all of Donna's plans. The walls were closing in: She had lost George, and her business was closer to filing bankruptcy.

All Gail's fault.

Near the end of the e-mail, Donna said she was thinking about killing herself "and the baby." Why should "we" live any longer? She had no reason to exist in a world, knowing that when she was gone, Gail was going to step in to take care of her child. It disgusted her.

45

WHAT MOST PEOPLE involved in these types of adulterous situations don't realize as things come undone is that, sooner or later, there comes a time when the unnecessary occurs. This sort of back-and-forth, pointing of fingers, making accusations, idle threats, curses and slurs, cannot go on forever without a *consequence*—sometimes several consequences. And when one is dealing with an irrationally thinking psychopath, one has to expect the unexpected.

On September 1, 1999, Donna e-mailed George. Unlike the e-mails she had sent up to this point, this one started off all business. She spoke of claims and audits, adjustments and payments. The tone was terse. Donna had always rambled. She'd start off talking about one thing—sex, for instance—and merge easily into how their future was paved in love. But here, after a tumultuous month (August) of disappointments and accusations on George's part, she obviously had other things on her mind. This person writing on September 1 was not the same woman who had written a few weeks prior. A good indication of when Donna had lost control came when, back on August 17, her forty-sixth birthday, she called George in Michigan out of the blue with a request.

"I need you to promise me that you won't have sex with *her* today!"

For some bizarre reason Donna wanted to know that George would not sleep with Gail on Donna's birthday. She claimed it was important that he did not have sex with Gail on this *one* particular day. If she could have peace of mind, she would be okay for that one day.

"Sure, Donna," George said.

They talked some more, but George had to go.

In the end this was not a hard promise for George to keep: Gail was in Texas visiting family.

Ten days after that bizarre request, Donna called.

"I need you here to help me sell CCHH."

George said he'd talk it over with Gail.

"Not unless I go with you," Gail said.

Donna called back and asked again.

George told her.

"Don't you *dare* bring that bitch down here!" Donna raged.

"I'm not going without her," George said.

George hung up, realizing those days of sharing any information about his family or future plans were over. Donna couldn't be trusted. Everything from her now was filled with hate. She even sounded different. Meanwhile, George was going to church with Gail again. His marriage was improving. Gail and George were talking again, planning trips together. Gail's birthday was just a few days away, September 6. George promised to take her to the Soaring Eagle Casino in nearby Mount Pleasant.

As George read through this new e-mail, it started off all about CCHH; yet Donna couldn't address George without including some of that fury boiling over inside her.

She felt scorned. It was apparent Donna was not going to walk away without making somebody pay.

Donna was running out of money as the summer came to a close—at least that's what she told everyone associated with CCHH. There were employees not being paid. Her rent was overdue. Many of the vendors she used were not receiving checks.

She said one of her employees had bitched and moaned about getting paid, so she cut the woman a $500 check, noting how everyone at CCHH believed she could save some money by not paying George because he had "another job."

Whenever Donna began to degrade George or Gail, it snowballed. Her rants spiraled out of control. For example, as Donna wrote about her money problems, she used it as a pathway to talk about how much she despised the idea George had suggested weeks ago about not coming down to Florida without Gail. It was something that grated on Donna's mental state. She said no "other businessman" would have let his "wife interfere." It showed how weak a man George had been throughout their breakup. Every reference to Gail was painted with critical remarks and pointless jabs. Donna said she should have known better than to ask George to come to Florida, anyway. Taking a swipe at Gail, she groused that "when you are a queen," who had been "raised with a silver spoon," you can get whatever you want in life.

She hated her rival for this.

Donna talked about doctors and how she couldn't understand why George believed one doctor so easily. She said all he had to do was take the trip south—*alone, without Gail*—and he could see for himself how sick she was and how big her stomach had gotten.

After another brief denunciation, focused on CCHH,

Donna signed the e-mail: Your Donna, who still loves you. . . .

"It was all a bunch of lies. All the stuff she said was lies," George later said.

Gail approached Emily one afternoon. It was close to Gail's birthday. George was out.

"What do you think?" Gail asked. She held up a pair of "sexy" black underwear—the silky, see-through type.

Emily didn't know *what* to say.

"Look," Gail said. A black push-up bra.

This was so unlike Gail, the very conservative Catholic. Here she was, standing in her bedroom, her daughter staring at these garments, an uncomfortable silence between them.

Had Gail Fulton changed *that* much to satisfy her husband's needs?

Gail was trying to "be more sexy" for George: If that's what he wanted, and it would keep him at home, why not?

Was Gail going too far? Or was she trying to conform to her husband's wishes and listen to his needs? If this—wearing sexy lingerie—was going to make him happy, why not?

Gail had a nervous laugh. She let it out as Emily stood in front of her, stunned, staring at the clothing.

"I cannot believe I just showed these things to my daughter," Gail said, flashing an embarrassed smile, dropping her arms, and tossing the clothes on the bed.

"Too much information," Emily responded. "You need to divorce Dad. He's not treating you right."

"I don't believe in divorce, Emily. Plus, I need to be here for you and your brother." Gail felt the only way she

could be a good mother to her children was by staying
married to their father and taking care of all three of them.

"You need to worry about *you*, Mom. Don't worry
about me and Andrew. We'll be fine. You need to go back
to Texas and be with your family. It doesn't matter. We can
come, too, and all be together."

Emily noticed that look in her mother's eyes—a single
moment when Gail thought seriously about it all, and how
less stressful life sounded. But then Gail snapped out of it
and decided that divorce wasn't something she ever wanted
to consider. She had married George for better or worse.
She would take those vows to her grave.

"My mother had turned into this needy child," Emily
observed later. "She relied so heavily on me and my
brother, and I had watched this situation with my dad destroy her. I thought, 'Divorce is the only way out of it all.'
It cannot be healthy for her to stay in this marriage. There's
no way this is right. No one person should have *that* much
power over another person. I was making an impact on her.
She was taking computer classes. She was thinking about
leaving. I had no idea to the extent of what was between
my mother and father then, and had realized later that it
would have taken a lot longer for me to turn her around."

On September 6, 1999, Gail celebrated her forty-eighth
birthday with family. For several days leading up to it,
George had been unable to get ahold of Donna and worried something was up. Donna was not returning his pages;
she had not sent any e-mails; his concern was that she had
gone and done something stupid.

George called one of Donna's friends. "Hey, was
wondering if you've seen Donna around? I haven't heard
from her . . . in weeks. This is unlike her."

"She's fine, George. In fact, she just threw a party the other night at her house."

A party?

Finally, near September 15, Donna returned George's page.

"Just wanted to know how you were, Donna," George said.

She laughed. The line was quiet for a time.

"I want to tell you what's going on, but you won't want to know," Donna replied.

Immediately George thought—based on the tone Donna used—that she "had moved on with her life" and she had "a new boyfriend." It was a relief and a shock. George had told Donna some time before this phone conversation that if she ever went out and found a new mate, "I don't want to know about it."

George had a feeling after this call that he and Donna, someday, might laugh at this entire episode of their lives. Maybe they could even work together again. All Donna needed was time to get over it. George could forgive and look toward the future. People said things under duress and depression they did not truly mean.

The next day George sent Donna a dozen carnations, wishing her luck with an upcoming audit that her company was going through. It was part of a new sale Donna said she was involved in. If the audit went well, a corporation was going to buy CCHH and dig Donna out of a financial hole.

I wish you luck, love, George, he wrote on the card accompanying the flowers.

46

DONNA WAS WORKING behind the scenes assembling a team—though not the trio one might have imagined. This was no dream team of businesspeople set to handle the sale. Donna was putting together a squad of killers. She had made a choice: Gail would have to be killed. It was the only way to win George back.

On September 26, 1999, at 10:26 P.M., Donna had Sybil Padgett—the team leader—phone George. He wasn't home—or he wasn't answering his phone. The answering machine picked up, instead: "Hey . . . George, it's me, Sybil. I'm just calling because [Donna's] real upset. I don't want nuttin' . . . but please call me back. I just want to talk to ya—just want to find out what's going on. She's havin' a really hard time, and she really cares a lot about ya . . . and I just don't understand what's all goin' on, and I just want to find out . . . because I am concerned for Donna. I just wish you'd return the call . . . and talk to me if you would. I'm out to dinner right now with a friend of mine, and Donna beeped me and she was all upset, crying and crying." Sybil said she wouldn't be home until later that night, but she stressed, "You know, please, George, just try to touch base and let's talk. I really care a lot about Donna, and I don't like seeing her like this. I've been with her a long time . . . and I—I just don't like seeing her like this. I want to talk to you, George." Sybil paused. Then: "Please call me." She left a phone number. "Good night, George. Sweet dreams."

Donna called George's home office the next day, over and over, all morning and afternoon long. Emily could hear from upstairs that the phone would not stop ringing.

When Donna finally figured out George was not going to answer, she called incessantly upstairs, the Fultons' home number.

Sick and tired of a ringing telephone, Emily picked it up: "*What* do you *want*?"

"I need to speak to him, Emily. Where *is* he? There's an emergency here at the office. . . . I need to speak with him now!"

"He took my mother to Mackinac Island," Emily explained. George and Gail were gone on a romantic weekend getaway.

This brought about a long beat of silence. If Emily's guess was right, Donna was furious.

Donna started screaming at Emily before becoming "very upset." Then she hung up.

When George returned, he called Donna. Not once during this call did Donna ever mention Emily had told her where Gail and George had gone that weekend. Instead, Donna sounded cheery and upbeat. She talked about CCHH and wondered if George was still willing to do some work for her.

Donna refused to accept that George was more devoted to his wife than her, said a law enforcement report. *The guilt leverage she placed on George's conscience had failed.*

Donna tried reasoning with George.

Begging.

Lying.

Bullying.

Screaming.

Crying.

The silent treatment.

None of it worked.

But now, that same law enforcement document reported: *[Donna] . . . had a final solution.*

III

———✦———

A VIEW TO A KILL

47

HELEN PADGETT AND her daughter were about as close as could be under the circumstances. Helen had watched Sybil's children, a little girl (nine years old) and a little boy (four years old), whenever Sybil went out, running around, doing errands for Donna. In late September, Helen was mothering her grandchildren more than their own mother. This greatly troubled Helen. She loved her daughter, but she wondered what Sybil had gotten herself into.

Helen did not like the idea that Sybil invited her nineteen-year-old boyfriend, Patrick Alexander, a skinny, lanky kid with no future, to live with her at the house Sybil rented on East Orange Street in DeFuniak Springs, Florida. Not for nothing, but Sybil was seventeen years older than Patrick. Same as with a previous relationship she had been in (and a husband who had, according to Sybil, beaten her up), the scent of trouble oozed from Patrick. What was a nineteen-year-old unemployed kid doing living with a thirty-six-year-old woman? Sure, he could be using Sybil, but she didn't have a pot to piss in. On top of that, Sybil's girlfriend lived in the house. Among them all, they could not afford to keep a landline phone turned on, much less take care of Sybil's children. The house was a pigsty; the yard was unkempt.

Sybil drove around in a green 1999 Malibu that her boss, Donna, had rented under the guise of Sybil needing a vehicle for work.

Helen once asked Sybil, what's going on? (Although Helen couldn't recall, when asked by police, the exact day.) Something seemed to be bothering Sybil. She was preoccupied. She hadn't been herself.

"You *know,* Ma," Sybil said.

"Don't get involved in that, Sybil," Helen responded.

Sybil stared at her mother. What was Helen talking about? Did she truly know what Sybil was planning and what she had been doing for Donna?

Helen had overheard Sybil and Patrick talking about "it." She wasn't supposed to hear the conversation. Helen asked Sybil what Donna wanted from her. If what she had eavesdropped on was true, Helen thought Donna was pressuring Sybil to get involved in something dangerous. ("She told me about it one time," Helen said later, "that Donna wanted her to kill Gail.")

"Don't do it, Sybil!" Helen said.

"Ma!"

Her mother wanted to know more.

"George was living with Gail *and* Donna, and George went back to Gail."

Helen later told police: "And Donna wanted her done away with."

Helen had no idea who these people were, other than the few details Sybil had given her, and what she had heard Sybil say during her conversations. This included the fact that there was $2,500 up for grabs for the person who completed the job.

"From whom?" Helen asked. Who was putting up the money to have another woman murdered?

"Donna," Sybil said.

Helen thought she knew her daughter well enough to

know she was never going to get involved in something so evil. Donna called the house one night. Helen, who lived four blocks away from Sybil, was there, watching Sybil's kids while Sybil and Patrick were out. Helen answered, saying, "Leave my daughter alone!"

"Sybil has been talking about committing suicide," Donna said, as if she had been there for Sybil as a friend, mentoring her, helping her, making sure Sybil didn't go through with it.

"Now *why* would she do that?" Helen asked. Donna seemed to be trying to take over the mothering role in Sybil's life. Helen had never seen any signs that Sybil was depressed enough to want to take her own life. What was all this talk about suicide, and Sybil being depressed and down and out?

Donna had a pathological, psychotic way of being able to come up with things on the spot. "Because of *you* and your *son*!" Donna snapped at Helen. "That's why she's so damn depressed. Sybil is sick and tired of taking care of y'all."

Donna was "calling and calling" the house. "She kept bothering Sybil." Sybil would come home from work, crying, never wanting to talk about it. That day, after Helen admitted she somewhat knew what Sybil was planning, she pleaded with her daughter: "Don't do it, honey."

Sybil left the house and they never discussed it again.

Then Sybil called Helen one morning near the end of September. "I need you to watch the kids, Ma."

"Sybil . . ."

"Just watch the kids for me next week. I need to go away for a few days with Patrick and some friends."

48

KEVIN OUELLETTE WAS on his way back to Florida from Ohio to meet his girlfriend, Stephanie Bowden, Sybil's roommate. Kevin had been living in Akron. He and Stephanie decided to get back together after a breakup. Kevin made a decision to ask Stephanie to marry him. This reunion in Florida was something Kevin had been looking forward to. Stephanie was a good woman. He'd been stupid to let her go.

"Hey," Kevin said over the phone as he rolled into Mobile, Alabama, "can you meet me? . . . I'm stuck. My car broke down."

Stephanie said sure.

"I done blew the motor, I think," Kevin reiterated. "Shit." He had a job lined up in Florida, but he needed his car to get there. Now this.

Kevin stood leaning against a telephone pole as Stephanie pulled up. DeFuniak Springs, Florida, where Stephanie lived with Sybil, was a 125-mile, two-hour trip through Spanish Fort, over Mobile Bay, into Mobile, Alabama, where Kevin left his vehicle. Still, they didn't have to go that far. Kevin had hitched a ride with a local truck driver into Marianna, Florida, an hour east of DeFuniak, not knowing he overshot the town where Stephanie lived with her roommate.

As they pulled up, Kevin noticed Stephanie had people with her.

"Hey," Stephanie said, jumping out of the car, embracing her man. Behind her was a large woman with long blond hair and piercing blue eyes. She stepped out of the car, walked over. "This is Sybil," Stephanie said, introducing her friend. "I'm staying with Sybil."

Then a tall, frail, punkish-looking young man emerged. He had dirty-blond hair, nearly buzz cut, a bit of peach fuzz for a beard and mustache. He was wiry and jumpy. Kevin didn't like him.

"This is Patrick," Stephanie said.

"Hey," Kevin said, nodding. "What's up?"

Patrick drove the 1999 green Malibu, which Sybil had been driving, to her rented house. Kevin had nowhere to stay. Sybil had told Stephanie he could live with them at the house if he wanted. There was plenty of room. Kevin had a job waiting for him, he explained, but since he had blown the motor of his car, and had no way of getting there, he was going to be fired before he started.

"Drop Stephanie and me off at a hotel," Kevin told Patrick.

"Wait," Sybil said, "just give me that money. . . . You can stay with us."

Kevin had a few hundred dollars on him. "All right," he said, trusting Stephanie's judgment about people.

It wasn't long after Kevin moved in with Sybil that he and Sybil were out on the porch one night, the sky a pinkish hue of cotton candy before them. Kevin sparked up a cigarette and started talking about not being able to find work without a vehicle. Without a car, he couldn't find a job, because he couldn't get there. He added, "I'm running low on money." He shook his head. Then he ran his hands through his hair and let out a long drag from his cigarette. He didn't know what to do. He felt like a loser.

"I know a way to make some easy money," Sybil suggested.

"What are you talking about?"

Sybil looked inside the house to make sure Stephanie wasn't around. With the coast clear she said, "I know somebody who wants somebody beat up."

Sybil heard Kevin had a past of beating people up for money, sort of like a bookie's muscleman. He was a big dude, at six feet, 235 pounds. Kevin had a pierced ear, tattoos, scars, and that rough "prison" look. He had once been a guy who broke flesh and shed blood for a price.

Kevin stared at Sybil, thinking. Then he turned his attention toward the setting sun, squinting, taking pull after pull from his cigarette. "Okay," he said casually, "I'll do it."

"Good," Sybil said.

Sybil walked into the house and called out to Patrick and Stephanie. "Come on, y'all, we're takin' a ride."

Sybil knocked on Donna's door, but Donna wasn't home. Donna had some "young guy" living with her, a boarder. The guy let them in and then went off and stayed to himself. They got comfortable and sat around having a few drinks. It was hours before Donna arrived.

Sybil greeted Donna as she came in and put her purse down on the counter. At first, Donna seemed startled, looking around, as if to imply, *Why the hell are y'all here?*

"Donna . . . Donna," Sybil said, "I want you to meet Mike." Kevin stood and walked over. Sybil smiled. It was as if she had gone out and found what Donna had been looking for. "This is Mike, Donna. . . . Remember . . . *Mike!*" (Wink-wink!)

Kevin looked at Sybil. *What is she talking about? Mike? What the hell?*

Sybil had promised to deliver a biker dude by the name

of Mike, who was going to take care of Gail, but Mike didn't want anything to do with "the job." Therefore, Sybil introduced Kevin as "Mike" in order to prove to Donna that she could deliver on a promise.

Donna looked at Stephanie and motioned for Patrick, Mike, and Sybil to follow her into her bedroom for privacy. Stephanie wasn't welcome.

"I'll be back, babe," Kevin told Stephanie.

After they got settled in Donna's bedroom, Donna opened with the familiar prologue that Patrick and Sybil had heard before: "I was dating this guy . . . and, well, he . . . left me for another woman!" She had an angry, vicious look about her. Blood had rushed into Donna's face, making her flush. The thought of it all had obviously brought Donna to another place. "I want this bitch taken care of—you *understand* me?"

"Taken care of"? Kevin thought. This was different from beaten up. *What is she asking?* But he didn't question Donna then and there. Instead, Kevin allowed Donna to continue.

As she told her stories of desperation and lover's anguish, Kevin was bored. The way he understood it, Donna was asking him to travel up to the state of Michigan and shoot—*kill*—a woman. Not simply rough her up. Quite a difference between the two.

"Five thousand dollars," Donna said—the price now on Gail's head.

Kevin liked the sound of that figure.

Patrick and Sybil sat on the bed, not saying much. Donna and Kevin talked.

Patrick, one law enforcement document stated, *knew Donna's plan was idiotic . . . but surrendered . . . so he could keep Sybil's sexual pleasures coming his way and please Sybil in general. Patrick had no direction in life other than what Sybil gave him.* Patrick was having the most incredible sex of his life, and nothing was going to stand in the way of it. He didn't care that Donna's plan, with all of these people knowing about it, would be figured out eventually. He was a victim of Sybil's manipulation, who, herself, was victimized and manipulated by Donna. Shit *did* roll downhill—Patrick Alexander's life was a good definition of the old cliché.

On the other hand, Kevin Ouellette, law enforcement explained, "had recent financial woes," which put Kevin in a position of weakness: *By nature, [Kevin] had a cold streak, which permitted him to engage in violence without much consideration for [the] reality of his conduct.* The guy was considering killing another human being for the price of a used car. Plus, he and Donna did not, for one moment, take into consideration the ramifications of their actions—the inevitable ripple effect of one murder affecting generations of Gail Fulton's family and friends. Additionally, this was nothing more than a *job* to Kevin. Employment. He didn't know what Gail looked like or, better yet, anything about her.

Kevin agreed to Donna's plan—with one hitch. "I'll do it," he explained after she made the offer, "so long as Sybil and Patrick help me."

Kevin was the solution to Donna's warped desires to maintain control of George Fulton, law enforcement reported. *Donna would* not *be denied.*

When they returned to Sybil's house, Kevin analyzed the crime in his head. Then he started asking questions.

"Yeah," Sybil said to one, "I went up to Michigan a couple of times already to case everything out and know the routine . . . the plan for everything." Sybil appeared confident. She knew Gail's schedule and could direct Kevin as to the best way to kill the woman. Sybil said she had a few ideas of her own.

"What are you thinking?" Kevin asked.

"The only time she's consistent," Sybil explained, going through Gail's week, "is Monday nights."

"What do you mean?"

"She works *every* Monday night and gets out at the same time."

Kevin liked the sound of that.

"It's a library," Sybil said.

On the following day Donna, Sybil, Patrick, Stephanie, and Kevin went out to eat. Then they went back to Donna's house to discuss the murder in more detail. Donna seemed to enjoy this part of the process, methodically going through it, focusing on specific aspects of the crime, as though getting off on how it would play out. Kevin had made it clear that he did not want Stephanie (who would later refer to Donna as "the boss lady") to know what they were doing. As far as she knew, Kevin was going to beat up someone.

Donna still thought she was dealing with a biker named Mike. No one had told her Kevin's real name. When they got back to the house after dinner, in fact, Sybil called Todd Franklin. Todd was that bed friend of Sybil's with whom she had first initiated the conversation about killing Gail.

"I'm sitting here with Mike," Sybil said, appeasing Donna, who was listening.

"What . . . Mike?" Todd asked.

"Your Mike."

Todd knew this couldn't be. He had never introduced Sybil to Mike.

"Well, let me talk to him, then."

Sybil laughed. She walked outside, away from Donna and the others. Whispering into the telephone, she said, "It's not *your* Mike. It's somebody *I* found—but Donna thinks it's your Mike."

Todd Franklin understood. He'd play along.

After the call Donna motioned for everyone to walk back into her bedroom; she had something she wanted to talk about with Mike.

Sybil, Patrick, Kevin, and Donna trekked into the murder room. Donna closed the door and walked toward Kevin slowly. Her eyes were on the ground, a hand on her chin.

"What's up?" Kevin asked. Patrick and Sybil sat on the bed and horsed around, as usual. They behaved as though this whole thing was like some sort of prank they were planning on a friend.

Quiet for a time, Donna finally spoke. She had something she wanted "Mike" to do while he was in Michigan. It was important. "I want you to kill *everybody* who comes out of that library with her—you understand me? It will look like a random thing, then. It won't look like you're *targeting* just the one person." Donna had thought long and hard about this part of the murder plan; she was willing to take out a slew of people—maybe four or five—just to claim her man. Donna, a woman running a business designed to help people and care for those who were sick, a nurse herself, wanted a mass murder so she and George could be together. She was willing to sacrifice a crowd of human beings for the sake of her passion.

"No way I'm doing that," Kevin said. No amount of money would change his mind. "Look here . . . I agreed to kill one you have this problem with"—he held up an index finger, even later recalling how he might have pointed it in Donna's face—"but I am *not* going to kill everyone that walks out of that library with her! No way."

"I'll throw in another twenty-five hundred," Donna promised, driving the total up to $7,500. She figured the guy was a killer. Every man had his price.

Kevin shook his head. "No . . . no . . . I am *not* agreeing to killing everyone that comes out of that library."

Donna changed the subject, talking about *when,* saying, "She gets off work every Monday at the same time."

Sybil listened, nodding in agreement.

"Okay," Kevin acknowledged.

"So the best day to do it would be on a Monday night," Donna said.

"Sounds good."

"Nine o'clock is probably, like, the best time," Sybil offered.

They decided Patrick would drive, Sybil would ride shotgun next to him, and Kevin, sitting in the back, would act as triggerman.

"We all good on that?" Donna asked, looking around the room.

A resounding "yes" echoed.

49

THEY ALL SLEPT at Donna's house that night. Kevin realized the following morning that there was a major problem that needed to be addressed immediately. He had been thinking about it ever since taking the job. He went to Sybil, who was just waking up.

"What is it?" Sybil asked. Kevin had this *look* on his face.

"A gun! I don't have a gun."

"Ah, I'll take care of that. I know someone."

"We'll talk later on about it."

"At home," Sybil said.

"Yeah."

That night Kevin walked out to the back porch, where Sybil sat, smoking a cigarette. Patrick wasn't home. He had gone out to a party.

"I got a problem," Kevin said. "I don't want Patrick involved."

"What? Why?"

"He's too young, Sib," Kevin answered, using Sybil's diminutive nickname. "He'll go out drinking, run his mouth some night, and get us all caught."

"I know," Sybil said. "I agree. But . . . you know, he already knows too much. Doesn't matter now."

Kevin had accepted $2,500 from Donna. She had paid him in cash. He gave Sybil $150 and told her that was the weapon budget.

Kevin had always wanted a fast car. It was a dream. After Donna fronted him half the money, he went and put a down payment on a 1974 Trans Am, which he had found in the newspaper.

Then the morning came—October 3, 1999, a Sunday.

"You guys ready?" Kevin asked.

"You bet," Sybil said. The night before, a "black guy," as Kevin later described him, "showed up at the house and brought a thirty-eight Smith and Wesson revolver." Kevin had been in the military. He grew up around hunters and guns. He knew his way around a weapon. This was a solid gun. It could do tremendous damage if fired at the right distance.

As they walked out to the car, Kevin spotted something. He asked out loud if anyone knew what happened to the back taillight.

"Shit," Patrick said. He explained how he had taken the car out the previous night to a party and backed into a tree on the way out of the driveway. "I put some tape over it. It'll be fine."

"Get in," he told them. "Let's go."

Kevin dressed in the mood of the crime he was about to commit: black leather jacket, black jeans, black boots, black do-rag. Sybil took an old winter wool ski mask (black) she had found inside her house and tossed it in the trunk. "Maybe you can use this?" she asked Kevin.

Kevin drove first. Patrick and Sybil sat in the backseat. They stopped in Birmingham, Alabama, so Kevin could grab a few things from his car. ("Some clothes . . . and a couple of photo albums," Kevin remarked later.)

From Alabama, Patrick took over. They drove into Ohio.

Kevin had a friend he wanted to meet up with so Patrick and Sybil could get some weed. It was a good place to stop and grab a hotel. Eat. Sleep. Then drive on to Michigan. Akron, where his friend lived, was not far from the library where Gail worked—they could make the drive in half a day. Plus, there was something else Kevin needed that he could get only in Akron.

50

IT WAS LATE that same Sunday, October 3. Cathy Baxter (pseudonym) was on her way out the door with her father, heading for the corner bar. She wasn't expecting the call.

"Hey," said a familiar voice from the past, "me and two friends are here in Toledo. Was wondering if we could come through Akron and hang out overnight?" It was a lie, obviously. Kevin, Sybil, and Patrick were not far from Akron, but heading north *from* the south. Toledo was northwest of Akron, right there at the western tip of Lake Erie.

"Kevin . . . my gosh," Cathy said, a bit startled. "How are you? Yes, sure. Come on over."

Cathy and Kevin had been friends for about three and a half years. At the time Cathy lived in Akron, which, arguably, was the tire capital of the world. It was a big city, with lots of nightlife and action.

When Kevin pulled up, Cathy could not, she later said, tell what type of car he was driving, because it was—literally—a "dark, rainy night. . . ." The car was a rental. That much she knew, because Kevin had told her.

"It was a four-door and wrecked in the rear quarter panel. That's all I remember."

Kevin wasn't alone. He had two other people Cathy didn't recognize with him. "This is Sybil," Kevin told Cathy. Sybil smiled and waved from inside the car. "That's Patrick," Kevin said, pointing to the skinny dude sitting next to Sybil.

Originally they had made plans to meet at Cathy's house. However, Cathy had gone down the block to a local gin mill with her father and ended up leaving Kevin a note at the house. The introductions between them took place inside the car after Kevin had gone into the bar and asked Cathy to take a ride. By now, it was "lights out" time in the bar, around 1:30 A.M.

"Last call. . . ."

As the four of them took off from the bar, Kevin asked Cathy if she could point them in the direction of a cheap hotel in the area, where they could park it for the night.

"Just down the road," Cathy said. "Go straight, make a right at the corner."

Kevin drove down Newton Street, then made his way closer to the main highway, Route 76. They stopped at a "couple different motels, trying to find the cheapest rate," Cathy explained, but they didn't have any luck. The Best Western on Gilchrist "was too expensive" for Kevin's tastes, Cathy said. So Kevin drove toward South Arlington under Cathy's direction, heading into the center of Akron.

"There's a Red Roof Inn there," Cathy said.

Kevin agreed that a Red Roof Inn was probably more within his budget.

"So what brings you guys out this way?" Cathy asked. "Wow, all the way from Florida!" They were getting out of the car, heading into the lobby of the Red Roof Inn. Cathy was thinking, *Geez, a thousand-mile trip, almost sixteen hours—why here? Why now?*

"Sybil works in the geriatric field and, um . . . her boss . . . she sent her to Toledo for some classes," Kevin, doing most of the talking, said. "Sybil done lost her damn license, so she paid me to drive her out here."

"Why come all the way to Ohio, though?" This seemed strange to Cathy.

Were there not any classes closer?

"I don't know," Kevin said.

("He just kind of blew it off, and I took him for his word. I figured that's what they were doing.")

"Okay," Cathy responded.

"Hey, listen, you mind putting the room in *your* name?" Kevin asked his old friend. They were almost at the lobby desk.

"What? No. . . . Why, Kevin? What's going on?"

"If anything happens, you know . . . I don't want anything left behind that would put me being here."

Cathy thought this to be an odd statement. *Why would he say such a thing? What in the heck is Kevin talking about?*

Approaching the desk clerk, Kevin reached into his pocket, pulled out a roll of cash, and paid for the room—probably not the smartest thing he'd ever done—and put it in his own name.

Sybil and Patrick unloaded the luggage. They all went up to the room. After unpacking, they sat around for a short time and chitchatted.

"You need to take me back to the bar," Cathy said at one point. "I left my purse in my dad's truck." Cathy and her father had gone to the bar together. She had taken off with Kevin and the others. "I didn't think we'd be gone this long," she added, looking at the LCD clock on the nightstand.

Kevin nodded. "No problem."

Cathy and Kevin took off.

After they stopped and picked up Cathy's purse back at the bar, Kevin said, "Hey, is there a Walmart round here?"

"Yup . . . right next to your hotel."

The store was one of those twenty-four-hour outlets. Kevin walked in. Cathy followed. He headed directly back to the "hunting area" of the store, as Cathy later put it, but "they were closed."

"When y'all opening up again here?" Kevin asked a store employee.

"In the morning," the guy said. "Six o'clock."

"What do you need back here?" Cathy asked.

"Bullets."

("I never thought anything of it," Cathy later said, "because he drove a truck, and it seemed logical to me." At times Kevin worked as an over-the-road trucker, hauling loads in one of those big eighteen-wheelers, or smaller box trucks, with sleepers. Having a gun meant getting a good night's sleep in his rig. And what good was a gun without any bullets?)

"Come on," Kevin said, "I need something else."

Cathy followed.

Kevin walked over to the medicine aisle and picked up some rubbing alcohol.

When they got back to the hotel room, Kevin, Patrick, Sybil, and Cathy were "all just sitting around" shooting the shit. Patrick and Sybil had some leftover food they ate. Kevin got up at one point, put on a pair of what Cathy described as "baseball batting gloves"—those stretchy latex types that golfers use, too—and pulled "something wrapped in a towel and T-shirt out of his coat."

What in the world?

At first, Cathy didn't know what it was; but then, as Kevin presented it in a proud gesture, as if displaying a prized fish he had just caught, she realized, "It was the biggest handgun I had ever seen."

There were two beds in the room. Cathy sat on one by herself. Patrick and Sybil, playing around like teen lovers, giggling and talking sexy, tickling each other, laughing and whispering, sat on the other bed. Kevin positioned himself at the desk chair, a mirror in front of him, marveling at this enormous weapon in his gloved hands.

As Cathy looked on, Kevin took out that rubbing alcohol he purchased back at Walmart and placed it on the desk in front of him. Then he removed "three or four bullets" from the chambers of the gun, wiped each bullet down with rubbing alcohol and a tissue, wiped the entire gun off, put each bullet back into its respective chamber, stared at the weapon admiringly for a beat, wrapped it back up in his T-shirt, and put it back in his coat pocket.

Kevin was ready—and so was his gun.

Cathy later talked about the utter look of fascination on Kevin's face as he sat and methodically went about cleaning the gun, bullets, and then wrapping them back up. It was as if he had entered into another realm. Kevin had that rebel-without-a-cause look, to begin with: searing blue eyes, dark hair, a bit of a boy-band beard and goatee, hair slicked back like Elvis. But with that gun in his hand, a cigarette hanging from the corner of his mouth, a look of darkness on his face, he resembled a young Marlon Brando—a "wild one" on a mission. Someone hired to do a job he loved.

"Does anyone want a soda?" Patrick asked. He jumped up from the bed, putting his hand on the doorknob.

They all said, hell yeah.

Patrick left. Sybil stayed.

"Too bad we had to bring him, huh, Sib?" Kevin said out loud. Patrick was out of the room by then, on his way to the vending machine.

"Uh-huh," Sybil answered.

"He's just in the way, ain't he, Sib?"

"He sure is, Kev."

Sybil turned to Cathy at that point and said, "We had to bring him, though, ultimately, because he *knows* too much." She smiled.

What? Cathy thought. *Knows what?*

Cathy had no idea what they were talking about. Still, she knew whatever it was, she didn't need to know, so she never asked or pushed the issue. Instead, Cathy Baxter nodded, playing along, as though she knew what they were referring to.

51

CATHY WOKE UP first the following morning, October 4, 1999. She had slept with Kevin, but she didn't "sleep" with him. Kevin had been a friend of the Baxter family for a long time. He even lived with Cathy's family for a brief period.

Cathy needed to rustle everyone up and get them moving so they could check out. While getting their stuff together, Patrick asked Cathy, "Hey, you know anyone round here who can sell us some weed?"

"I do," Cathy said.

Patrick looked at Kevin, the de facto leader of the group, almost as if to ask for permission.

They drove to Cathy's connection and "waited there for probably two hours or so, until they got it."

"You know where I can get me some more bullets?" Kevin asked Cathy, who had become like some sort of intern. She could tell by now they had stopped in Akron to use her to get the things they needed for whatever they were up to. But she didn't want to say anything, obviously.

"There's a pawnshop nearby," Cathy said. "They probably sell them. Let's check it out."

"Let's go."

Patrick, Sybil, and Cathy sat in the car while Kevin went into the pawnshop.

"He came out," Cathy later explained, "with a brown paper lunch-size bag that had a box in it."

Kevin drove. Cathy requested to be dropped off. "I need to get back home, Kevin. It was nice seeing you."

"Sure," he said.

Kevin, Patrick, and Sybil dropped Cathy off at her apartment in downtown Akron, said their good-byes, and headed northwest, toward Lake Erie. They had about a four-hour drive ahead: up and around the left tip of Lake Erie, through Toledo and Detroit, and then finally past the Rochester Hills region of Lake Orion, where Gail Fulton was at home preparing to go to work at the library for what would be the last day of her life.

About six hours before Gail was murdered, Donna Trapani e-mailed George and asked if he had billed a company for several claims CCHH processed back in September. According to Donna, the claims amounted to "lots of money." She listed seven of the actual claims George was supposed to have billed. The e-mail was all business. Nothing personal.

George responded at 6:38 P.M., saying he didn't have all of his notes in front of him in order to bill the company accurately—and that was it.

Gail was at work by then.

Donna Trapani was at home in Florida.

A band of murderers was on its way to Lake Orion.

52

BACK AT THE pawnshop in Akron, where Cathy Baxter brought Kevin, Kevin went inside the shop by himself and asked the owner if he had a speed loader for his .38-caliber weapon. A speed loader allows the shooter to load all the rounds at once into each chamber, instead of one bullet at a time. In asking for this speed loader, what was Kevin planning? Did he have a change of heart? Was he going to mow down everyone who walked out of the library with Gail in order to make it look like some nutbag had "gone postal" in Lake Orion? Surely, six shots were enough to take out Gail. Why would he need to reload the weapon so quickly?

The pawnshop clerk said he didn't have a speed loader for that six-shot model .38.

At this point of the trip, Kevin later remarked, he did not even know the name of the town they were heading into to commit the murder. All Kevin knew, he said, was that it was near Detroit. So as they passed through the Motor City, breezing by the seat of Wayne County, Kevin pulled over and parked the Malibu at a gas station. Before stepping out of the vehicle, he leaned over the seat and looked at Patrick. "You drive from here. I have to go get some cigarettes."

When he came out of the gas station, Kevin was looking at the back of the Malibu as he walked toward the car, shaking his head. "Shit . . . that's great. Just great."

Sybil and Patrick heard him and looked at each other.

That damn broken taillight.

Kevin walked back into the gas station and bought some tape. The taillight was hanging. During their trip north, the tape Patrick had put on in Florida had come undone. During the entire time he did this, Kevin had his .38 packed in the side pocket of his leather jacket, as if he were some sort of professional hit man.

After he finished taping the taillight back together, Kevin sat in the backseat, and Sybil moved into the front with Patrick. Patrick and Sybil had been up here already; they knew where they were headed. Kevin didn't even want to think about it. He was focused.

"We're close," Sybil said. "Lake Orion is right up the road. Let's get ready here." She got out of the car. Patrick followed. Sybil popped the trunk and took out that ski mask. She handed it (and a map) to Kevin, who was still sitting inside the car. Sybil and Donna had written notes all over the map, plotting out Gail's every move: where she went on a certain night, where she lived, where she worked and went to social events. It showed the systematic nature of planning this murder from Sybil's and Donna's perspective. Kevin, a male, was more focused on the mission—getting there and committing the kill; Sybil and Donna, however, were fixated on the mechanics of the murder: the intimate ins and outs of every possible scenario, as if they enjoyed the choreography involved in plotting and planning.

"Here," Sybil told Kevin, "take the mask."

"Right," he said, staring at it on his lap. "Let's go."

An eerie silence took over inside the vehicle as they drove toward the library. It was near eight o'clock at night.

Gail didn't leave work until nine. Sybil wanted to case the parking lot, though, and Kevin wanted a handle on how many people were still around. Additionally, they needed to find out if Gail was actually working. For all they knew, she might have left early or called in sick.

After some time Patrick took the right on Joslyn Road into the Orion Township Library parking lot and drove around the inverted J-shaped entrance drive. Pine trees as perfectly straight as arrowheads lined the lot. When they took the corner and the parking lot appeared before them, closer to the building, where patrons and employees parked their vehicles, Kevin was shocked to see how many people were still there this late into the night.

"There was a whole bunch . . . there," Kevin said later.

Kevin had no idea what type of vehicle they were looking for, but Sybil and Patrick had stalked Gail. They knew her van. Where was it?

Patrick drove the Malibu through various lanes, passing white-lined parking spaces. It was dark, even though there were plenty of overhead lights. The southwestern portion of the parking lot was surrounded by dense, thickly settled woods; the northern side was lined with a row of pines in front of the South Newman Road neighborhood adjacent to the parking area. There was a long, multiple-acre field directly in the back eastern portion of the lot. So there was good cover all the way around. The only witnesses they had to worry about were people coming out of the library, or anyone pulling into the parking lot to pick up someone.

"There it is," Sybil said, pointing out Gail's van. "Pull up over there."

"No way I'm doing this with all these cars and people around," Kevin said from the backseat, his eyes darting side to side. "No way."

Patrick stopped the Malibu near Gail's van.

At first, they stared at Gail's van without speaking. Then Kevin and Sybil started talking, figuring how it could be done.

Sybil got out. She walked over and checked to see if Gail's van was unlocked.

"Patrick, you go into the library," Kevin ordered from the backseat. "You find out for me how many people are still working."

"Yup."

Patrick walked into the library.

Kevin got out of the car, and he and Sybil spoke.

"If it's not locked," Sybil said, "you can get in, and as she leaves, do it then."

Kevin liked that idea. Come up from behind Gail while she drove—and pop her in the back of the head. No one would see a thing. Just a flash of light inside a van. Gail wouldn't have a clue it was even coming.

"It's locked," Sybil said after trying all the doors. "Damn."

"Shit."

Patrick came back. They all sat inside the Malibu.

"Any ideas?" Sybil asked. "What's the best way?"

Kevin didn't say anything. He was thinking. Patrick knew his place by now and kept his mouth shut.

"I got it," Sybil said. "Cut one of her tires. She'll get stuck there after everybody else leaves."

Kevin remained quiet. Then he got out, looked around the parking lot, took out his knife, and slashed the back passenger-side tire of Gail's van.

A loud *hissssss* . . . and the van sank to one side.

"Gail's working now," Patrick said. "There's four or five employees with her."

"Leave," Kevin said. "Go. Get out of here."

Patrick took off out of the parking lot.

53

KEVIN NEEDED TO make certain some of the people cleared out. So he had Patrick drive around the town of Lake Orion for "about a half hour." Patrick took a right out of the parking lot onto Joslyn Road; then he headed toward South Newman and Square Lake, just around the corner.

Patrick Alexander originally thought of this plot to kill Gail Fulton as some sort of "crazy idea" Sybil had cooked up with Donna: a revenge-driven pipe dream that would never happen. Sybil was always going on about her wild side, Patrick later said. She was an idealist, easily manipulated by Donna, who knew Sybil's weaknesses and insecurities better than anyone else, and used them against her. Sybil was her own worst enemy.

Still, Patrick Alexander went along with Sybil's plan simply because he was having great sex and did not believe half of what she said.

"It blew my mind," Patrick later told police, "to think that stuff like this—something you usually see on television—and there it was before my own eyes and . . . something that happened in real life." Not so much a wordsmith, or confident while explaining himself, but Patrick made his point. "That was my exact thought—'Man, here it is in my life and it's happening to me!'"

The first time it occurred to Patrick that he was involved in a bona fide conspiracy to commit murder was when he stood by and watched Donna offer Sybil money to find someone to kill Gail, or do it herself. He knew then that they were serious about the plan.

"Here is somebody offering me money to go kill someone and stuff like that. . . . I used to see this stuff on TV. That's what blowed my mind."

According to Patrick, Donna's first offer was $15,000. She had made the offer to Sybil, but Sybil said she would think about it. Before she agreed to anything, Sybil wanted to discuss it with Patrick and see what he thought.

"I would tell her 'No, it's not the right thing. You've got kids. You have to think about that kind of thing.' But as time grew on, it got harder, to where we were having to scratch and scrape to get money to buy the kids food and everything. So we decided to do it."

"We." Patrick admitted he and Sybil were equally culpable, had made this decision together. And yet, same as Kevin and Sybil would soon bullhorn, Patrick was also saying that Donna Trapani was the mastermind behind it all.

Donna had been badgering Patrick and Sybil for a month, Patrick claimed, before they took off to do the job, begging them, frosting the situation with the idea that the money they made ("You won't get caught . . . trust me. . . .") would take care of Sybil's kids for quite a while. Donna kept harping on it and asking them to go through with it, but Sybil couldn't do it by herself, she said, and certainly didn't want to have Patrick do it for her. The guy could barely do laundry by himself. So to get Donna off her back, Sybil told Donna about Mike, the biker, explaining how Mike was the right person for the job.

The pressure Donna put on the both of them, Patrick

later said, became sweeping and all-consuming. They could not get away from Donna. It was as if Donna had had some sort of hold on Sybil.

"Very much to the point where, see, that was her boss lady, you know, and she (Sybil) couldn't work nowheres else, so she pressured us to the point, you know, to where . . . I mean, sure, we had other options we could have taken, but we didn't feel like that, you know, 'cause she had, more or less, had us hanging by a string . . . 'cause she *controlled* Sybil's money and everything. . . . It was basically a long, drawn-out process."

So they drove around Lake Orion, near the public library, for a half hour and returned.

"I'll drive," Sybil said.

"Yeah," Patrick said.

"No, I don't want to now," Sybil said.

"Come on," Patrick said. "I'm tired of it."

"Shut up," Kevin shouted from the backseat. "Just pull over." They were a few miles from the library entrance.

Kevin hopped into the front seat and drove. When he got to the entrance, he pulled over and told Patrick to take the wheel. Sybil did not move. She sat in the front seat and kept her trap shut. It was not yet nine o'clock, so they sat on the side of the road until it was a few minutes before the hour.

Then Patrick drove the car into the parking lot.

"Pull over there," Kevin directed, "to the back end of the parking lot and *park* the damn car." Tension was taut. Nerves were frayed. Kevin knew the time was coming to play this thing out. He needed to produce. They had come all this way.

Patrick parked. Kevin got out and placed a white T-shirt over the license plate of the Malibu, in case someone heard the shots and came running out. Finished, he walked over to the car, hopped in, and told Patrick, "Go inside and *find* her." This time (according to Patrick's recollection), Kevin handed him a photo of Gail, which "Donna had given him."

"Make sure she's still working," Kevin said.

Patrick got out and walked inside the library.

When he came back a few minutes later, he said, "Yup. She's in there."

"Pull up and park a few spots away from her van," Kevin instructed, taking complete control. At times it sounded as though Kevin found himself dealing with two idiots who couldn't get out of their own way.

Patrick did what he was told. Sybil wasn't saying much of anything.

"Now we wait for her to come out," Kevin said, sounding like a boss.

As they sat and watched the employee entrance, workers emerged just past the nine o'clock hour. They walked out of the employee doors and into the parking lot; they all reached into their purses and jackets to fetch car keys.

Then they all got into their cars and left.

"That's her," Sybil said, pointing to a woman walking out of the door by herself. The parking lot was clear by now. Gail was alone.

Perfect.

Here was Gail: slowly and unknowingly walking toward her death.

"Stay put . . . ," Kevin said. They agreed she would get into her van, realize the tire was flat, and then stop. Kevin had the mask Sybil brought for him. He put it on. Sybil coiled her long blond hair up and stuffed it inside a baseball cap.

Gail did exactly what she was supposed to do, right on cue.

"Now you pull up behind her," Kevin told Patrick, who

started the car and drove around one of the islands as Gail pulled back into the same spot she had just pulled out of.

They were now directly behind Gail's van.

Gail got out. She walked toward the back of her vehicle. She looked down at the back tire. Then she turned to see who was driving up on her.

Kevin stepped out of the car. He walked hurriedly toward Gail.

She realized immediately what was happening.

"I shot four times," Kevin said later, describing that next moment.

Gail looked directly into his eyes.

The first shot was aimed. "In the head," Kevin explained. The next three were shot at random. It was over in a matter of seconds.

Kevin jumped back into the car. "Go . . . go . . . go!"

Sybil and Patrick said nothing.

Patrick took a sharp left out of the library's entrance, chirping the tires, speeding toward Route 24 to make the connection with Interstate 75. The plan was to make it to a truck stop near the Ohio border as soon as possible, head through Toledo, then make a fast track south.

As they sped down the street outside the library, Patrick pulled into an apartment complex and parked.

Kevin jumped out and ripped the T-shirt off the license plate.

"Go, man . . . drive."

They made it to a truck stop near the border in good time. Kevin was in need of some alcohol to calm his nerves. He sent Patrick into the store to get "some change," he said, but did not explain further why he did this. Nevertheless, as Patrick walked around the store, Kevin and Sybil spoke outside.

"He can probably keep his mouth shut," Kevin said to Sybil, meaning Patrick.

"Yeah."

Patrick returned and gave Kevin his change; then Kevin went in to get some booze.

Kevin took over driving from there. They made it, he said, "all the way down to Kentucky" without stopping much.

"I'm too tired to drive anymore," Kevin said as they crossed the border. "You want to get a hotel or drive?" he asked Patrick.

"I'll drive," Patrick said. He'd had his fill of Sybil by now. As Kevin drove from Ohio down toward Kentucky, Patrick and Sybil had had sex in the backseat several times.

As Patrick drove, Kevin lay down in the backseat and slept.

"You know," Patrick said a while later, "I think I'd like to stop and get a hotel."

It was close to five in the morning. They grabbed a room and slept until checkout at ten. Then they got back on the road, grabbed some breakfast, and headed toward Birmingham, Alabama, where Kevin's car had been parked.

"I had a cooler in there, some CB equipment, and some tools, and various odds and ends," Kevin later said. He wanted to pick that stuff up before they returned to Florida.

"Find a pay phone," Kevin said to Patrick after they drove away from his abandoned car.

Patrick spotted a phone up the road and pulled over.

"Page Donna," Kevin ordered Patrick.

"Okay."

Kevin went into a nearby convenience store to grab a coffee and some smokes. They all sat in the car, "sitting there, waiting for her (Donna) to call . . . waiting and waiting, and it didn't seem like she was going to call back."

Donna knew what the call meant as her pager went off.

She had spoken to the police over the phone just a few hours before.

Patrick and Sybil walked back to the car and took a load off. They were tired of waiting for Donna. Kevin waited by the pay phone, smoking cigarettes, thinking about what he had done. There was no turning back now. He had killed a woman. He wanted his money.

The pay phone startled Kevin as it rang.

"Yeah?"

"It's Donna."

"It's all done," Kevin reported.

"I already *know* that. I got a call from the police. They questioned me about George's whereabouts—I was on the phone with him when it happened."

Covering her own self, Kevin thought.

"Well, we'll be in town in a few hours—have my money ready. You got that?"

He hung up.

Instead of driving to Sybil's, Kevin instructed Patrick to drive straight to Donna's.

"Mike," Donna said as they all walked in, "how did it go?"

"I just want my money," Kevin answered.

"She kept on asking me questions about how it—you know, what happened," Kevin said later. "She wanted *specific* details. And I told her, 'Don't worry about it. It's done. Give me my money.'"

It wasn't that Kevin did not want to assuage Donna's demon seed and provide those violent particulars and images of Gail's final moments, which Donna so deeply craved, but, Kevin explained, "The less she knew, the better."

Donna realized Kevin wasn't going to talk. Anyway, she could get the details she wanted from Sybil later on. So

Donna took out some cash and counted out $1,000, slapping the bills on the table for Kevin to see.

"What is this?"

"What do you mean?"

"Where's the rest?"

"I'm waiting on a check to clear," Donna said. "It's supposed to come into my business, and I'll pay you when it comes in and clears."

Sybil started to say something. Donna cut her off. She had an idea. "Sib, I can write you and a few of your friends personal checks and you can cash them and give the cash to Mike."

A little bit of a harder paper trail to follow, Donna suggested (but one, she didn't quite realize, cops would have no trouble figuring out).

Donna flipped open her personal checkbook and started writing.

They left Donna's and stopped at the Waffle House for something to eat. Then they drove to one of Kevin's favorite retail outlets these days.

Walmart.

54

KEVIN OUELLETTE HAD KILLED a woman whose family was suffering now, and would continue to suffer as the long days and nights of mourning carried on. While Emily and Andrew Fulton wiped tears and learned the specifics of what had happened the night before, Gail's killers shopped for stereo equipment, hygienic and household items at a local Walmart near Fort Walton, Florida. Kevin had about $1,400 cash on him to spend on whatever he wanted. Donna had promised the remainder in a few days.

"So I picked up a new stereo for my car [that Trans Am he had purchased before the murder] and a couple of other small odds and ends."

Kevin had ditched the gun the previous night while driving over a bridge in Tennessee, later saying, "We went across a body of water, and I rolled down the window and I threw the gun out."

The only problem, as Patrick later told it, was that the gun hit one of the pylons or guardrails on the bridge and bounced back onto the busy road.

"It didn't make it quite over the guardrail," Kevin added. "It hit the guardrail and came back onto the highway and slid across the bridge."

"You better go back and grab that," Sybil had suggested. Patrick agreed with his girlfriend as they watched the gun slide into traffic.

"You kiddin'—no way!" Kevin said. "The road's too busy."

So they left it.

After leaving Walmart, Kevin drove to Sybil's. They were all exhausted, physically and—one would only imagine—emotionally.

It was a few days before Donna came over to the house to see what was going on and deliver some more money.

"She came over," Kevin recalled, "with a bunch of printouts from the computer from the paper. . . ."

Donna brought the articles and stood inside Sybil's bedroom, where she talked to her about the content. Kevin was shocked to see Donna had blown right past him without mentioning his money, so he followed her into Sybil's bedroom.

"What's going on?" Kevin asked. "You bring my money?" He looked down at the folder in Donna's hand. It wasn't one article about the murder Donna had with her, but an entire file.

Kevin took one and read.

"You did a good job, Mike—the papers call it a 'professional' hit," Donna said. She had a cocky smile and calm presence about her. Clearly, Donna was very happy with the result.

Donna rifled through the articles, looking for one in particular. She wanted to show Sybil something. Among all the patting on the back and celebrating, there was one little problem. As professional a hit as it might have come across as, there was this teeny-weeny issue of the entire murder being caught on videotape.

"What?" Sybil snapped. "What are you *talking* about?"

Kevin was startled. "Videotape?"

"Yeah. The library has cameras."

"Son of a bitch," Sybil said. Breathing heavily, she paced.

Donna calmed her and then headed for the door, saying, "I'll be back in a few days."

Kevin sat on the porch as Donna got out of her car and walked up to the door. She stopped before going into the house and took a look inside to make sure no one else could hear. "I have an idea to get the heat off," Donna said quietly.

"What?" Kevin asked.

By now, it was clear from the newspapers that the OCSD was busily investigating the case and would eventually tie Gail's murder to George Fulton and Donna Trapani. Undoubtedly, they would soon be in the state of Florida banging on doors. Kevin was no dummy. He understood when dominoes began to fall, names were as good as years shaved off your sentence. Sybil and Patrick would roll over like bloated fish.

Donna sat down. "Listen," she said in a whisper, "I will type up a note saying something . . . like . . . sometimes people see the wrong people, and the wrong people are taken out. I want you to find some druggie off the street up there [in Michigan], kill him, and plant the note on him."

The master manipulator wanted Kevin to commit a *second* murder to cover the first, so the cops could pin it all on a street junkie. That's what Kevin understood Donna to be suggesting.

"I'll pay you what I owe you, *plus* an additional five thousand dollars," Donna promised.

Kevin thought about this as he took a pull from his cigarette. *She wants me to drive all the way back to Michigan—the scene of the crime—and find some dude and kill him.*

"Yeah," Kevin said. "Sounds like a good idea."

Kevin had another plan, however. Take the additional $5,000 and tell Donna to go for a long walk off a nice Florida pier; he wasn't killing anyone else.

"Really?" she said.

"I want the entire five thousand up front."

They made plans to meet in a few days.

At some point later, Kevin was out. He paged Donna.

"Yeah?" she said, calling him back.

"Let's meet up."

"Where?"

"Tom Thumb."(This was a convenience store near Sybil's house.)

Kevin parked near the entrance. He sat and waited for three hours.

Donna never showed up.

"That kind of got me mad," he later said.

Kevin drove home and found Sybil. "Hey," he snapped, "you tell your friend that it ain't too smart to hire someone to kill somebody and *not* pay them! You understand!"

Donna paid Kevin in small amounts, none of it adding up to what she had promised. During one of her trips to Sybil's, as she walked into the house, Donna noticed the Malibu had a banged-up taillight. She was livid.

"Patrick," Sybil explained.

"What?" Donna went over and found Kevin. Patrick was gone, out somewhere. "Mike, how much would it cost me to take out Patrick?"

Just then, Patrick walked in. "Hey," Kevin said, "Donna here wants me to kill you for what you done to that car of hers she rented!" They laughed.

Patrick knew Kevin by now. That wasn't going to happen. Donna was panicking, falling apart, wanting to kill anyone and everyone who got in the way.

Kevin waited a few weeks and decided it was time to

make a move—just not the move anyone would have expected him to make.

Sybil came home one day and Kevin was packing his things.

"What's up?"

"She's not paying me, Sib," Kevin said. "I need to do something. I called my old boss. He's giving me my job back. Now that I got myself a car, I can get to work."

It was just before Thanksgiving. The OCSD was closing in on Kevin, Patrick, Sybil, and Donna. Kevin stopped by the house after completing one of his over-the-road driving jobs. There were a few things at Sybil's house he had forgotten. He wanted them back.

"You seen my photo album and road atlas around?" Kevin asked Sybil.

"I haven't seen them. How you been?"

Kevin shrugged. Then he left without saying much more.

Driving away from Sybil's that day, Kevin thought about the past few months. He was preparing for a long-haul job that would take him into New Jersey, New York, and Connecticut. Donna was on his mind—how cold and contemplating she had been throughout it all. Kevin had murdered a woman. Yes, he knew how malicious and evil that was, in and of itself. But Donna had truly shown herself to be a merciless, coldhearted woman.

"I can't remember when it happened," Kevin later told police, "[but] Sybil and Patrick told me Donna talked to them about trying to poison [Gail] or kidnap her and bring her back. . . ."

That was Donna's first plan: Sybil and Patrick were to toss Gail into the trunk of the Malibu and drive her back to Florida so Donna Trapani could, in Kevin's words, "take care of her, herself."

55

GEORGE FULTON WAS home when the doorbell rang. It was October 31, 1999. Gail had been dead three weeks.

It was a delivery driver. The guy had a box in his hand.

George signed and accepted it.

Inside the house George opened the box.

Donna has sent George a dozen red roses. She wanted to celebrate, the card said, their two-year anniversary of meeting.

George took the flowers and drove them down to the church Gail attended; he did not want them in the house.

IV

CARRYING
CROSSES

56

HIS **WIFE HAD** been dead for six weeks. For the Fulton family, life had gone on, as tough as it was for George and the kids. Gail was gone. There was nothing anyone could do but honor her memory and make sure her killers were caught and brought to justice.

George was once again corresponding with the woman who had ordered his wife's murder, although George had no idea at this time that Donna had been behind the crime. In all fairness to George, it was Donna's relentless obsession that was behind much of the back-and-forth between them.

On November 20, 1999, Donna e-mailed George under the ruse of needing information about several reports he was working on for her. In a postscript to this short e-mail, she added how nice it had been to hear his voice yesterday. (They'd chatted about work issues for a brief time.) She said she "greatly missed" talking to him on a regular basis. She "wanted to cry," just thinking about his voice over the telephone. She said she "must be crazy" for continuing to want him, even though he didn't want her. Foolishness, she said, "comes with old age."

George wrote back immediately. He said his life had been a "roller-coaster ride" since his wife was "brutally

murdered." He mentioned the house being searched (for
five and a half hours), burying Gail, and "having all sorts
of things said in the paper/TV" about him and his wife. He
talked about the media badgering him and driving by the
house, his blood pressure being "erratic and high," his feeling "sick all over," and here was Donna with the nerve to
ask how he felt.

How do you *think?* George wrote bitterly in the e-mail.

There was some indication at the end of the note, however, that George was not yet finished with Donna, although in what capacity was not obvious. He asked Donna
to try and understand what he had been through and "what
still remains, who knows?" It was clear George wanted
space. He needed to focus on his life and rebuilding the re-
lationships he had with his kids—not on the claims that
Donna was sending him to work on, as though it was business as usual.

A week later, Donna sent George a "cutie," as she called
it. It was an Internet, holiday-themed joke she believed
would make him smile. Bizarrely enough, it dealt with
conditions of the mind: schizophrenia, multiple personality disorder, dementia, paranoid delusion, and mania. Later
that day she sent a long story she thought might help to lift
his spirits. At the end of this e-mail, Donna inserted her
own little wish for "my dearest George," which included
thoughts and hopes of all his pain being replaced with
mercy, and self-doubt being a precursor to confidence, and
all sorts of other self-help advice. To read this and the additional e-mails Donna sent near this period—knowing
what she had done—is to look into the mind of a desperate woman who truly thought her plan—as long as she
pushed hard enough—was going to come to fruition one
day. Gail was gone. Donna was trying the best she could
to work her way back into the good graces of her lover
and bring George back around. She wanted to make sure

her presence was felt; so if he decided he wanted to get back with her, she was there, waiting.

Donna ended the e-mail, saying if she could have just "one wish," it would be to "ease" George's "pain and suffering." She said she'd "give anything" to help. She wanted so bad for George to "get over" it and "calm down" and "get some rest." She wanted George to know he was forever in her "thoughts and prayers." If he ever needed anything, all he had to do was ask.

In light of this correspondence, there was an obvious part of Donna that just wasn't getting it—or wanted to get it. Donna believed that if she persisted enough, that happily ever after she saw with George would happen.

57

WHEN DONNA'S E-MAILING campaign failed to win back the heart of her old flame, she tried a different approach, which could be considered more diabolical, maybe even evil. The idea that Donna thought she could do something such as this—and believed she was going to get away with it, or that it would work to her benefit—proved that Donna's extreme narcissism was growing as each day passed. The longer Donna got away with having Gail murdered, the more brazen she acted.

On November 29, 1999, the fax machine in George Fulton's Michigan basement office rang. After a few brief chirps, a fax scrolled out from the bottom of the machine addressed to *Dear George.*

Within the first few paragraphs, the *anonymous* writer—ahem, giving herself away almost immediately—said she "was a friend of Gail's," and there were certain things about Gail that George should know. The writer believed that now was the appropriate time. Enough time had passed since Gail's death for the truth to be exposed. And this truth about Gail, the fax author warned, was not going to be peachy keen and easy for George to accept. Yet he needed to know.

Much of what was going to be shared, the fax said in its

opening paragraphs, had been told to this person "in confidence" by Gail, and it was still difficult for this person to pass it along. There was no way around it anymore. The writer claimed to be a married female, who had discussed with her husband the prospect of sending the info to George, and decided—what the hell—to see what happened after she let it fly.

She couldn't reveal her identity because her husband didn't want the authorities to track them down and start asking questions. One day, she said, she would come out from behind the curtain.

For the next few paragraphs, George's anonymous pen pal said she had known how George felt because she, too, had gone through something similar with her husband. A lifeless marriage, she called it. Needs not being met. Affairs. Falling in love again with someone else. Having a new lease on love. It was all something, she explained, that had saved her from total soul annihilation.

And here was where Donna gave herself away: the fact that the fax was setting up an argument that it had been "the lover" who had made life blissful. And even though George had lost his wife, karma was at play. She intimated that perhaps a celestial plan had opened up the opportunity for him now to pursue his *true* love . . . the woman he had so deeply connected to down in Florida—whom Gail had told the fax writer all about.

This was a weak and rash attempt—maybe even stupid!—to win George back, now that Gail was completely out of the picture. Did Donna think George was an idiot? Did she, for one moment, believe the guy could not figure out it was Donna sending the fax?

It didn't take long for the fax writer to begin bashing Gail. She explained—in methodical, elliptical prose, pure pathological and psychotic—how Gail had manipulated her children in order to keep George at home. She mentioned how Emily had given Gail trouble, so Gail shied away from her and focused more on Andrew.

Quite brazenly, she wrote that if George had divorced Gail, Gail would have gone home to Texas and "would still be alive." She couldn't look away from blaming George for Gail's murder—another giveaway that Donna was writing the fax. Furthermore, George was rarely attacked in this eighteen-page, single-spaced document.

The fax writer went on to say George was "stupid" to think he could "will" happiness into his life. She warned the only way George would find happiness he had been searching for all his life was to reunite with his "true" love.

This "person" writing to George knew things about him that only Donna (or Gail) could have known. For example, she talked about how Gail would creep down the stairs while George was in his basement office, crying and listening to Celine Dion or Roy Orbison, thinking about Donna.

According to the fax, Gail had all of his phones "bugged."

Then she scorned George for not getting Gail professional help. If George would have gotten Gail help, the fax stated: *She may still be alive!*

That meeting George set up in July between Gail and Donna, the fax explained, had not been a disaster, after all, as George had been led to believe by Gail. Gail had stood in that hotel room and witnessed for herself the adoring glances George had given "the other woman"; Gail knew right there where his heart belonged.

According to the fax, Gail's biggest problems were that she "watched too much TV" and "read too many books." This behavior made Gail antisocial and unable to connect with anybody besides George. She couldn't function without him.

As the fax focused on why George never moved out of

his house, it almost got to the point where Donna came out and identified herself: *You should have gotten your own place. . . . Then she could have moved up there . . . and the three of you would have been together. . . .*

The writer said "three"? Meaning a child, too?

You knew you wanted very much to be with this other woman and . . . your unborn child, the fax claimed, and went on to say that a "real man" would never turn his back on his unborn child and the sick mother.

The writer went on to say Gail had told her about "the other woman" and now she—the fax author—knew why George had been so enamored with her: *Now I see why this woman is so admired by you.* She called the other woman "very diplomatic and businesslike" and "smart."

Apparently, according to the fax, there had been times when George had fallen asleep after having sex with Gail while muttering the words: *"I love you, my Donna. . . ."* This idea of mumbling Donna's name and terms of endearment and affection for her had been going on since George had moved back home.

Most interesting, the author of the fax claimed to have told Gail to go to a herbal store and pick up a certain concoction of herbs and then put them into George's drink at night before he went to sleep. Then, as he was falling asleep, she should ask him questions, sort of like giving him an injection of Sodium Pentothal, the so-called truth serum.

Gail did it, the mad faxer claimed. And, *You know what—it worked.*

She listed some of the questions Gail had purportedly asked George while he was asleep and under the influence of the herbal "true serum" remedy.

Interestingly, George supposedly was able to reply to

these questions, in great detail at times, while sleeping or nodding off to sleep:

> ***Did he wish to still be in Florida?***
> *Yes.*
> ***Was he glad to see Donna when she visited him in New Mexico unannounced?***
> *Yes.*
> ***Was George glad to see Donna in New Mexico?***
> *I missed her so much.*
> ***Was George happy with his present job?***
> *Not really. But it paid the bills.*
> ***Did you make love to Donna on New Year's Eve (1998–99)?***
> *Twice.*
> ***How did George feel about being home after leaving Florida?***
> *Sad.*
> ***Why did George like talking to Donna so much?***
> *I sleep better.*
> ***Was the reason he called Donna in Florida so much because he wanted to?***
> *Yes.*

These mock questions and answers went on and on for an entire page. Thirty in all. It was silly, ridiculous, and desperate.

After that, the fax became all about Gail. She wasn't pretty enough, according to the fax author. She didn't take care of herself. She didn't believe she could live without George. There was page after page of demeaning comments and snide remarks focused on Gail. Then the fax abruptly took a U-turn and went back into Gail and George's sex life.

The fax author claimed that Gail hated having sex with George, that the positions George chose to perform on his wife "hurt her," but she didn't want to tell him. On top of that, Gail supposedly hated the new sexual tricks that George tried on her sexually after he returned to living with her. Those new sexual maneuvers were supposedly taught to him by Donna.

Heading toward the final three to four pages, the "friend" concentrated on the baby. She said Gail (with some money that her mother had given her) had hired someone to look into the validity of Donna's pregnancy claim. She said, since Gail and Dora and Emily had spent all summer telling George that Donna was not pregnant, Gail decided to find out for herself and looked into it in more detail with the help of several professional people.

And you know what, the faxer said, *the reports came one by one. . . .*

Yes, George, you are going to have a little girl!

The proof, she said, was in numerous written documents, including sonogram reports, doctors' papers, lab reports, consultant reports, copies of insurance claims, legal documents, and so on.

Then there was a long explanation regarding the problems associated with the pregnancy, along with some guilt tossed in at the end of the rant, asking George why he didn't feel sorry for Donna and his little girl.

Finally, a page later, the supposedly anonymous source posited: *Do you know if this woman loses the baby it will be . . . your fault.*

At the very end of the fax, the last line gave the writer's agenda entirely away: *If you really care at all for your little girl, you better do something fast.*

58

I T TAKES ONLY ONE card at the bottom of a house of cards to topple the entire deck. That ace of spades, in this case, had a name: Todd Franklin, Sybil's old flame, the father of one of her two kids.

On Monday, November 29, 1999, Detective John Meiers, Detective Sergeant James A'Hearn, and Special Agent William O'Leary interviewed Todd Franklin in Florida. He had given them a rundown of the murder from Sybil's point of view. Now the team was meeting with Okaloosa County investigators to discuss how to go about locating Sybil and her co-conspirators. OCSD detective James A'Hearn gave a briefing regarding the information they had, how they had obtained it, and how they were going to bring down Donna's house of cards. The main focus of this meeting was that rented green Malibu. If they could locate the car, a key piece of evidence would be in hand, and, depending on who was driving it, a key player in custody. By now, they had the name Patrick (but Todd was not certain of Patrick's last name), along with Donna Trapani and Sybil Padgett.

The first thing the team did was station a few investigators outside Helen Padgett's house to watch for Sybil. They hung out all morning, but they failed to locate Sybil or the green Malibu. Back at the Walton County Sheriff's Office (WCSO) later that morning, an alternate plan was hatched.

An investigator working for Walton County popped into the room, where the team was talking, and said, "I have a last name—Alexander. This might be who we're looking for. He's Sybil's boyfriend, claims my source."

And just like that, things started coming together.

Two investigators drove out to Patrick's mother's house.

No one was home, so they headed over to where she worked.

After pulling Patrick's mother aside, one of the investigators said, "We have a warrant for your son, ma'am, and need to know where he's at."

"I don't know . . . ," she said nervously, "but when I—I get off work, I can go looking for him and then bring him to the sheriff's department."

Leaving that building, investigators drove into DeFuniak Springs. As one report noted, *Continued to look for the rental car.*

"Let's try Sybil's mother's house," one of them said.

Helen Padgett told investigators her daughter was home.

As they pulled up to the house, there was that now-infamous green Malibu parked outside.

They parked next to it and got out.

That broken taillight told the story.

Sybil answered the door. She had a look of despair on her face. This was it—the game was over.

"Sybil," OCSO lieutenant Grady Anderson said, "we need to talk." Anderson showed Sybil a summons.

As Anderson stood on the stoop talking with Sybil, Helen Padgett and Sybil's brother arrived.

Helen looked distressed. Frantic. She knew what was happening. She had foreseen it all. "Sybil, we'll watch the kids. . . . Go," Helen said.

Sybil and Lieutenant Anderson walked toward his cruiser. "Listen," Anderson said, "we have some investigators here in town from Michigan and they're investigating a homicide. They need to talk to you, Sybil. You going to be okay with that?"

Sybil looked at the ground. Her shoulders slumped. "I understand," she said. "I'd like to talk to them."

Anderson drove Sybil to the "Old Stuckey's Building" on Highway 90 in DeFuniak.

The OCSD team was waiting there. Anderson made the introductions.

"Would you be willing to come with us to the Ramada Inn on Okaloosa Island and talk with us?" James A'Hearn asked.

"Yeah . . . ," Sybil said; then she turned to Anderson. "Would you come, too? I don't know these detectives."

"Certainly," Anderson said.

They Mirandized Sybil and she agreed to talk and answer questions about the Michigan homicide (without a lawyer present).

This is never a good idea if you're a murder suspect.

Sybil Padgett talked for quite some time about her relationship with Donna Trapani and how she had met Donna through a job at CCHH.

After a time Sybil seemed comfortable with the investigators. From the questions they asked, it was not hard to tell that they had a source fingering Sybil in the murder. She was caught. After taking a deep breath and a long pull from a cigarette, Sybil said, "Look, Donna asked me to find someone to kill Gail Fulton."

Sybil paused.

"Me and Patrick . . ."

"Patrick who?" one of them asked.

". . . Alexander, my boyfriend. We went up to Lake Orion, Michigan, and we went to where she worked at the library."

Sybil talked them through meeting Kevin Ouellette and how she introduced Kevin to Donna and how the plan came together inside Donna's bedroom, with Donna directing it all.

They sat for over an hour and she talked through everything. Then the OCSO took Sybil Padgett into custody and booked her.

Patrick sat inside the WCSO nervously awaiting the arrival of Detective Chris Wundrach and Sergeant James A'Hearn. By now, Patrick knew the end was near. He had spoken to several OCSO investigators about his rights. Talking to them, Patrick understood the bottom line: The more he helped, the better off he'd be in the end.

For the next few hours, Patrick talked about the entire plot to murder Gail—and the most important aspect of the interview for the team cracking this case became, with the exception of a few minor details, Patrick's story was identical to Sybil's.

"You know where we can find Kevin Ouellette?" investigators asked Patrick.

He shrugged. "No. He's driving a truck now, I think."

On December 1, 1999, two investigators located the company in Alabama that Kevin Ouellette had been working for since he had murdered Gail and left Florida.

"He's on the road," said Kevin's boss. "Headed for Branford, Connecticut."

Kevin's boss explained that the truck Kevin was hauling

had a GPS satellite and the company could find out where he was, at any given time.

Both investigators made arrangements to head out to Connecticut, where Kevin would be dropping his load and making the trip back to Alabama, unaware of a warrant for his arrest on murder charges and a hunt for his truck was under way.

With that tile in place, the final domino sat at home in Fort Walton Beach, Florida, deciding how to go about convincing George Fulton to come back to her. Donna Trapani was going about her business, oblivious to the fact that sheriffs from Walton County and investigators from Michigan were gearing up to take her in—and, boy, would she ever have a story to tell when they interviewed her.

59

HE HAD LIVED with Donna for the past few months. Brad Adams (pseudonym) had paid Donna $200 cash each month to help her with the rent. He knew nothing about Gail's murder, save for a day when Donna approached him with a question. It was "the first week of November," Brad recalled.

Donna popped into Brad's room and asked, "Can I use your computer?"

"Sure," Brad said. "What's up?"

"I'm looking for info on the Internet about my bookkeeper being charged with murdering his wife."

The investigators were hovering around Donna's place, following her, looking for the right opportunity to begin questioning her. One of the questions they asked Donna's boarder was if Donna had ever mentioned to him that she was terminally ill or pregnant. Brad had lived with her. He would have known.

"No," Brad said to both questions. "I didn't know that."

Two detectives watched Donna's home on December 1, 1999, beginning near six in the morning. Donna believed she had surrounded herself with a coterie of people who, when the walls tumbled down around them, would protect and preserve her role in Gail Fulton's murder. She thought she wielded power. She thought she had control over anybody under her grasp. But, wow, was she ever misleading herself!

After not seeing much movement near the house, one of the detectives, Steve Pearson, got out and peered in through a garage window to see if there was a vehicle around.

Donna's Lincoln Town Car was parked inside.

So Pearson and his partner, Detective John Meiers, knocked on Donna's door.

No answer.

Meiers left his business card in the door.

The investigators parked down the block and "established a position to observe activity" at Donna's house. Was she dissing them? Or was Donna out with someone?

Nothing happened for quite some time.

At 12:40 P.M., Donna phoned Meiers. She wanted to know what he wanted. Why had he left his card in her door?

"We're here from Michigan investigating the murder of Gail Fulton—we'd like to talk to you," Meiers said. "Can we stop by?"

"Oh, geez. So sorry I missed y'all earlier. I had an OB/GYN doctor's appointment. Sure, you're welcome to come to my home and talk with me."

An open invitation. Just what they'd hoped for.

"Okay, then."

Donna opened the door. "Come on into the family room," she said, leading the way. "We'll be more comfortable in here."

Meiers didn't notice Donna had a baby bump of any

sort; she wasn't showing in the least. Maybe she wasn't pregnant? She didn't seem like a terminally ill patient, either.

They sat down on the couch.

Meiers introduced himself and Pearson. "Would it be okay if we tape-record this conversation?" Meiers asked. "You're not under arrest or anything like that . . . and you can ask us to leave anytime you want to."

"I understand, sure," Donna said obligingly. "Yes, you can record. I don't have a problem with that."

Meiers did a brief sound check to make sure everything was working right. As he did that, Pearson took a Miranda rights card from his wallet and read from it.

Donna came across as comfortable and natural. She said she had spoken to her lawyer and he advised her to "see what y'all had to say. Look, I'm an adult. I understand my rights and certainly know how serious this interview is. I'd be more than happy to answer your questions." She paused, but then she made a bizarre statement: "Besides, attorneys are expensive—and I ain't about to pay one to just sit here." She laughed.

"Right," one of the detectives said.

They talked. Donna went through her vitals: where she was born, raised, schooling, marriage, how she came to Florida.

"Hold on," Meiers said. He looked down and noticed the spindles on the tape recorder not spinning. "Would you mind if we start over?"

"Sure, sure," Donna said. And she went through it again.

For the next ten minutes, Donna talked about her life in general terms. There was a "poor me" tone to it all, Donna trying to draw as much empathy as she could. After she finished, Meiers asked about George and how they met.

Donna was frank. She talked about the Seagull Bar, how they had sex after that second meeting, and how the affair went from zero to one hundred overnight.

"He fell in love with me, and I fell in love with him."

No one said it, but the thought was there between the detectives: *And now his wife is dead.*

Donna couldn't help herself, apparently. She started in on Gail and even Gail's mother.

"[George] said his mother-in-law was a well-respected member of her community in Corpus Christi and knew lots of influential people," Donna explained, after telling the investigators how she and George discussed business and how George had expected to be rolling in money from clients provided by Dora Garza. "He said he thought his wife would get her mother to give him some connections in Texas with doctors and lawyers, and that he would be well on his way. He said help never came, and that he never got any help from his wife or her mother."

Donna said she had given George the opportunity to duck out of the relationship whenever he wanted. The way she made it sound was that she had never put any pressure on him.

"George went home for Thanksgiving [that November 1997] and went to confession and said he wanted to cut off the relationship that [we] had. I told him if that's what he wanted . . ."

Then George returned to Florida, Donna claimed, after Thanksgiving. He told her he couldn't forget her and they started up again. The line George gave Donna that won her over, she said, was "'I've never had these feelings for my wife.'"

As Meiers flipped over the tape, and Donna continued to talk openly about the affair, it seemed George was the one begging her to come back, after repeatedly going back to Gail. The way Donna framed it was that she could not have cared one way or another if George came back to her every time he took off for Michigan and into Gail's arms. It was as if it had never bothered her. She didn't realize, of course, the OCSD was working on a search warrant as they sat and spoke—a warrant that included her computers, eventually revealing all those e-mails between her and George. At this time she carried on about how nonchalantly she viewed the affair.

"I used to have to force him to call home," she said, explaining how George never wanted to talk to his kids or Gail while he was in Florida. "He even said to me once, 'It's almost as if they don't exist up there [in Michigan].' He said the whole time he was in Florida, he didn't even think too much about up there. He said being down in Florida was almost like a dream . . . that it was like a fantasy."

"Did Gail ever find out about you two?"

"Sure. George called his oldest daughter and she checked on the number, as it showed up on her caller ID. [Melissa] didn't waste any time calling her momma!" Donna laughed at that. "Gail called almost immediately and asked George if he was living with somebody. I gave him his privacy while they talked. Then he came to the back of the house and told me, 'Gail knows. . . . She knows that I am living with you. . . . She's crying, talking about ending her life, talking about leaving, talking about me coming home right now. . . . She wants to know what I want to do. I'm moving out. I knew she would someday find out. Gail is devastated.' So I began to cry—but I was, you know, not crying for me. I was crying for Gail."

Donna said the entire Fourth of July fiasco was George's idea. The version of what happened inside the hotel room Donna gave police was incredible. Donna said that after

George left the room, she and Gail talked, but Gail "went into a rage."

Donna blocked the door so Gail couldn't get out of the room and "hurt herself." Donna said she put her arms "around Gail tenderly and calmed her. Gail was crying, and I was trying to soothe her by stroking her hair. I then told Gail, 'George has had other affairs,' and she ran from the room."

The next morning, July 5, George showed up at the hotel with his bags and claimed, "'Gail threw me out,'" Donna told officers.

She told the investigators that she said to him, "'I don't want you —get out of here.'" And so George left the hotel and went back to Gail.

At one point during the interview, Donna said she realized a while later that she was going to have to break off the relationship for good—it was just too chaotic. Gail and George Fulton were too crazy for her.

Then Donna brought Sybil into the scenario. She came across as Sybil Padgett's mentor and savior, telling detectives Sybil had been abused by her husband and kicked out of her home. She said that Sybil had trouble taking care of her children. But Donna was there for her, loaning her money, giving her and the kids a place to stay, bringing her to a women's shelter for counseling.

"I gave her a job, and she always had a job with me. And then I started telling her about my problems with George and our relationship," Donna stated.

Over the due course of time, Donna said, she turned to Sybil because she was there: a person to confide in. They were two girlfriends helping each other through life's bumps. As she talked with Sybil about George, Donna told investigators, and involved Sybil in the day-to-day problems and arguments more, Sybil became another person—someone who was full of revenge and wanted to help her friend make the man who had hurt her pay for it.

Donna returned once more to the subject of George Fulton and his family. "George loved his kids," Donna said, "but he never said, he *never* loved Gail. He said some bad things, but never said that he *didn't* love her."

Donna said that when cops called her on the night Gail was murdered, she "thought he said shootings" (with an *s* on the end), and assumed that there was more than one. "I just figured it must have been drugs or something. I wondered what had happened."

Eventually, while talking to police that night, she considered it "might have been a prank. . . . I asked how George and the kids were doing. I wasn't really concerned with George so much that I was more concerned with the kids."

They asked her when she next heard from George.

"After Gail's death I never heard from him. I would have liked to have offered my condolences to Emily. I did call George a few weeks ago about business, and I realized what I said must sound like, and I asked him how he was doing. We e-mailed things back and forth," she said, "but it was all business-related material. I could detect anger in George's e-mails directed at me or my company. I sent George some roses and told him that roses represented beauty and that I hoped that the flowers and the card would bring a smile to his face and brighten his day."

60

DETECTIVE JOHN MEIERS popped in "tape #4" as Donna continued talking. They could not shut her up, actually. She wanted to talk about everything and anything, including her sex life with George, which she described as "wonderful." Yet, Donna added for no obvious reason, that "the sexual relationship George had with Gail was *not* good. I hope this doesn't come out in court because it will embarrass him, but he told me that in twenty-five years of marriage to Gail . . . [she] would not touch him. We had dated only a month or two, and George said that I had touched him more in that time than Gail had in twenty-five years."

Donna was proud of that badge, telling her tales with a smile.

"Can you give us a list of the problems in the Fulton marriage, as you saw them?" Pearson asked.

"Sure," Donna said. "The main problem was that Gail should have gone back to school and gotten herself a job. She needed a job. She needed to get out and socialize and meet people. Then there were the kids. Gail always seemed to have time for her kids, but *never* [for] George. Her whole life was as a mother, *not* a wife."

"Did you ever tell George you were pregnant?" Meiers asked.

"Um-hm."

"Are you pregnant?"

"Um-hm."

They assumed she meant yes.

"How far along are you?"

Donna hesitated. Then: "Almost there . . . almost there! To be perfectly honest, though, they don't think I am going to make it. I was in the ER last Monday night. I'm probably going to lose the baby. I should have had an abortion, according to my doctor. I'm bleeding a lot. They've been packing me."

"When was the last time you went to the doctor and had an ultrasound, Miss Trapani?"

"I saw my doctor this morning. I've had *many* ultrasounds."

The interview had crossed a threshold. Donna shifted in her seat and became progressively more uncomfortable. There was an accusatory tone to some of the questions and Donna picked up on it.

"What did your doctor say about the baby this morning— is the baby okay?"

"I don't think so," Donna answered, drooping her shoulders, dropping her head, lowering her voice. "I don't think she has a left kidney."

"How does George feel?"

"Huh! He doesn't believe me and hasn't done *anything* for the baby."

"What's your due date?" Meiers asked.

"Three weeks," Donna said, holding up three fingers. "December thirteenth. I'm in that phase right now . . . and they're trying to get me to hang on."

Meiers and Pearson carefully observed Donna as she spoke, later noting, *It did not appear . . . that Donna was pregnant. Certainly not since she indicated that she got pregnant in January or February.*

The math alone didn't add up. As she sat there, Donna would have been ten or even eleven months into her pregnancy.

As they talked, Donna's cat jumped up on the couch and walked across her midsection. Both detectives noticed the cat had left footprints, as if walking on sand, on Donna's stomach.

Indentations were left by the cat, said Meiers's report, as if the animal had walked across a Posturepedic mattress.

The detectives looked at each other.

Donna had packed something underneath her clothing to make it appear that she had a bump. And even then, she wasn't showing the same way a woman about to give birth any day would have been. Plus, her face was not puffy. She had not appeared to have gained any weight, and she had no trouble moving around easily.

"Do you know anyone who would want to kill Gail?" Meiers asked.

"I don't know anyone that would want to have her killed," Donna said.

Pearson and Meiers thought this to be an odd response.

"What type of person would kill a woman like that?" Donna said next. She paused for a moment and then answered her own question, as if thinking out loud: "I don't know. . . . Somebody that . . . I don't know. . . . A drug addict, alcoholic, criminal? . . . I think she was killed by mistake or something. Or she was in the wrong place at the wrong time. Or something was going on."

But that first reply: "want to have her killed." Donna had let out a Freudian slip without realizing it. She had said, "want to have her killed," both detectives realized. They had asked about someone *killing* Gail.

Donna opened a door.

So they asked about rental cars and if Donna had rented a car for one of her employees.

"Sybil Padgett, yes, but I took the fees out of her paycheck. The last time Sybil worked for me was October, but she still has the car. . . . In fact, I wanted to ask you, why [was] the car recently impounded and taken to Pensacola? I got a call from the rental company."

There was a bowl of pretzels on the table in front of them, which Donna had not touched since they sat down, almost three hours before. It had been a long conversation. Donna had weathered it well, stood up to each question, and had an answer for everything.

Or so it seemed.

"We believe that reason for Gail's murder was a love triangle," Meiers tossed out, looking to see how Donna reacted.

Donna became subdued. She turned "quiet and soft-spoken and began to eat pretzels," Meiers later explained. She became anxious.

They struck a nerve.

Meiers continued, "We think you went to a group of people to have Gail killed."

"That's not true!" Donna said sharply. "I've never said that!"

Meiers took out a photo of the redbrick LAKE ORION TOWNSHIP LIBRARY sign positioned at the parking lot entrance. He showed it to Donna. Then he took out a newspaper clipping, with a photo of Gail and George sitting on their front porch, smiling. Above the photo was a headline indicating Gail's murder had been caught on video surveillance, capturing Gail's final few moments of life. After that, Meiers showed Donna a photograph of the green Malibu that Sybil had been driving around (which

Donna herself had admitted to)—the same car, he noted, captured on the video of Gail being shot to death. Then he showed Donna a picture of Gail lying in a pool of blood by her van. The next photo was a close-up of Gail. Meiers's report stated: *[There were] massive amounts of blood on the ground around her head and an air tube down her throat. . . . The victim's eyes and mouth were open and the gunshot to the forehead was very evident.*

There in front of Donna was a photo array of the crime she had masterminded.

Donna sat up. She stared at the pictures, but she would not—at first—look at any photos of Gail.

Meiers held up the photos of Gail. Donna indicated she wanted to look at them closer. She held them, one in each hand, and studied each snapshot, close to her eyes.

As Donna peered into these gruesome images, Detective Meiers said, "Look, Miss Trapani, we have arrested Patrick Alexander and Sybil Padgett, and both have confessed to the murder of Gail Fulton."

Donna didn't say anything; instead, she stared at the photos and continued to munch on pretzels. It was entertainment to Donna, like a movie she had not only scripted and starred in, but one she was taking pleasure in watching.

"We know about the two trips to Michigan and how you gave Sybil one thousand dollars for the first trip."

Donna again said nothing, said Meiers's report, *but continued to eat pretzels.*

There was a long pause. Donna put the photos down. Then: "If this is all true," she said, using a finger to point to the photos and what detectives had accused her of, "why did I have to sit here and talk into this recorder for the past four hours?"

It was a good question: If they had the proof to make an arrest, why would they waste time interviewing Donna at her home and not inside the confinement of a police station?

Meiers stuck to the focus of the interrogation, saying, "We know about the meetings in your bedroom. . . . It's time for you to tell the truth, Miss Trapani."

"It's not like how you're sayin'," Donna said, shaking her head.

"Then how *did* it happen?"

"I don't know."

Meiers's report explained how Donna reacted next: *She continued to eat pretzels.*

Meiers looked down and noticed the tape running low. They had Donna against the ropes. Maybe she was going to cop to the crime and make things easy on everyone. Forgo a long, drawn-out trial and cut a deal.

He put in the fifth tape of the day and quickly hit RECORD.

"You don't have any remorse, do you?" Meiers asked. "You don't have *one* ounce of remorse—do you, Miss Trapani?"

Donna didn't respond.

Pearson said, "You can tell us the truth."

"I just can't," she said. "I don't know all the truth."

"Why can't you?"

"I just can't. . . . I have never really said that I wanted her dead or out of the picture. I know one thing—"

"This is your opportunity to tell us the truth."

"And then what?" Donna asked.

Meiers brought his tone down a notch, to give the impression they were not there to quarrel or play good cop/bad cop. There was common ground among the three of them. "Listen," he said, "I tell you what, you are going to feel a hell of a lot better."

"Why?"

"Because you'll be able to sleep at night, and it's the right thing to do!" Pearson said. "Because I really don't think—" Pearson tried to say as Donna interrupted.

"But what's going to happen to *me*? What would happen to *me*?" Donna took on that all-too-familiar role of the narcissist, worrying about herself and how it would affect her. She'd had an opportunity to show some compassion for the victim, but she had waived that direction long ago. She was concerned only for her well-being.

"What's going to happen to *you*?" Meiers uttered.

"Um-hm. I mean, if I *did* do this, I mean, if I *am* guilty and I did do this, then why can't I just be killed and put under, too? If I did it, then I need to give my life if I did it! I cannot say what you want me to say. If I sat here for the rest of my life, I wouldn't be able to explain it to you. I don't know how to say it."

If this was a confession, it had to be one of the most unique and obscure these two cops had heard. What was Donna Trapani saying?

Accusations were made by us detectives, Meiers's report explained, *and little response was given. It appeared that she was experiencing some guilt but she continued to eat pretzels.*

Donna finally said, "I don't want to talk here. I don't want to talk into this machine. I want to call my attorney, and I am not sure if I can do that or not."

The conversation had become, by Meiers's observation, "frozen." So he said, "I understand it's hard for you to say something that would put you in prison for the rest of your life."

"It would put me in prison for the *rest* of my *life*?" Donna asked as if shocked by the revelation. "I'm having a hard time because some of that . . . like if I say anything like what I want to say, what I'm trying to say, 'cause I

don't know what I'm trying to say, it will make me sound . . .
It's nothing like what was supposed to ever happen." Donna
took a breath.

Was she ready to come clean?

"I got duped," Donna said, implying she'd been burned
by her co-conspirators. "But not by the people you think.
It was never supposed to happen."

Was she admitting her involvement?

Donna started and then stopped. She was finished talking. She had invoked her right to an attorney moments
before and meant it. She was done.

So Meiers and Pearson stopped the interview and told
Donna they were going to have to take her down to the
Okaloosa County Sheriff's Office to be booked on charges
of murder and conspiracy to commit murder.

Donna did not balk at the proclamation, almost as
though she had expected it.

Steve Pearson and John Meiers handed Donna Trapani
to Detective Larry Ashley as soon as they got back to the
OCSO. In the meantime they'd have to file the paperwork
to transport Donna to Michigan so she could be booked
there, where the murder had taken place.

Ashley took Donna into the processing area to fingerprint and formally charge her.

"I need to pat you down," the detective explained, "and
check you for weapons."

Donna looked at the tile floor nervously.

Ashley felt something soft stuffed into Donna front
pants as he patted her down.

"What the . . . ?"

Ashley asked Donna to lift up the front of her sweater.
There, stuffed down her pants and around her waistline,

Donna had placed several place mats to make it appear as if her belly and midsection had been growing. There was another place mat deeper down into her pants.

"I have another in my pubic area," Donna admitted.

"Go into the bathroom and take it out," Ashley ordered.

61

KEVIN OUELLETTE WAS taken into custody without incident in Branford, Connecticut, on December 2, 1999, as detectives from the OCSD headed north, from Florida, back to Michigan with Donna Trapani and the others.

Kevin sat inside a cell at Troop G in Bridgeport, Connecticut, awaiting Lieutenant Joseph Quisenberry and Sergeant Michael Elliott, of the OCSD, along with Special Agent Rich Teahan, of the FBI, to question him. Kevin had been arrested at a rest stop along Interstate 95. For all investigators knew, he could have additional information. Were others involved?

As he spoke, Kevin had a defeated tone to his voice. He knew there was no getting out of this now. In fact, maybe he should have thought it through a bit more before committing such a violent crime with three idiots. Kevin considered himself smarter. He never thought himself a killer.

But he was.

That personal demise began, Kevin explained, when his wife died suddenly (he never said how) and he was left to care for their young child.

"I let my sister watch him," Kevin said of his son. "She

got divorced, and the kid ended up being taken by the state and is now in their ward. I don't know where my son is right now."

He looked greatly concerned.

They asked him about life in general.

"I graduated high school and did a small stint in the army, but got out with a general discharge. It was mutual. The army wanted me out, and I wanted out."

No one told Kevin why he had been dragged into Troop G. He had been roused from his truck and asked to take a ride. So he asked: "Why am I here?"

They read him his Miranda rights. They pushed a piece of paper across the table and asked Kevin to initial the questions, which Kevin did without a problem. With that, he had waived his right to an attorney and indicated he wanted to talk.

It took a matter of four questions before Kevin, the report stated, *admitted he knew the facts about the homicide of Martha Gail Fulton . . . and went on laying out the scenario of the killing in a taped statement.*

In ninety minutes Kevin told the story from beginning to end. He talked about being broke and living with his girl at Sybil's, and then the request by Sybil and meeting Donna and being paid by Donna to kill Gail. It really was that simple, he said, when it all came down to it: Donna Trapani had initiated this murder and paid him to commit it with two misfits.

End of story.

62

PUTTING THIS CASE together was not that much of a challenge for the OCSD and the Oakland County Prosecutor's Office—once the pieces were in front of them, that is.

APA Paul Walton, the man in charge of seeking justice for Gail Fulton and her family, knew from experience that if a suspect had three people pointing a finger at her, well, maybe she should try to cop a plea and count her blessings that there was no electric chair in her future. Most murder-for-hire cases included capital felony charges, which generally resulted in a trip to death row. Donna was charged with first-degree murder, a capital offense in Michigan. But what saved her life was that a conviction for a capital offense in Michigan meant life in prison. Michigan does not have a death penalty and was actually the first in the country to abolish the death penalty in the late 1800s.

Regardless, Donna Trapani wasn't interested—not that Paul Walton was offering, anyway—in rolling over and playing the part of the guilty mastermind. If nothing else, Donna was ready to fight. As she had proven with her past (obsessive) behavior, she wasn't going down without taking a few good swings.

The public got its first glimpse of the state's case against

Donna and her three criminal cohorts in March 2000 as Paul Walton presented his case before the Honorable Nancy Tolwin Carniak at the 52/3 District Court in Oakland County. Carniak had been appointed to the bench by the governor in January 2000. A beautiful woman by any standard, Carniak's attractive looks or general greenness to the bench should not have fooled those who might have perceived her to be a bit standoffish. Carniak had attended Michigan State University, where she received a Bachelor of Arts in business administration in 1979; she acquired her Juris Doctor from the Detroit College of Law in 1985. She had served as an associate and partner in private law firms for fifteen years prior to putting on the black robe. According to her bio, the judge's passion for law and education spread into the community when *[Carniak] initiated the Mock Trial program for fifth-grade students . . . [who] learn about the legal system firsthand by participating in a mock criminal trial . . . [and] take a tour of the Oakland County Sheriff's substation and observe actual criminal proceedings in the courtroom.*

Paul Walton had his hands full with facing not only Donna Trapani, but also Kevin Ouellette, Sybil Padgett, and Patrick Alexander. This preliminary examination was set to prove that there was sufficient evidence to send all four to trial on felony murder charges. (Some states call it a probable cause hearing; and only under rare circumstances in Michigan is a grand jury summoned.) The preliminary exam is the most efficient way to make certain a defendant is getting his or her fair chance at justice. Each defendant was represented by his or her own attorney. There was some banter about Sybil and Patrick wanting to "talk," but those discussions had broken down as the preliminary exam began.

For the state's case the motive and cause of Gail Fulton's brutal murder was clear-cut: rejection had spurred

Donna into a plan to have her rival killed—a plan she had promised to pay $15,000 to see put into action by her three co-conspirators, all of whom rolled over on her as soon as cops put the squeeze on them. It was George Foster's move back home in April 1999 that pushed Donna over the proverbial cliff—not only to have Gail killed, but to make up that entire pregnancy and terminal illness plot, which culminated in a meeting between Gail and Donna at a Rochester Hills, Michigan, hotel. When that fell apart and Donna realized her chances with George were finished, she decided murder was the only "shot" she had at winning him back. Walton made the state's argument clear and precise in the accompanying documents and charges, one of which summed up things quite frankly: *This case clearly shows the capabilities of human evil when unchecked.*

Walton graduated from Detroit College in 1991 and passed the bar that same year. His first real job, which he had started while in law school, was with the United States Attorney's Office in the Eastern District of Michigan. Then he moved on to the St. Clair County Prosecutor's Office and was shortly thereafter working for the Oakland County Prosecutor's Office, a job he had stepped into and had not left. Walton had experience in major crimes and felony trials, including numerous jury trials involving murder.

Part of winning at trial began with hitting hard and fast within this preliminary hearing atmosphere. It was a lawyer knowing his weaknesses and understanding that although he may walk into a courtroom certain of a conviction— with evidence as taut and obvious as he could ever hope— there were always surprises. As a trial lawyer, an attorney can never underestimate the value of having too many witnesses and too much information at his disposal. For Paul Walton, he had a stellar team of investigators in the OCSD who had worked this case, covered every possible aspect of it, documented it about as well as it could have been, and had never once—as far as he could see—headed down a road that might have put additional suspects outside the confines of a biased set of blinders. These cops seemed to have left no stone unturned.

Or had they?

When a person looked at it on paper, this seemed to be nothing short of a blowout for Paul Walton and the state. After all, he had suspects' confessions; the crime—appearing grainy and blurry—was captured on video surveillance; a map of the Michigan area where Gail had lived, worked—and was actually murdered—was marked up by the *alleged* murderers and full of fingerprints; these pieces of evidence sketched out the crime. There was a detailed affair between the victim's husband and the purported mastermind and, perhaps more important (which prosecutors are not required to prove), a clear and present motive, the oldest one on record: love, obsession, revenge. When blended together, these three are all potential deadly poisons.

Opening the preliminary hearing, the first responding officers to the crime scene testified about how they received the call to head out to the library and found Gail Fulton barely breathing, fighting for her last breaths, a pool of blood all around her head. The drama and heartache these two police officers brought to the courtroom was humbling for most, terrifying for Gail's family, but important to the scope of the tragedy and how four people conspired to murder an innocent woman. For the mastermind in murder-for-hire schemes, the crime becomes almost like a dream, a fantasy, simply because the person sanctioning the murder is not usually there to see it happen. This takes the architect out of it and allows the person to convince himself or herself that he or she either played a lesser role in the murder, or none at all. Nearly everyone has seen those "exclusive" surveillance tapes on *Dateline, 48 Hours,* or *20/20* of men or women paying off undercover agents for murders that never happen. Viewers have seen how those people react to being shown the tapes: They almost give off the sense that they might have been kidding, or that they really didn't mean what they suggested. And then they are brought into a court of law, and all this evidence is placed in front of them, and they still don't get it—they still want to convince themselves it was all some sort of misunderstanding. That's what Donna Trapani had tried to tell detectives Meiers and Pearson in her living room. She could talk until she was blue in the face, but they would never understand what she meant.

Paul Walton was a smart prosecutor, and he had reviewed the case and knew how to combat Donna's argument. With old-fashioned circumstantial evidence, as well as state-of-the-art forensic evidence, Walton was going to prove how Donna Trapani knew damn well what she was doing, what she was asking of her co-conspirators, and the results she was hoping to achieve by paying that money.

With the murder scene set, Walton called the one witness who could put the entire motive and affair into context. For the first time the public was going to hear from the one man who had not spoken to anyone, save for cops, since the time of his wife's murder.

George Fulton.

63

GEORGE FULTON WALKED into the courtroom; he was wearing a crucifix hanging from his neck (outside his shirt, over his necktie) to show that he had his convictions and his mind back on the cross, where they belonged. This definitely was what Gail would have wanted. This symbol of Christ crucified seemed to suggest that George's faith might have been tested, but it had not been shattered.

Some viewed the cross as a feeble attempt to conjure images of a still-grieving husband who wanted the public to think he was a God-fearing man who had stumbled.

Either way, George was here to tell his side of the story.

After George gave Paul Walton his vitals, the prosecutor introduced the dynamic of Gail and the crumbling Fulton marriage. Gail's last day on earth—October 4, 1999—became known between the witness and the prosecutor as "that day."

A life and marriage of twenty-five years boiled down to *that day.* . . .

Within minutes Walton asked George about the phone call he received from Donna Trapani on *that night*.

"How do you know Miss Trapani?" Walton asked.

"I used to work with her as her chief financial officer,

chief operations officer for her business, Concerned Care Home Health in Fort Walton Beach, Florida," George said, adding, "And I also had a business where I processed her claims for her health care company."

Where was the unbridled affair he had with Donna in all of that?

But George never mentioned the affair without being prodded. Maybe he assumed the court knew already and he didn't need to get into it any further?

Walton encouraged George to talk about how he and Donna met.

George discussed October 1997.

That bar. That first glance. All the chitchat. Donna's Lincoln. The kiss. The hotel room. The sex. The sex. The sex.

Of course, George never mentioned any of it. He gave generic responses.

"Sir, at the time that you met Miss Trapani, were you . . . married?"

"Yes, I was."

"When you first met Miss Trapani, what type of relationship did you have with her?"

"Physical and emotional." Straight answers. Light on detail. Heavy on snappiness.

A few questions later: "You indicated that you had a romantic relationship with her, correct?"

"Correct," George said.

"How long did the relationship with her continue?"

"Until July 1999."

One year, nine months.

Walton pushed his witness and got him to talk about how he ended up living with Donna. George said he eventually told Gail about the move.

Then the assistant prosecutor asked about the pregnancy. When was it George first heard about it?

"Around the end of March 1999," he said. "Maybe [the] first of April."

"At that point, sir, what was going on with your relationship with Miss Trapani?"

"I was fixing to leave. I'd given my letter of resignation [to CCHH], because I was not getting paid. So I'd accepted another job in Michigan. . . . So I was leaving because I wasn't getting paid."

"What was your *relationship* with Miss Trapani at that point?"

"It was ending" was all George said.

"Had you discussed it with her?"

"Yes."

"Now, sir, did she indicate to you who had fathered the child?"

"Yes."

"And who'd she say fathered the child?"

"Well, we both knew it was me. I accepted it."

Then came a rather interesting exchange, offering an intimate look into the way in which George viewed his marriage and how much control he had over his wife. Walton asked if he had decided, after Donna made it known that she was pregnant, to "remain married, or . . . go through divorce proceedings?"

"I had a change of heart initially. I thought I wanted a divorce, but I changed my mind. Even though I still continued seeing Miss Trapani, I changed my mind, and I fluctuated back and forth. But basically, it ended several times . . . finally in July 1999."

There was no mention of what Gail wanted, or how Gail felt. Or how much this back-and-forth had weighed on poor Gail's emotional well-being. It was as if whatever George Fulton decided, George Fulton got. George called the shots.

They talked about the letter "allegedly written," George said, "by our [CCHH] medical director, Dr. Bevins, that said Donna . . . had stage-four lymphoma, was terminal, and had less than a year to live, and she was also pregnant." George explained how he showed the letter to Gail when he got back from Florida one day, and the contents of the letter became, essentially, the impetus for that meeting between Gail and Donna, which George had facilitated. Yet buried inside his explanation was a heaping amount of vanity. Even as he sat in the courtroom as a prosecution witness against four people who had conspired to murder his wife—*that day*—George Fulton continued to talk about his own needs and wants: "I was struggling with what my responsibilities were to [Donna] and my family. . . ." Because of this moral struggle, George implied, he decided it would be best for his lover to meet his wife and, apparently, allow the two of them to work things out between themselves. The goal, he decided by that point, was to have Donna move to Michigan down the street from where he lived with Gail and the kids.

George explained how the debacle at the hotel turned out.

Then Paul Walton brought in some of the actual evidence. One particular piece was a photograph. Gail had made a photo album for George to keep by his side while he was in Florida; it was sort of a keepsake so he could look at it and think of his family back home. There was one photo in particular of George and Gail together, sitting. They looked happy. They looked like a couple. They looked as if life had dealt a few blows, but they had weathered it well. But there came a time, Walton explained during his questioning—"Am I right, Mr. Fulton?"—when that photo had been cut in half; Gail's part of the picture went missing. The implication was that Donna had cut Gail out and had given it to her hired killers so they could identify Gail Fulton and not end up killing the wrong person.

George said yes. He explained Donna was the only person to have a key to his apartment in Florida, where the photo album had been stored.

Another important factor Walton needed to establish was how George's fingerprints ended up on the same map the killing team used to find the library and track Gail's movements. It was the same map Sybil and Patrick used to find Gail's home and stalk her during their first trip north.

George admitted he had circled several locations on the map for Donna. He told the court he and Donna had purchased the map together.

Throughout his answers here, however, George never once mentioned why he circled all those places, including the exit ramp leading into an area of Lake Orion where he lived and where the library was. He never said why Donna wanted to know these things.

Walton moved on in his questioning.

They talked about how George discussed the schedule Gail kept, where she worked, the type of vehicle Gail drove, her habits, how Gail liked to watch television and read.

By the end of his direct testimony, there was a strange feeling in the courtroom that George Fulton had unknowingly helped Donna Trapani—his lover—plan *that day.*

64

DONNA TRAPANI'S LAWYER, Lawrence "Larry" Kaluzny, was a sharp-dressed, experienced trial attorney. Kaluzny knew he needed to approach George Fulton with the white-glove touch, a smooth hand of locking George down to his story and finding out if there were any holes that could help his client. The only defense available to Donna was to scream ignorance and claim her co-conspirators had done this horrible deed on their own after she made a few snide, off-the-cuff remarks about her archenemy, Gail Fulton. White-haired Kaluzny knew this was not going to be an easy task, suffice it to say his client was sitting in a courtroom with three disloyal codefendants, who had thrown her under the bus. Kaluzny had to be careful: George Fulton, regardless of how he had treated his wife, was not on trial. The guy's moral turpitude was not in question. No matter how one framed this picture, calling George a cad, a Lothario, or a serial cheater, who had made promises to Donna he had not fulfilled, did not take the onus off Donna Trapani and the overwhelming evidence against her.

Kaluzny started with dates. Then, as he got into the mechanics of the affair, an important point emerged: the pain Gail Fulton must have endured as she clung to this

man as though her entire identity relied on staying married
to him.

"Approximately when was it that your wife became
aware of your relationship with Donna?"

"Probably September, October of '97, after she found
out I was living with [Donna]." Then George rethought his
answer and added: "She suspected, but didn't know."

"And did you tell your wife it was just a relationship or
it was more than that—that you *loved* Donna?"

Smart lawyering: Kaluzny was walking George—
slowly—into his wife's demeanor and emotional state
during the affair, having him explain what he had put his
wife through.

"It was more than that," he answered. "I told her that."

"That you loved her?"

Pause. "Yes."

They spoke of how George found out about Donna's
pregnancy and how George realized the letter Donna had
sent him was a forgery. This was not a subject Kaluzny
wanted to harp on too much.

Kaluzny established when—"July fifth!"—the affair
supposedly ended. He asked George to walk the court
through it one more time.

"Was that a significant date," Kaluzny asked, referring
to July 5, 1999, "because that was the date that she was up
here and met Gail?"

"Yes," George answered. "That's when I decided I really
wanted my marriage. I needed to work on it, and that's
when I told her it's over. It *has* to be over."

"Now," Kaluzny said, seeing an opening, "was that
before or after you stayed with her at the inn?"

"*After* I stayed with her."

"So you stayed with her at the inn. You had sexual rela-
tions that night?"

"Yes."

"And then the next day you told her it was over?"

"Yes." George coughed. "Yes."

The next ten minutes was consumed with George talking about—after Kaluzny quizzed him incessantly about it—the type of work he had done for Donna and how their intimate relationship had allegedly ended. Still, after their breakup, George continued speaking with Donna, e-mailing her, and exchanging letters for the sake of Donna's failing company. George painted this period of his life—July 5 through *that day*—as strictly business, but Kaluzny stealthily got George to admit there was plenty of personal talk inside that employee-employer dynamic. There was no indication where Kaluzny was heading with his line of questioning. It almost felt as if he wanted to ask George if he was involved in Gail's murder.

But he never did.

"[Had] Donna ever told you she thought it was wrong that you were having this relationship with [her] while you were married to Gail?"

George had a strange look on his face. He stayed silent.

Kaluzny waited.

"The question again, please?" George asked.

The defense attorney obliged.

"No," George responded.

"Did [Donna] ever indicate at all that it wasn't fair to Gail what was going on?"

"She might've . . . but it was totally from a selfish perspective—her *own* perspective."

In George's opinion, that is.

No objection.

Kaluzny touched on the maps. George admitted he and Donna bought them during the Fourth of July weekend. And finally, George was asked why he was involved in purchasing these maps. What was the purpose? Why would George buy a set of Michigan maps for his lover, not long before his wife was murdered?

"At that point," George said, looking down, then up, having a little trouble getting himself together for this one, "I thought Donna would move up here because she said she was dying, that she was going to have a baby. She needed a place to come, because she had nobody to take care of her."

The woman owned a home health care business, but she had nobody to take care of her?

Odd.

Paul Walton never brought up this point as George continued, stating emphatically, "And the purpose of those circles"—referring to the markings on the map— "was to find areas in and around where I lived where she could try to find a place to live."

Pause.

Then: "Apartment hunting."

This was exactly what Kaluzny wanted to hear. Those maps might have looked—circumstantially—like some sort of murder-plotting device. However, in actuality they were nothing more than common apartment-hunting tools that Donna needed to find a place to live. She needed to be nearby so George could take care of her, and Gail could take care of the child. George was setting up his mistress with an apartment near his home.

But the situation, George explained further, wasn't what it seemed. George made a point to talk about the fact that he believed Donna was terminally ill and his child was going to need a family. It was the only reason why he decided to set up Donna in her own apartment so close to his home.

To further bolster Kaluzny's point, the lawyer asked George whose idea it was, in fact, to purchase the maps.

"It was *my* idea," George answered.

"Okay. . . . Mr. Fulton," Kaluzny said after looking at his notes, clearing his throat, "at any time did Donna discuss with you killing your wife or getting rid of her in any way?"

George leaned into the microphone: "No."

Lawrence Kaluzny asked several more inconsequential questions and passed the witness to Kevin Ouellette's lawyer, Michael McCarthy. Kevin, Patrick, Sybil, and Donna sat in front of the witness-box. The fearsome foursome. Beside each defendant was his or her lawyer. It was an extreme situation in many ways: Four defendants faced each witness.

For the most part McCarthy backtracked and had George reiterate several points he had made already. There was no silver lining here; there was no bombshell that would exonerate Kevin Ouellette. It almost felt forced, as if McCarthy was belaboring issues for no reason.

The next day, March 10, 2000, Paul Walton faced off once again with his four main suspects in Judge Nancy Tolwin Carniak's courtroom. First up, Walton brought in two investigators to tell their stories of putting the case together and heading down to Florida to round up suspects. After they got each suspect into a room, it became a matter of shining a light in his or her eyes and asking if he or she did it. To bolster the conspiracy aspect of his case, Walton brought in Kevin Ouellette's girlfriend, his former roommate from Akron, Ohio, as well as Sybil's mother, Helen Padgett, who had a few interesting insights to offer.

Sybil, Patrick, Donna, and Kevin sat staring at Helen, who came across as nervous. Like many people called into court, she did not necessarily want to be there testifying, especially against her own daughter. This was definitely one of those I-told-you-so moments. Back when Gail was murdered—you know, *that day*—Helen knew in her gut that Sybil was up to no good. She even confronted her daughter about it.

One of the more interesting exchanges between the prosecutor and his witness came when Paul Walton asked, "Do you ever remember sitting down with your daughter and telling her, at one point, not to get involved in something?"

"Yes."

"Do you remember about when that was?" This was an important question.

"No," Helen said.

"What were you telling your daughter not to get involved in?"

Gail was still alive then.

That day.

"Not to kill Gail," Helen said with a stoic sense of not comprehending, truly, what she was admitting to: knowing about a murder before it happened.

"Why did you think your daughter would go and kill Gail?"

"Because I heard her talking at one time. . . ."

"I'm sorry, who was she talking to?"

"She told me about it . . . ," Helen answered, not entirely sure of how to respond.

"What do you recall her saying about it?"

"That Donna wanted her to go kill Gail. I told her not to do it."

With that response Helen had admitted publicly that she—same as two previous witnesses before her—had known about Gail's murder *before* it happened.

No one had gone to the police, however.

* * *

Concluding the hearing, the assistant prosecuting attorney Paul Walton brought in three more law enforcement witnesses. With George and the others, Walton had made a good argument for probable cause. All of these defendants were heading for trial, Walton was certain.

Then again, courts were finicky. Judges could come in on either side and surprise everyone. All one could do—as an attorney working the case, or a defendant waiting on the decision of his or her life—was wait and see.

65

PAUL WALTON WAS happy with the outcome of the preliminary examination. His charges stuck. Four defendants were headed to trial to face a jury for the murder of an innocent woman. That said, the tenacious prosecutor knew he still had plenty of work ahead of him. The goal was to convict Donna Trapani, Sybil Padgett, and Kevin Ouellette. Nothing less would suffice.

Patrick Alexander came forward after the preliminary exam and wanted to deal. If the prosecuting attorney was willing to agree to charge him with a felony that included a non–life sentence, Patrick said through his lawyers, he would trade his testimony. Here was an eyewitness to the murder—and more important, the conspiracy—coming forward to give up the others.

Second-degree murder, it turned out, was what Patrick Alexander wanted. It was quite a step-down from first-degree murder. It meant Patrick would likely get out of prison one day.

"After reviewing all of the evidence in the case," Paul Walton said later, "we decided to extend that offer to Mr. Alexander."

Why not? There's that whole "cut off your nose to spite your face" comparison. Bottom line: If one removes the loose leg of a table, it will topple over. If Patrick had never met Donna through Sybil, so goes the argument, he would not have been involved in this murder. Paul Walton had to think about cutting his losses and going after the mastermind to be certain justice was served. Paul Walton made it clear that Donna Trapani was never going to be offered such a deal.

On Tuesday, October 17, 2000, after a three-day trial, a jury of his peers convicted Kevin Ouellette of first-degree murder. It took jurors two hours to reject Kevin's argument that he was "so mesmerized by accused murder plot mastermind Donna Trapani" that he "wasn't acting of [his] own free will."

Yes, ridiculous. Kevin was saying Donna had *made* him do it; and because of her expert manipulation skills, he had gone through with it.

Kevin was thirty-three on the day he was convicted. He faced a mandatory life sentence under Michigan law, but the judge held off sentencing the convicted murderer until Donna and Sybil's cases were adjudicated. Kevin's lawyer, Michael McCarthy, an attorney Paul Walton respected greatly, told the *Detroit News* shortly after the verdict, "It was clear that [Donna Trapani] had a hold on George Fulton." McCarthy called George an "educated man," who was, despite his intellect, under Donna's spell. The fact remained that Donna, McCarthy continued, was able to "get him [George] to do things that a rational man wouldn't normally do."

There was no mention of the fact that George was also getting his feverish sexual needs met by Donna and was an equal contributor and partner in the affair.

"Likewise with Mr. Ouellette," McCarthy added, "she

pulled the strings. He didn't really make a conscious, freewill choice."

Perhaps driving to Donna's house and demanding his money right after the murder, and then heading out to the local Walmart to purchase stereo equipment and deodorant, was somehow part of Donna's wicked spell, too? And that taped confession Kevin gave police, which Walton had played for jurors—that must have been Donna still controlling the poor guy as well.

To say that Kevin Ouellette was being forced to do things by Donna Trapani was ignorant and patronizing to the jurors—not to mention laughable.

In response to Ouellette's defense, Paul Walton put Kevin's explanation in perfect context: "Each [defendant] was culpable," the prosecutor noted, "in [his or her] own right."

With two down, Paul Walton got back into trial mode as November dawned. November in Michigan is akin to the dead of winter anywhere else in the upper part of the country: cold, damp, bare-naked trees; the ground hard and suede-colored; the skies routinely threatening snow, which is measured by the foot.

Part of securing Donna Trapani's and Sybil Padgett's convictions was going to be asking Kevin Ouellette to testify. With his conviction on the books, and an absolute surety he was going to appeal the verdict, Walton didn't think he had a chance of getting Kevin to agree to take the stand against Sybil and Donna. Why would he? There was nothing in it for him.

However, when asked through his lawyers, Kevin said, "Sure, I'll do it."

Part of the deal, a source later said, included a promise that if Kevin testified against both (Sybil and Donna were set to be tried together, simultaneously), he wanted the Assistant Prosecuting Attorney's (APA) office to write a letter on his behalf to the Michigan Department of Corrections (DOC) indicating a desire to be moved to a prison closer to family and friends.

"It was highly unusual for him to want to testify, because anything he would ultimately say in either case would, ah, be used against him during his appellate process," Paul Walton—a bit baffled by Kevin's willingness to testify—said later.

It was a simple case from where Paul Walton prosecuted it. Donna's defense, he later said, was weak, but basically it was all she had left if she hoped to stage a fight.

"It was twofold," Walton commented, analyzing Donna's strategy. "One, those witnesses who were testifying against her misunderstood her anger and took it upon themselves to kill Gail." It was similar to the argument Donna had made during the preliminary exam. "This was a convoluted [stance] that seemed to lose its message a little bit as her trial proceeded. She kept trying to control which way the evidence came in. Her lawyer was trying to, in my opinion, mitigate all of this by trying to get her convicted of a lesser offense." Walton called it a smart move, and the only ploy the attorney had available.

"Our second problem, if you will, was that we were trying a woman—Donna—with murder [who] wasn't even in the state at the time."

Donna was on the phone with George.

That day.

Her alibi, apparently.

Factual challenges, Walton viewed. To him, after studying the reports, looking deeply into Donna's life, he could clearly see he was dealing with a "very manipulative, very single-minded, extremely egocentric, and narcissistic" female who believed that all she had to do was give an explanation and she was going to get out of it.

As far as murder trials went, Walton considered the case not to be as easy as it might have seemed from the outset.

"We had four cases," he said. "Initially we were going to do two trials. It's always a juggling match. You have to be on top of your game and watch as the evidence is presented because juries are ushered in and out of the courtroom depending on whose case is being talked about." It can get maddeningly confusing for jurors. "You always want to make sure you're giving a consistent version or that the evidence is coming into the cases consistently."

How am I going to convince a jury that this woman was a murderer if she had not left the state of Florida? Walton pondered over and over again. *How am I going to convince a jury that Sybil wasn't some sort of undereducated, manipulated person who was easily led, and that maybe the jury should have some sympathy for her?* These were the number one anomalies that kept playing in the APA's mind.

The driving force Walton had going for him in that regard became, as he put it, that "the case was thoroughly investigated, and I was confident we had *every* piece of evidence we could squeeze out of it. It came down to making sure we presented a consistent and cohesive train of evidence."

66

NOT YET OFFICIALLY winter, it had been one of the worst she could recall since moving to Michigan from Texas almost five years prior. Emily Fulton left work early one day to catch the afternoon session of jury selection, and the snow came down in a whiteout. It seemed there was a foot on the ground already as she drove. To begin with, she did not want to go to court. Here was this crazy snow coming down and driving was hazardous. It was too much: the pressure of hearing the details about her mother's murder, her father being there, the anxiety of the weather. Emily started crying.

"Someone once told me that, sometimes, when it rains, it is our loved ones from Heaven looking down at us and crying because they miss us," Emily later reflected. "I think the same is true of the snow, because during this time I felt so much sadness and anger, and the snow seemed to be a physical manifestation of it all."

Voir dire had begun on November 21, 2000. Those asked by mail to serve their community were ushered into the courtroom in groups, asked questions, and ultimately a jury of Donna's and Sybil's peers was chosen. Donna and Sybil were being tried together (and also sat together inside the courtroom). It was a smart move. Why go through this process twice?

Many in Gail's family had come to Michigan for the trial. They all sat together and settled in for what was going to be a bumpy, emotional ride.

The jury was in place by Monday, November 27, and Judge Richard Kuhn gave Paul Walton the go ahead to address the men and women chosen to hear the case. Walton was a fair man who understood the subtle intricacies of a courtroom that only an experienced trial attorney could. More than that, Walton was a realist with matters of the court; he was not one of these prosecute-regardless-of-the-evidence types of hardnosed DAs looking to climb a political ladder. Walton wanted justice served, regardless of whether it tasted good to his palate. The case he had built against a woman who had been romantically burned, and had come back to seek revenge on the wife she saw as the sole source of all her anguish, was simple in terms of *why:* Donna Trapani viewed Gail Fulton as an obstacle in the way of her man.

Sybil Padgett and the others were the means to that end. *Their* motive was monetary. Donna's was more cerebral and psychologically deep-seated.

After explaining how Gail walked out of the library unknowingly into the hands of her murderers, this straitlaced, loving, charming, devout, and caring woman had no idea she was going to be the "victim of a contract killing. A murder," Walton said loudly, "that was masterminded and put into motion by *this* woman"—he pointed at Donna, who looked down and away—"Donna Kaye Trapani!"

Walton listed the reasons why Gail was murdered. One of which turned out to be the "dedication to her family," he said.

He called Donna the "rebuffed and aging lover to George." And when George decided to return home and rekindle his relationship and marriage, watch out! Donna took that as Gail Fulton crossing a line in the hot Florida sand.

"Failing in her bid to win back George," Walton said, shaking his head, reacting to how silly it all sounded, yet how evil and spurious, "immediately I think of a quote when talking about this case . . . and it goes something like this: 'Heaven has no rage like a woman—a woman's love turned to hatred. Nor hell knows no fury like a woman scorned.' Failing in her manipulation to win George back, she decided she was going to kill Mrs. Fulton. A plan [that] was executed with deadly precision. . . ."

Walton talked about how the murder went down, step by step. He mentioned details. He spoke of those chilling moments when Gail looked down the barrel of a gun and into the eyes of her killer—but undoubtedly saw Donna's face. He mentioned how Sybil and Patrick and Kevin tore out of the parking lot after mowing Gail down in a hail of gunfire and quickly drove back home to seek their monetary reward. He called Donna the mastermind several times to implant that image in the minds of jurors. He called Gail's death a "contract killing"—maybe more times than he should have—but he made the point that this murder was the plot of *one* woman.

When they returned to Florida from Michigan, Walton explained, pausing first to allow the jury and gallery to focus on what he was going to say next, the well-spoken prosecutor lowered his voice and described how Sybil, Kevin, and Patrick went directly to Donna to "collect their money for a job well done."

His point was made: These were vile creatures that killed an innocent woman who had done more good for more people within twenty-four hours of her life than they had likely done combined throughout *all* their lives. These killers, Walton implied, were selfish people who took it upon themselves to judge and condemn a woman for nothing more than loving her husband. And even among those who had admitted to the crime already, remorse or sympathy was hard to find. Kevin said he'd killed Gail in cold blood. Patrick said he'd planned and watched. Neither said it had made him feel bad or that he was the least bit sorry for committing such a violent act. It was as if by admitting to the crime, each should be rewarded.

Walton took a moment to go through the charges and make sure jurors understood each count and how his office had legally reached those charges. This was where Walton broke down that one bothersome aspect of the case he felt he faced going in: making sure jurors knew exactly how a woman could commit a murder and yet be in another state when the act took place. He used words like "aided" and "abetted." He explained the legalese behind "intent to kill." He outlined the cool contemplation, scheming, and measured acts of violence Donna had planned methodically, making a solemn point, giving everyone in the courtroom a closer look into Donna's mind-set and thought process as she began planning Gail's death: "The intent to kill was premeditated and deliberate. This simply means that the defendant considered the pros and cons of the killing and thought about her actions *before* choosing."

Donna Trapani had gone up to Michigan and proclaimed her pregnancy to Gail. She said she was dying. That didn't work. Then she drove home. She sent George e-mails begging him to come back to her. That didn't work, either. So she carefully and evilly decided Gail would have to pay for George's decision to diss her. And maybe, when George finally woke up, he would come crawling back to her.

Ending his opening statement, Walton went through the day-to-day mechanics of the affair and how Donna became a marginalized woman hell-bent on revenge. Most were probably sitting, listening to how this relationship unfolded and then fell apart—and how George brought Donna (who claimed to be pregnant and dying) up to meet his wife—and thought why in the world did Donna kill Gail if she had felt so betrayed? Why not put a cap in the back of George's ear? If Donna was truly a woman belittled by a man she had devoted her heart to, why had she taken revenge on his innocent wife?

Simple: Donna Trapani hated Gail. That argument was made by the recurring criticisms and hasty gestures and mean-spirited remarks Donna had made about Gail whenever she mentioned her in a letter, fax, or e-mail. Donna got off on the idea that Gail would suffer. Donna felt fuzzy inside thinking about Gail being taken out of the picture so she could then move in and pick up the pieces of George's shattered life.

Larry Kaluzny began by asking the jury why they were in the courtroom, pointing down at the table he stood near.

Kaluzny answered his own question by paying respects—as infinitesimal as they were—to the one person who is generally forgotten once a murder trial gets under way: the victim.

"We are here," the highly regarded attorney said, "obviously because Gail Fulton was killed." But also, he added decisively, "Because Donna says, 'I'm not guilty.' Make no mistake about that. Whether she testifies or not, she tells you," he said, pausing, looking at each juror, "'I am *not* guilty.'"

As many defense attorneys will do during opening arguments, Kaluzny broke into a canned speech about the *facts* of the case and how jurors should judge a defendant on those *facts* alone.

The problem with this argument is that most juries judge a defendant by her appearance, demeanor—if a defendant smiles, if she laughs, if she scratches herself the wrong way, if she whispers to her lawyer too many times, if she testifies, if she closes her eyes when she's not supposed to, if she cries or doesn't cry, and so on. Juries do this first. And then, maybe, when they begin deliberations, only then do they talk about *facts* and evidence. But judgments are made first, no doubt about it. No matter what any potential juror says during the voir dire process, he or she is judging a defendant the moment that defendant sits down. Jurors are human beings, obviously, and people like to judge other people. Everyone draws conclusions about others based on a list of personal hang-ups, reservations, insecurities, self-esteem issues, and makes immediate decisions. This does not change because a person has sworn an oath. Yet defense attorneys—many of them—refuse to address this concern in their openings. Instead, like Larry Kaluzny, they belabor this idea of sticking to the *facts* of a case and basing the verdict on those facts.

"We ask that you be conscientious," Kaluzny told jurors, "as you listen to the *facts* of this case—of credible evidence"—and here came the defense hammer walloping the prosecutor—"not of just *theory*. Of believable facts. Not anger. Of reliable facts. Not vengeance. A precious life is gone, other lives have been touched by that, and another life is at stake here as well."

Then came a little preachy rhetoric all defense attorneys spew when speaking about how juries should never, ever *presume* guilt (yet they all do). Leave that to the cops and prosecutors, Kaluzny jabbed, almost laughing. They, he added, *always* presume guilt. They have to whenever they step into a case.

"Juries presume innocence," he said, slowing down. "That presumption is strong, and it exists as we sit here now."

Thanks for pointing that out, there, Mr. Defense Attorney.

Kaluzny went on and on, trying to stay as far away from those *facts* as he could. Because, when anyone studied the bare bones of this case, it was inside those *facts* that Donna was going to meet the iron lock of the steel door closing in on her freedom.

67

SYBIL PADGETT'S ATTORNEY, Raymond Correll, mimicked Larry Kaluzny's arguments. There was not much difference between the two cases—albeit one defendant was now accusing the other of acting on her own, while the other was saying she had been programmed to kill because of the threats and manipulation of the other. Donna Trapani manipulated Sybil Padgett. She hung things over her head. She dug up rotten things about Sybil at work, threatened to go to the authorities and report Sybil for falsifying records, and forced the weaker woman in the friendship into finding her a killer. One could argue all day why Sybil did not go to the police, but it would not solve the situation of bringing Gail back to her family and her killers to justice.

Walton started with Barbara Butkis, the library worker who first spotted Gail lying in the parking lot, bleeding to death. This image of a librarian gunned down in the parking lot of what is a solemn, peaceful, nonthreatening public space was disturbing and chilling. It brought tears to Barbara's eyes as she recalled those violent memories now embedded in her psyche. Those in the gallery swallowed lumps, twisting and turning in their seats, as Barbara described Gail's final moments and the panic Barbara developed as she realized Gail had been shot.

"You said you noticed an injury to her head?" Walton asked several questions into the testimony.

"Yes," Barbara replied, "because I kept looking all over to see if there was something I could do for her. And noticed"—she paused, caught her breath—"and noticed . . . there was a hole at the top of her forehead."

Many in the courtroom gasped.

"About how big was the hole?"

"It was just a . . . Well, I guess it was just a small one that I could tell."

And so Barbara set the stage, giving jurors a clear picture of the end result: Gail Fulton lying in a pool of her own blood, wheezing for her last breaths, undoubtedly praying to God. But even more, Barbara was also able to interject Gail's working schedule into the trial, which proved it was not a normal nine-to-five, Monday-through-Friday, working-class routine. For someone to know when Gail was at work, he or she would have had to know Gail or have stalked her.

OCSD sheriff's deputy Guy Hubble was next. Hubble, a fourteen-year veteran of the police force, walked jurors through the crime scene as he came upon it. The most damaging piece of testimony here was, again, those images of a dying woman. However, Hubble brought something else to the table before stepping down: that videotape of the murder and scores of photographs depicting Gail dead in the parking lot, a pool of blood the size of a garbage can lid around her head.

Then OCSD sergeant Alan Whitefield took the stand. Whitefield talked the jury through the phone conversation he'd had with Donna early the next morning.

* * *

On cross-examination Lawrence Kaluzny questioned Alan Whitefield about the call, not adding anything to the "facts" of the case other than belaboring an issue that was truly not something the prosecutor had put all that much thought in, to begin with.

End result: Whitefield had called Donna and she never asked why; she never wondered what might bring the OCSD to phone her in the middle of the night; she had not asked if anything had happened to George.

Why? Whitefield's testimony made clear: Donna *knew.* There, in that subliminal part of her brain, she knew. Donna never asked certain questions to the investigator because she already *knew* the answers.

Donna's lawyer got into a Q&A with Whitefield regarding personal checks and the *fact* that the OCSD had not found a paper trail linking Donna to paying off Kevin, Sybil, or Patrick.

No, they did not. Because Donna had made sure to cover her tracks in that regard by having others cash the checks and also paying Kevin with cash she had pilfered from her company.

Sybil Padgett's lawyer, Raymond Correll, took a crack at Alan Whitefield by harping on how long that phone call he'd had with Donna lasted. Correll, however, realized he was getting nowhere, and sat down.

It was closing in on the end of the day, so the judge suspended proceedings until the following morning, giving jurors the usual don't-listen-to-radio-or-TV speech and don't-talk-among-yourselves dictum.

Gavel.

68

THE NEXT DAY, November 28, everyone was back in court, now ready to hear from one of the state's chief witnesses.

George Fulton.

Mostly, Paul Walton had George stick to the same testimony he gave during the preliminary examination. Here, though, George was asked to go into greater detail regarding certain matters, and Walton introduced several tape-recorded voice mail messages that Donna and Sybil had left on George's voice mail. One depicted the rage and hatred Donna had for Gail; jurors heard Donna call Gail a "bitch" several times during the message, warning George not to bring her down to Florida. It was that same "Florida is my state, Michigan is her state" voice mail that Donna had left after she heard Gail had insisted on going to Florida with George if he went for business. The jury heard straight from Donna's mouth how nasty, vile, and vulgar she could get when she felt the least bit slighted.

George did not hold back, although his answers borderlined on being snobbish and intentionally patronizing at times. For example, after being asked when his and Donna's relationship "changed" between the first night they had met and the second, when they ended up inside

Donna's Lincoln Town Car necking like teenagers, George said, "We engaged in sexual intercourse." Leaving it there.

Hour after hour went by as George talked about every aspect of his life with Donna while he was in Florida and his world slowly crumbling back home in Michigan. Time and again, Paul Walton asked if Gail knew what was going on, and George Fulton said no, "not then," meaning the first year he and Donna were together. What became clear was that George was living two separate lives for a long period of time, and it didn't seem to matter to him (morally speaking). It was stressful. Sure. It was wrong. Most definitely. But George had no qualms about continuing for as long as he could get away with it. Not until Donna started acting a little wacky and possessive did George take a step back and review the relationship. The more Donna pushed George into making a choice, the more he backed off. This was something Donna never realized: All she had to do to keep George was, essentially, cut him off sexually and tell him not to call until he left Gail. Yet, by the time that light-bulb went off for Donna, George had been emotionally cooked and had made the call to leave Donna already.

Walking away, according to George's testimony, had made Donna furious. She grew angrier by the day.

What was respectable about Walton's questioning of George early on was how the prosecutor asked questions about Gail and her life, in effect, humanizing her. Having George talk about Gail—her dreams and loves and dislikes—drew a connection between Gail and the jury. She became a person, not just a murder victim or a headline. This was smart trial lawyering on Walton's part and explained the type of person Paul Walton was inside a courtroom. Giving jurors a reason to love Gail would help them to draw the same conclusion as Walton had: Gail Fulton, truly, was an innocent victim, who had been killed by a lying and conniving female obsessed with the idea of doing whatever it took to get back her man.

For a time Walton had George describe the relationship between Donna and Sybil, and how George had gotten to know Sybil. He talked about the problems Sybil often got herself into at work, and how Donna covered for and gave Sybil second chances, even when the integrity of the business was at stake.

Another important *fact* George brought out was how Donna had not made it common practice at CCHH to rent Enterprise rental cars for employees other than Sybil. The way Donna made it sound to police was that she had rented cars routinely for her employees because they traveled so much for care visits.

Interestingly enough, George told jurors, when he first received that letter from Donna's doctor indicating she was pregnant and dying of stage-four lymphoma, he had a sense he recognized the handwriting on the envelope as Donna's.

"I thought it was hers," he said.

Lawrence Kaluzny objected.

A brief argument ensued.

But again, a bell had been rung. It didn't matter now.

When asked why George thought it would be a good idea for his mistress to come up to Michigan to meet his wife, George responded, "At that time I thought, if my wife met her, she would see she was a person like she was. If, in fact, she was dying, and if, in fact, she was pregnant, what would happen to the baby and what would happen to her?"

"Did you discuss with your wife some plans about this?"

"Yeah . . . we had talked about it, what to do. And I was not sure what to do."

Walton had George talk about the maps he and

Donna had purchased while she was in town. George had unknowingly helped Donna plot his wife's murder. He felt disgusted by the thought of it.

He talked about his life with Donna, how Gail found out George was planning a trip to Florida, how Donna began to badger George (after the breakup) about work, and how he had gotten to a point where he didn't want to work for her any longer.

As the noon hour approached, the judge stopped the questioning, explaining that the court had "things" (unrelated to the case) to do, and recessed until Thursday, November 30, 2000.

Emily Fulton sat and listened to her father testify, not really hearing what he was saying. "I don't remember what my dad said as much as his tone of voice and how he looked," she recalled. "My dad has been more of an emotional person over the years . . . but at this time he was not, and so his voice was more monotone and devoid of emotion. . . ."

George alternated crosses he wore during his days in the courtroom.

"The cross," Emily said, "was honking huge. My dad wore white shirts with some sort of tie and then the huge wooden cross on a leather strap thingy that hung down to the middle of his chest, almost down to his stomach. I believe that someone from church gave that cross to my dad, as it was not something he purchased himself. See, my dad has always felt as if he was being persecuted and that he was the one on trial, since he had to tell so many personal details. . . . He always said the media persecuted him, tarnished his character, and made him into this bad person. So, in my opinion, he wore the cross to show he was religious and to symbolize he was almost being persecuted like Jesus. Now, of course, there is no comparison between Jesus and my dad and this comparison is just [from] me, but that is how I remember seeing it. . . . [He] could never see what he did wrong and the pain he caused to his family."

When they returned two days later, Paul Walton made a point to enter into the record several documents, giving the jury an idea of how Donna Trapani could have gotten hold of Gail Fulton's schedule. Certain work documents Donna had asked George to fill out for CCHH were revealing in that regard. It seemed no matter what Paul Walton and George Fulton talked about, the pendulum swung toward Donna Trapani and her desire to erase Gail out of their lives.

There was no indication how Lawrence Kaluzny was going to treat George Fulton. Arguably, George was Kaluzny's biggest obstacle to overcome. If Donna Trapani was going to argue that Sybil Padgett and the others acted on their own behalf, was it really necessary to contest George Fulton's direct testimony?

Kaluzny got right to the point: How was your marriage with Gail before you met Donna?

George said it was okay. He and Gail had "disagreements" and there were "small things." In no way was the marriage in trouble.

Then they talked about CCHH and the dynamics of how the company ran.

Then, after saying it was not his intention to embarrass George or smear his reputation, Kaluzny made a point to have George tell the jury he had been lying to Gail for quite some time. That every day he spent with Donna was a lie.

George was asked about all the traveling he did.

Then he was questioned about "opening up to Donna" and if that was what attracted him to her.

George agreed.

Kaluzny asked George if he was thinking of divorcing Gail.

He said he was, back then.

After that, Kaluzny started in about Gail's schedule and how it might have been George who had inadvertently given it to *other* employees at CCHH.

Sure, that was possible, George agreed.

Sybil Padgett became a hot topic. During his questioning Kaluzny was able to paint Sybil as a derelict employee whom Donna felt sorry for and had given chances to because of Sybil's children. Donna felt sorry for her, the questions suggested.

"Was there any resentment detected toward you," Kaluzny asked, trying to drum up a motive on Sybil's part, "because of the salary you were earning, the position you were taking in the company?" George had already made it clear to the court that he and Donna were the highest-paid employees. Could this have sparked enough hatred on Sybil's part, along with George coming into the fold and taking Donna away, to want to go and kill George's wife on her own?

69

THERE CAME A time during George Fulton's cross-examination when jurors and trial observers developed a look of fatigue. Not that anyone was particularly tired. But George's answers to what seemed to be baseless questions were beating on an issue that could be beat no more. It was almost as though the more George talked, the more jurors despised Donna Trapani and her weak attempt at blaming someone else for a crime she had planned, plotted, facilitated, paid for, and, clearly, enjoyed seeing played out. Alienating a jury is not hard to do during a murder trial. And once a juror crossed that threshold of scratching reasonable doubt off the table, he or she was finished.

"At some point you decided," Larry Kaluzny asked George, "that Gail had to know about what was going on between you and Donna, correct?"

"Yes."

"Did you tell Gail, or did she find out about it?"

"She found out."

"What time period are we talking here?"

And this was how it went: rehashing regurgitated information that meant absolutely nothing to Donna Trapani's or Sybil Padgett's end result.

Donna's lawyer then brought his line of questioning back to Gail threatening suicide, as if her state of mind had anything to do with Donna's guilt or innocence.

George opened up; he said he cheated on his wife. Deceived her. Lied to her. Treated her like garbage. What else did the attorney want to know? There was an indication that maybe George did not have any feelings about how he had treated Gail. That he was perhaps cold. So he turned the tables and questioned Kaluzny, asking sharply, "How do you *think* you would feel, Mr. Kaluzny? *Tell* me."

"I think we would all understand she might be suicidal."

"She *wasn't* suicidal. She just *mentioned* it, Mr. Kaluzny. My wife had great faith. She wouldn't do that, because she had the children. Also, if she did that, she would hurt the children, and she knew that was *not* the right thing to do!"

George was tired of having to answer for Gail, a dead woman.

So Kaluzny went back to the Fourth of July. He asked George to describe his approach to the two women meeting, saying, "Was there some idea in your mind that Gail and Donna had many things in common about education, themselves, not just you?"

"I think the things they had in common, Mr. Kaluzny, were me, and that they were women. That was about it."

"Well, certainly, Mr. Fulton, you were in love with Gail during *some* time?"

"Yes, I was."

"You were in love with Donna as well?"

"Yes."

"So—and you are painting her out to be a monster, and I understand that, we all understand that . . . but during a time period—"

Paul Walton interrupted, "That's argumentative."

Kaluzny continued, not paying any mind to the objection.

"Sustained," the judge said. "You may continue."

George responded by saying he did not think Donna was a "monster," because, at that time, "I *trusted* her."

As the cross-examination became somewhat heated between the two men, Kaluzny asked George if he had any way to truly know whether anyone else tried to copy Donna's printing or handwriting in any of the notes she had supposedly sent him. How could George be so sure, in other words, that someone else wasn't forging Donna's hand and sending George all those notes? If Sybil was the killer and had wanted to set up Donna, how could George be so sure Sybil had not forged those notes and letters?

Without breaking out laughing at the question, George made a good point, agreeing that he had no way of knowing if someone had forged Donna's handwriting, but that her style, George testified, her demeanor in those letters, the words on the page she chose to use, gave her away. Donna's character could not be forged.

"She writes, and writes, and writes, and writes," George said. "Just like she talks, and talks, and talks, and talks."

Donna was her own worst enemy.

Kaluzny saw a window. "By the way," he asked, "did you send a card to Donna at the jail in Oakland County?"

"Yes, I did."

"You also sent one to the other defendant?"

"Yes, I did."

"Now—and I don't want to mislead anybody—it was basically in the nature of a religious connotation rather than personal?"

"Yes, it was," George answered.

"All right, I want to give you a chance to explain it. *Why* would you send a card to the people"—Kaluzny stopped himself before he put Donna into that mix of "people"— "one that had already been convicted in killing your wife, and the other people involved in this case?"

"Mr. Kaluzny, I truly believe love is greater than hate. Mrs. Trapani and her three co-conspirators tested that philosophy or belief. I also, after what I went through . . . I wanted to learn to forgive myself for what I have done to my family, my wife, my mother-in-law, and everybody, and the people that did this, because I cannot feel without forgiving. If God can forgive me for what I have done, I have to forgive them. Otherwise, I cannot heal and get on with my life."

The questioning reverted back to how George felt about Donna on the Fourth of July and those e-mails he wrote telling her how much he loved and missed her.

Another aspect of Kaluzny's strategy became apparent after the attorney asked George a series of questions pertaining to the first interview George gave police. During that interview George had said he and Gail did not have any marital problems; and so Kaluzny tried to point out that here was a man and a woman who had just ended an affair, his wife had been murdered, and he was in no way thinking that his mistress had anything to do with it.

But again, George was honest; he might have been an adulterer, his testimony implied, and treated Gail badly at times, but he damn well knew—once he had a chance to sit down and see it all clearly—that Donna had hated Gail enough, and been obsessed with him, to the point of wanting Gail out of the picture. No matter how hard Kaluzny tried, he could not crack George and get him to admit to anything even remotely redeeming for his client. The evidence against Donna was too solid. He could attack George's character all day long, paint him as a cad and a Lothario, but it didn't change the fact that Donna Trapani had hired someone to whack his wife with the hope of winning back the man's love.

Raymond Correll, Sybil's attorney, had a few questions for George after Kaluzny finished. They seemed at best trivial; at worst, nothing more than a waste of everyone's time. When he was done, Correll passed the witness back to the judge, who asked Paul Walton if he had anything (he didn't), and then if Kaluzny had anything additional for George (he didn't).

"You may be excused, Mr. Fulton."

Gail's husband walked out of the courtroom.

The remainder of the day was consumed by Dr. R. Ortiz-Reyes, who talked jurors through Gail's autopsy. Again, the courtroom was hit with a dose of sobering reality when the doctor spoke of how those bullets ricocheted inside Gail's body. By the time he finished, the jury understood Gail had bled to death, a long and slow process, and suffered greatly before she expired. And there could be no doubt, as Gail slipped away, she knew her attacker had been sent by her rival, Donna Trapani.

Kevin Ouellette's girlfriend at the time of the murder testified. She had dated Kevin and lived with him inside Sybil's house. She told stories of meeting Donna, and how Donna and Kevin and Patrick and Sybil retreated into Donna's bedroom at various times. She explained how she knew what was going on, although her belief then was that Kevin was being hired by Donna to beat up somebody.

A friend of Sybil Padgett's testified. The guy met Sybil as she showed up one day to nurse his father. They struck up a friendship. Within a few questions it was apparent why the man was on the stand: Sybil had gone to the guy weeks after meeting him and asked if he could find her a gun.

"Were you able to get her a gun?"

"Yes."

Next, Kevin's friend from Akron, Ohio, came in and gave her version of that part of the murder—detailing the night Kevin and Patrick and Sybil showed up looking for bullets and weed.

By Friday, December 1, 2000, Todd Franklin had given his version of turning Sybil in to the authorities after making that call to police and breaking the case open. As each of these material witnesses came forward, stood, held up their right hands, sat and testified, the one result was that Donna Trapani had been the woman behind the curtain in Emerald City the entire time. If nothing else, it became obvious that Sybil and Patrick were not smart enough to pull this murder off on their own—and anyway, why would Sybil Padgett, Patrick Alexander, or Kevin Ouellette want to kill a woman located over a thousand miles away from Florida—and one whom they had never known?

Gail Fulton's mother—bless her heart—sat down and talked jurors through the life of her daughter and those disturbing phone calls Dora had received from Donna. Dora mentioned how she had confronted George and gotten no response from him when she asked about his having an affair. It was heart-piercing testimony, humanizing Gail, bringing jurors into the life of a woman who suffered under the umbrella of a loveless marriage for so many years. However, Gail was, as of September 1999, coming around, feeling better about her life and husband. Gail was, Dora said, in "good spirits."

70

THERE WAS A certain boyish immaturity that fit Patrick Alexander well. He donned peach fuzz, a kindergartener's first-day-of-school haircut, and a tired look of defeat in his eyes. Patrick was a kid, in so many ways. With the right deal he could get out of prison and still have plenty of life left to live.

This was the one plus Larry Kaluzny had going after Patrick: Patrick Alexander would say whatever he needed to get out of prison as soon as he could.

Maybe even lie.

There was some talk among the lawyers regarding Patrick's criminal record coming in. The jury was asked to leave the room while Patrick answered questions. Yes, he was a career criminal. He had been busted for grand theft, breaking and entering, destruction of county property, and, as he put it, "several thefts." He also had broken his probation so many times he had lost count. On top of all that, however, Patrick had come forward and bartered a deal for his "truthful testimony" for one reason: a reduction in his sentence.

After several sidebar conversations among the lawyers, the jury was brought back in and the trial resumed.

It wasn't quite love at first sight, Patrick explained, when he and Sybil hooked up.

"One weekend I went to stay at her house with her brother," he said, "and when Miss Padgett came in, after the weekend was over, I asked her permission to stay with her. . . ."

Why?

"Because the person I was staying with," Patrick explained, "had attempted to run me over with a truck, so I needed a place to stay."

One thing led to another, and Patrick started sleeping with Sybil.

Patrick talked jurors through their early relationship and how, by driving Sybil to work every day, he eventually met Donna.

Not far into his direct examination, Patrick gave up the goods. Paul Walton asked when the first time was Donna had brought up hurting someone.

"On the porch," he answered.

"What do you remember about that—what was said?"

"We had set on the porch for maybe an hour or so, and Miss Trapani, she was discussing how she was having problems with her boyfriend and her boyfriend's wife. And she initially stated that she wanted to find someone to commit a murder."

Walton asked his witness to be more specific. Did Donna say "commit a murder"?

"To kill someone," Patrick clarified.

At first, Patrick and Sybil didn't think Donna was serious, so they "blew it off." But Donna brought it up again, not long after that first conversation. They were poolside at Donna's house one night. Patrick and Sybil were drinking. Donna started to riff on having someone murdered. She talked about it incessantly, almost as if she was bullying Patrick, who had told Donna by then he was not the right person to go around hurting people for money.

"Miss Trapani stated that, once again, that—she talked about her problems with her boyfriend and his wife. She then stated that the wife's name to be Martha Gail Fulton . . . [and] that she was going to make a trip to Michigan, which is where Mrs. Fulton and Mr. Fulton resided. She then stated a sum of money of fifteen thousand dollars to have Miss Fulton killed." (Throughout his testimony, Patrick would occasionally refer to the married Gail as "Miss Fulton.")

Patrick said he and Sybil were paid $1,000 to drive to Michigan and stalk Gail.

From there it became a matter of going through the story and having Patrick recount his and Sybil's roles in the murder. The thought that kept coming up for anyone listening to this testimony was how close Patrick's story was in terms of Kevin Ouellette's. There was not a lot of wiggle room here for a defense attorney to poke holes in. And that's the funny thing about the truth: If you speak it, it never wavers or suffers from lack of integrity. It is, as they say, what it is. The truth will not change. Lies become tangled in a mesh of additional lies. They don't add up. Liars are caught within the tiniest details: times, places, colors, words, and those odds and ends that prevaricators never think of when lying.

Patrick went through it all: the maps, the masks, the gun, the bullets, the rental car, the walk through the library to find Gail as she worked, Kevin slashing the tire of Gail's van, the crash and boom of the weapon rounds going off in Kevin's hand, the getaway.

He didn't miss a beat.

One chilling moment came when Patrick explained Donna's initial plan, saying, "Her first suggestion was that Miss Padgett and I kidnap Miss Fulton and bring her to Florida so . . . [Donna] could deal with her. Another suggestion she made was to inject [Gail] with antifreeze, or have her swallow antifreeze."

Donna had even drafted a suicide note for Patrick and Sybil to leave on Gail's body after they were finished.

Imagine . . . Donna had gone as far as to use Gail's own emotional fragility against her to have her murdered and cover it up. That spoke to the sociopathic mind-set Donna had tapped into as she planned and plotted Gail's demise. Antifreeze. Suicide. It was all alarmingly cruel punishment Donna was willing to dole out for the sake of winning.

For the sake of taking a man away from a woman.

For the sake of control.

Another revelation Patrick laid on everyone was that he and Sybil had not only gone up to Michigan in September to stalk Gail, but also to kill her.

"What changed your mind?" Walton asked.

"Seeing [her] in the person, herself, and also seeing [her] children coming and going from the house."

When they returned to Florida and explained to Donna they didn't have the nerve to kill Gail, Donna had a fit.

"She was outraged. She got mad, started storming around her house, slamming dishes into the sink. She was just violent."

Hell hath no fury . . . indeed.

Donna confronted both of them as if they were children, Patrick explained, screaming:

"'I sent y'all to do *one* simple job for me and y'all couldn't even do *that*!'"

Enter Kevin Ouellette.

The way Patrick described the murder, a listener would think he was talking about a day at the races.

"Miss Fulton falls to the ground. And Mr. Ouellette returns to the vehicle and we leave."

Walton pushed Patrick to talk about the "expression" on

Gail's face when she realized she was going to be shot "in the face."

"Look of fear. A look of, 'Why is thing happening to me?'"

By the end of the day, Patrick finished his direct, explaining Donna's reaction to hearing the details of the murder: "Excited! Like she had won the lottery. She complimented Mr. Ouellette."

A job well done.

Donna's and Sybil's attorneys were unable to rattle Patrick during cross-examination. His testimony added to what Kevin Ouellette and Sybil Padgett had said already. Which led to one conclusion: If one person calls another party a killer, she might walk away, shunning the person with a shush of her hands. Two people call that same individual a killer, and she will probably turn and listen to what they have to say. But when three people—all of whom were there at the time— call that woman a killer, that person had better start thinking about how she is going to decorate her cell.

The court recessed until nine-thirty the following Monday morning.

Several additional witnesses testified on behalf of the state: crime lab specialists, detectives, experts in ballistics and in handwriting. All of these folks outlined a forensic case for Paul Walton. Each piece of evidence pointed to the one person whom jurors had not heard from, as of yet— Donna Trapani.

And the look on her face as each witness walked in and heaved a shovel filled with dirt into that hole she found herself falling deeper into spoke to the one option she had left.

On December 8, 2000, Larry Kaluzny stood. Walton

had rested his case. Kaluzny asked the court if he could call his first witness.

"Your Honor," Kaluzny said, "we would call Donna Trapani at this time."

It was Donna's only shot.

"You may," the judge instructed.

Before Kaluzny allowed Donna to testify, he put on record something that shocked many in the courtroom—and led several to believe that maybe the entire story had *not* been told. Perhaps Donna should be given the benefit of the doubt?

Donna's defense attorneys asked if they could put a "stipulation on the record."

The judge said sure.

"Your Honor, after a discussion with the prosecutor . . . we stipulate that Donna Kaye Trapani's diagnosis of cancer has been confirmed by Dr. Bruce G. Rudman on November 7, 2000."

"Thank you," the court said.

"So stipulated, Your Honor . . . ," Paul Walton responded.

71

DONNA TRAPANI HAD NOT changed much since her incarceration. The only glaring difference was a recurring problem she'd always had with facial hair. In prison Donna couldn't get to the spa and have her mustache waxed, so it grew uncontrollably, and she did little to groom herself. Her hair, too, was frayed, a mishmash of split ends. She looked, well, beaten and worn.

While listening to witnesses, Donna had taken notes and whispered to her attorneys and even to Sybil Padgett. And there were times when she'd actually turned around and stared at Gail Fulton's family: mainly George and Emily.

"Donna would spend long periods looking at us, with almost a blank look in her eyes, and I could not for the life of me think what was going on in her mind," Emily recalled.

Donna had gawked uncomfortably at Emily, while Emily thought: *Why is she staring? She is sad and creepy, all at the same time*.

According to that stipulation submitted by Larry Kaluzny, Donna had not been lying when she said she'd had cancer. As her trial with Sybil headed into its final phase, a doctor had diagnosed Donna with the disease. And the predominant feeling became: If she'd had cancer, what was there on record to prove Donna hadn't been pregnant, too? It wasn't unheard of for a group of criminals to band together, conspire to commit a murder, and drag an innocent person down into the abyss of guilt with them.

Others, though, had different opinions: "My recollection is that she was scanned for cancer," Paul Walton later said, "but nothing [was] found."

All that aside, here was the one woman at the center of this double (defendant) murder trial, raising her hand, stating a belief in God and His Truth, ready to sit in the witness-box and explain her role.

As they began, Donna had to be told repeatedly to keep her voice up. She spoke low and slow. The idea was to come across as nonthreatening. The thought that Donna Trapani could not keep her voice at a level where she could be heard was preposterous. Donna was all about being the center of attention—the one that people listened to and took orders from.

After talking about her education, and where she grew up, and how she came to start CCHH, the first opportunity to take a poke at George Fulton came when Donna was asked to talk about the financial situation of her business "before George Fulton," as if somehow, by his presence, George had disrupted what was a multimillion-dollar business.

"My financial documents," Donna said nastily, as though she despised George for it, "for 1997 was [for a] one-point-five-million-dollar business!"

"And after?" Kaluzny asked, as if they'd rehearsed it. "Let's put it that way—until fairly recently, what was the status of the business?"

"It was on the verge of bankruptcy."

According to Donna, her failure had nothing to do with her incompetent business management, which just about every single one of her employees would later swear to. No. It was hiring George and the shadow of "big government" coming down on the poor woman.

They moved on from her failure in the business world to Donna's "friendship" with Sybil Padgett. Donna portrayed herself as an intelligent and successful mentor to a more backwoods-type hick, who needed someone to show her how to live a more healthy life. Then Donna mentioned how Sybil falsified records and lab reports and turned in slips for seeing patients she had never visited. Yet, even though George didn't want to, Donna said, she convinced him they should "give Sybil a second chance"—which was probably a mistake, Donna realized.

As her direct examination moved forward, it appeared Donna Kaye Trapani had an answer for everything. Something juries never want to hear. When a witness can put a shine on every part of her life, she's obviously hiding the scratches somewhere. When she hit on George, after talking about how they met, not disputing anything he had said in his testimony regarding those days, Donna sounded hurt, adding, "We fell in love with each other. And he eventually left Michigan and came down, came to work for me, and moved in with me." She paused for effect, hoping to perhaps dredge up a bit of empathy before delivering what was to her the final blow: "He promised to marry me."

Unsurprisingly, everything Donna said seemed to fit into her theory of the murder.

"To your knowledge," Kaluzny asked, "did the staff [at CCHH] know that George was married?"

"Only one person."

"Who was that?"

"Sybil."

From there, Donna broke into—as if anyone cared—a long, drawn-out conversation with Kaluzny about the computer systems she had purchased for the company under George's urging. Some $30,000 worth. It was hard to gauge where Donna was going with this. Was she still on the sinking-ship metaphor of a business spiraling out of control and blaming it on George?

Then she talked about those e-mails. "Every day," Donna admitted, the two of them communicated through e-mails, phone calls, and faxes.

"Were you pregnant at any time during 1999?" Kaluzny asked.

"Yes, sir."

"When did you become pregnant?"

"March '99."

"You have heard some testimony that when you were arrested, some cardboard"—actually, they were dinner place mats—"fell out of your clothing. Can you explain that?"

"Yes, sir. I really didn't want to have to file bankruptcy. And I had found, by way of a friend, through a management company in Memphis . . . they were trying to find a home-health agency in Florida. And he [my friend], had a potential buyer [for my company]. The potential buyer, the two of them, were dragging their feet. They—and I needed to get it off my hands in a hurry."

Kaluzny picked up on Donna not making sense and asked: "Donna, excuse me, Donna"—he closed his eyes and put his head down for a moment—"I don't want you to just ramble. Were you *pregnant* when the officers arrested you?"

"No, sir."

"Why did you have cardboard in your clothes?"

"Because I was still pretending to be pregnant to try to hurry up and get the sale of the business over with so I wouldn't have to file bankruptcy."

She carried on from there, giving jurors an exhausting

explanation regarding how being pregnant would affect the sale of CCHH and speed up the process.

"Did you try to deceive George?"

"No, I told him I was pregnant. I showed him the paperwork."

"In July, did you tell him you lost the baby?"

"When I [came] here in July, I told him that I wasn't going to share any information about the baby with him anymore."

That was a lie. Her letters and e-mails after that visit to Michigan were littered with fabrications about this so-called baby.

She was asked if she had "authored" the notes in this case—i.e., some of the e-mails and letters found inside her house under a search warrant. Donna responded, "Those three notes that were showed in here (court) yesterday. The three letters that [were] read . . . on the stand. Those three letters I *did* write. I wrote those right after my miscarriage when I was an emotional wreck."

She talked about Gail next: how she never wanted anything to happen to Gail, how she wanted to meet Gail and talk to her. She wanted to help the woman. She cared about Gail enough to want to see Gail have a psychological exam.

Nonsense. There was plenty of evidence to the contrary, including Donna's voice on tape chastising and degrading Gail to the point of calling her vulgar names.

The reason she had left that nasty message about Gail coming down to Florida, Donna had the nerve to tell jurors, was because she did not want Gail around the office if potential buyers were going to be coming in.

"I was very angry," she said of that phone message. "I didn't want him to bring her down and flaunt her in front of my potential buyers and cost me the sale of my business."

She then proceeded to give an explanation for those key pieces of evidence the state had against her.

The map? George gave it to her so she could find her way around Michigan.

Saying she wanted Gail dead? It was a joke, of course—that someone took too far.

The photograph of Gail? She never had one.

"Donna, did you do *anything* at all to assist in killing Gail?"

"No, sir."

"Did anyone threaten you over Gail's death?"

"Yes."

"Who was that?"

"Kevin!"

"And why was that?"

"One reason. . . ."

"Why? . . ."

"He wanted money out of me."

So Kevin Ouellette came up with this grand plan to drive one thousand miles north, kill George Fulton's wife, and then blackmail Donna Trapani into paying him off? Seemed as though Donna had been watching too many Lifetime Television movies while waiting for her trial to begin.

"Did you hire him to kill Gail?"

"No, sir, I did not."

"I have no further questions."

72

PROSECUTOR PAUL WALTON WORKED from a trial notebook he prepared for each case. The goal was to have all the police reports and exhibits contained in a "murder book," with an index and easy-to-locate list of bullet points. As he prepared for trial, Walton reduced his notes into an outline. He liked to stand at the lectern with a single sheet of typed bullet points in hand, each one hitting on a different aspect of the evidence. Those points would then be checked off as the trial moved toward a close. In this way Walton could be satisfied he had covered every base.

As Walton approached the lectern to question Donna Trapani, he had his trusty yellow legal pad with notes he had taken during Donna's direct examination. This court, in particular, did not allow for the lawyers to acquire daily transcripts of testimony, so the attorneys relied heavily on note-taking and memory. Donna had said some pretty crazy things. From the moment she began, she'd had a theory for everything except who shot JFK. As those in the gallery looked on, and Paul Walton got himself ready to ask the first question, Donna Trapani appeared nervous. She shifted in her seat, as if preparing to take a blow.

Walton opened by asking Donna if, when she sat down with detectives from the OCSD, she told them she was pregnant.

"Yes, sir," she answered.

"Were they buying your business?"

"No, sir."

"And when you sat down with the [OCSD] and spoke with them in your house, you actually gave them the name of a doctor who was treating you, correct?"

"Yes, sir."

"Didn't you just tell the jury here today that you didn't have any [Medicaid] or insurance?"

"Insurance, yes, sir."

"Okay. So you didn't have a doctor, did you?"

"No, not at that point in time, no."

"Did you give the sheriff's department the name of a doctor?"

"Yes, I did."

"What was the name?"

It sounded like Donna replied, "Dr. Mats."

"As in *place mats*?" Walton asked, smiling. The courtroom made some noise, seemingly ready to erupt into laughter. Had Donna had a Freudian slip, caught in a blunder of the mind?

Donna quickly corrected the prosecutor: "Dr. Metz! *M . . . E . . . T . . . Z*. Metz!"

Walton produced hard evidence against Donna—all of which showed, by example, how Donna had not only lied on the stand, but she was at the center of a campaign not just to have Gail Fulton murdered, but also to wreak hell on the woman's life. Walton showed Donna a note investigators uncovered inside Donna's home. She had written to Gail as Donna's ex-husband, Charlie, calling Gail a "stupid, helpless woman." The note went on to ask Gail why she would stay with a man who didn't want her.

Donna admitted writing the letter, but not without reason. She made a point to say she had never mailed it—as though if the letter had not been sent, well, it didn't really exist.

Walton went through several additional notes in which Donna had presented herself as someone else. He smartly used the term "pretended" while questioning her about them.

Donna was forced to admit that, yes, she had written those letters and notes.

One of the notes seized from Donna's house was, in fact, a suicide letter written from the point of view of Gail Fulton. Donna had written it, the prosecutor was getting at, because she had, at one time, planned and plotted to kill Gail and make it look like a suicide.

Walton wanted to know if Donna had told the police about this story of Kevin Ouellette threatening and blackmailing her, adding, "So you have never told *anyone* this story except for today?"

"Well . . . yes," she answered.

After a few more questions, Walton asked Donna if she had told anyone else besides her lawyer.

"Sybil," she answered.

Of course.

Shocking everyone with his brevity, Walton asked Donna a few more inconsequential questions and walked toward his seat, saying, "Nothing further, Your Honor."

Sitting down, staring at his notes, Paul Walton rethought his decision. He asked if he could have a few more moments with the witness.

"During the pendency of this trial," Walton said, standing once again, staring at Donna, after the judge had agreed, "while you were in the Oakland County Jail, did you *not* ask another—a number of inmates—to come in and lie for you?"

"I asked a number of people to testify for me, but not to lie for me."

"Did you promise [an inmate] two hundred dollars to write a letter [for you] and to take care of her when she gets out of jail?"

Donna Trapani could not just say no. Instead, "Not like that. We were planning, if I got sent to prison, that we were going to try to be roommates, and I told her I would help her if we were roommates, and I also told her that I would try to help her get a TV when she got there. That, you know, I had a friend that I was writing that had volunteered to get me a TV, and if we were going to be roommates, obviously, she could share it. . . ."

She went on and on, trying to talk her way out of what amounted to several inmates coming forward to snitch on her. She called all of the inmates "very poorly illiterate" women who needed some sort of "psychiatric medication."

Walton gave up. He had made his point.

Lawrence Kaluzny had several redirect questions, trying, in all due respect, to plug a hole in a ship that was three-quarters of the way underwater. It was like using a mop and a bucket to bail out the *Titanic*. The situation was beyond repair. Donna had been caught lying so often it was hard to tell if *anything* she had said beyond her name was true.

As Donna Trapani stepped down, the judge asked to see

the attorneys in chambers. When they returned a while later, "Would you bring the jury back in?" the judge asked the clerk.

"The court is going to recognize Mr. Walton," said the judge, "for the purpose of a closing argument." He paused. Then he looked toward the prosecutor. "Mr. Walton."

73

PAUL WALTON BEGAN his closing where he felt the trial, with all of its drama and media exposure and focus on Donna Trapani and Sybil Padgett, belonged: "Martha Gail Fulton was a loving mother to Melissa, Emily, and Andrew."

The case came down to the murder of a mother and wife—an innocent woman who had done nothing to deserve the torture she had gone through during the final few months of her life, along with that hail of gunfire she received as a sentence for loving a man she had been with for a quarter century. And it was that love of family, Walton explained, "a dedication and devotion, that ultimately cost [Gail] her life."

He talked about the law and "the counts" the jury was going to be judging Donna and Sybil on. Then he went through the long lead-up to the murder and the actual crime itself, telling jurors how Donna had committed this vicious crime with the help of Kevin Ouellette, Patrick Alexander, and Sybil Padgett. It all went back to Donna Trapani, however. She had masterminded the entire plot. She had put her pawns in play. It was as if Donna were there herself, in the parking lot of that library, pulling the trigger.

The prosecutor next mentioned the phone messages

Donna had left at George and Gail's house. Then he played the tapes.

It was powerful evidence. Direct. In your face. It showed how Donna could turn from a calm and articulate woman, well-spoken and somewhat intellectual, into an evil, calculating, and angry witch—all within the snap of a finger.

The voice of the killer, in all its rawness and vulgarity, was on that tape. There was the woman scorned—whom Paul Walton had opened his case with—ready to take revenge on the one person she saw standing in her way.

Gail Fulton, Walton said, making a great point, "represented *everything* that Donna Trapani wasn't!"

After talking about the videotape, Walton keyed on the bullets and how each projectile had entered Gail's body, where it landed, and how each added to a painful and bloody death.

He talked about the various ways in which Donna had first planned to kill Gail, adding, "When you started this case, you took an oath. . . . The evidence in this case is overwhelming. The evidence in this case clearly points that this woman"—he turned and directed all of his attention toward Donna, who sat writing something, a smirk of sarcasm on her face—"is a murderess, and that she not only is a murderess, she *planned* the murder. Conspired with others. Brought others into her warped sense of reality. And it is because of this that Gail Fulton is no longer with us."

Walton used the best that technology had to offer: PowerPoint, with photos and graphics. He put on an illustrated show that jurors could relate to as facts.

The prosecutor took a breath. He stood silent for a brief moment. There was stillness in the courtroom. Then, without another word, he walked back to his seat. It was smart to keep his closing brief and to the point. An attorney never wanted to belabor an issue. Paul Walton had that experience behind him to know the difference between saying too much and the power of leaving certain things unspoken.

The judge took a short recess. Then: "Mr. Kaluzny?"

Donna Trapani's lawyer stood. He put a hand in his right pocket. He walked toward the jury box, without saying anything, deep in thought. Lawrence Kaluzny was a clever, experienced defense lawyer; he had decades of experience behind him. He knew this case was an uphill battle from the start.

"Good afternoon, everybody," Kaluzny said, sounding as though a friend to each juror. By no fault of his own, Larry Kaluzny was running up an escalator the opposite way. Backpedaling. Trying to fix not what his client had broken, but rather shattered.

He decided to start by taking a poke at Paul Walton, noting: "I thought I was pretty high-tech when I got a pen that had a soft feel to it, but after *that* presentation, I don't think it is so high-tech anymore." He stopped short of laughing. Trying to, one would guess, speak to jurors on their own terms. There would be no PowerPoint presentation for Larry Kaluzny. No gadgets. No "high-tech" computer graphics explaining his case. He was old-school all the way. There would just be the powerful words of a lawyer pleading his case. "Donna did not want Gail dead. The relationship with George, in her mind, was not over. George was still communicating with her. Even after the Fourth of July weekend."

If Donna Trapani had not killed Gail Fulton, who had? Larry Kaluzny needed to solve this riddle.

"Other people were opportunistic. They preyed upon [Donna's] vulnerability, thinking they could benefit from a woman who they thought had a lot of money."

Kaluzny called Donna "a woman who, by all practical

purposes, was emotionally destroyed, physically devastated, and financially destroyed."

He warned jurors against putting "sympathy, pain, anger, [and] outrage" ahead of, or interfering with, "the facts of the law."

He next went through that common cornucopia of defense attorney reasons for finding his client not guilty: reasonable doubt, of course, being at the top of the list. He couched it as "proof beyond any doubt." He mentioned how jurors needed to be "one hundred percent" on board with a guilty verdict. And all of this, he realized, for each juror, was "certainly something much greater than the civil test, but . . . the prosecutor has to *prove* the case beyond a reasonable doubt."

"Matlock" was on fire. For about twenty minutes Kaluzny talked about George Fulton ("He is not to blame here!") and the relationship between the two lovebirds, noting, "What *does* make sense is, that group that came up here and killed Gail were looking for an *easy* way to make money."

Then it was on to Sybil Padgett. He called her Donna's "friend, employee, someone that Donna helped . . . someone Donna trusted . . . someone who cheated on her reports, filed false work claims. . . ." That very person, he stated, could be the same person trying to extort money from Donna and involved in trying to frame her for a murder conspiracy. Kaluzny added that Sybil was "the key" to getting this entire ball of killing Gail Fulton rolling. Sybil had taken out of context a few stray, anger-inspired comments by Donna (for instance, "I wish Gail was dead"). Donna had been mad and had been spouting off at the mouth, Kaluzny insisted, and Sybil put these idle threats into action. Kaluzny called Sybil "not a brilliant person."

"She is the one that gets the gun. . . .

"She is the one that gets Kevin. . . .

"She used Donna, and she wanted more money. If you're going to kill somebody, do you say, 'Give me a few thousand dollars now, and you can pay me the rest later'?"

A pause for a beat.

Then: "Well, maybe if you get enough!"

Kaluzny went on to call Patrick by the wrong name: Brian Alexander. He called him, the "young kid." The liar. The impish hick who had read the police reports in the case and then fingered the others to get out of serious jail time.

"Is he someone you want to believe?"

Kaluzny went on and on for twenty additional minutes; then Paul Walton stood and rebutted some of what Kaluzny had said.

In that hodgepodge of rebuttal comments, Walton came up with the line of the trial: "This crime was conceived in hell . . . [and] when you are going to conceive a crime in hell, you don't go to Heaven for the actors."

Lawrence Kaluzny had rattled Walton's cage, because Paul Walton felt the need to go on for ten more minutes, arguing many of the weaker points Kaluzny had made.

The bottom line here was fairly obvious as both lawyers finished, and Sybil's lawyer took a crack at saving her ass: For Donna Trapani, it was all over. For Sybil Padgett, well, that was a different matter. If she was lucky, Sybil was going to see a second-degree murder verdict and maybe, just maybe, she would feel the free light of day on her back again in the distant future.

74

I T DID NOT take long for either jury to come back with guilty verdicts. On December 12, 2000, a dreary preholiday Tuesday, as the Bush-Gore fiasco continued in Florida and the presidential race was still up for grabs (and a few new buzzwords—"hanging chads"—were enmeshed into the lexicon of pop culture), Sybil Padgett and Donna Trapani were convicted of first-degree murder, in addition to conspiracy to commit murder.

This meant bad times ahead for the dynamic duo.

When it came to sentencing, there was no other choice for the judge but to hold each woman accountable under the parameters of state law. Thus, Sybil Padgett and Donna Trapani were sentenced to "concurrent terms of life . . . imprisonment without parole for the murder conviction and life imprisonment for the conspiracy conviction."

Eternity.

"She didn't say anything," Larry Kaluzny told reporters after the verdict, referring to Donna's reaction to hearing the rest of her life spiraling down a prison drain. "I had her pretty well-prepared for the verdict. When she was trying to decide whether to testify, I told her she shouldn't stick her head in the sand, that there would be a good chance she will be convicted."

At least the guy was a realist.

Donna might not have said anything to her attorney as the verdicts were read into the record, but her wheels were spinning. She had plenty she wanted to discuss. Just not with Larry Kaluzny or the court.

After her conviction (moments, not days or weeks later), Donna Trapani informed her attorney that she wanted to sit down with Court TV, which had been in the courtroom during proceedings, asking for interviews while filming portions of the case. Donna wanted to give the network an exclusive sit-down.

Given that an appeal in any murder conviction is almost a guarantee, what was Donna doing?

For whatever reason Donna needed to have the last word.

As he was collecting his things to leave court, Paul Walton heard what Donna was up to. For Walton, one-half of the case had ended. He had won. Yet, it wasn't about jumping up and down, pumping a victorious fist in the air; it was about Gail Fulton. Walton had obtained justice for Gail and her family.

Still, Walton couldn't believe Donna was sitting down to talk about her case so soon.

"Listen, if she's going to be in there talking . . . before her appeal comes back," he told Larry Kaluzny, "I want to be there. I need to hear what she has to say."

Walton walked into the room. There was Donna. Teasing her hair. Dabbing her lipstick. Asking about her eyeliner. Making sure she looked good for the camera.

Donna Trapani's big network debut.

The woman had just been told she was going to spend the rest of her life in prison and here she was gearing up for an interview, as though she could talk her way out of it all.

"Donna, don't do this," Kaluzny warned her. "This is *not* a good idea."

The convicted murderer shrugged it off.

"This is surreal to me," Walton said.

"How is my lipstick?" Donna asked one of Court TV's crew members (according to Paul Walton). "Does anyone have a mirror?"

At one point during the interview, Donna stopped. She turned to Paul Walton after saying something into the camera and asked, "Can this be used against me later on appeal?"

"I'm sorry, Miss Trapani . . . but . . . um . . . I cannot give you any advice."

Duh!

Donna asked another question of the APA. By then, Larry Kaluzny had left the room.

"Miss Trapani, I *cannot* answer you."

In all his years of lawyering, Walton had never seen such a display of ignorance and ego from a defendant whom he had just put away for life.

With a broad smile on his face, the Court TV reporter who was emceeing the videotaped interview with Donna called it, "The murder-for-hire trial . . . that had more twists and turns and shady characters than *Pulp Fiction*." This "deadly three-ring circus," the announcer added, was loaded with high drama like what one only sees in Hollywood.

As for Donna Trapani, what can be said about this Court TV interview? Well, while wearing a neatly pressed pumpkin-orange prison jumpsuit, she once again rambled her way through what she referred to as the "facts," giving Court TV only one good grab it could use to lure viewers into what was, in the end, a worthless interview.

"I hated him—and I still do," Donna said, referring to

George Fulton, the man who, when all was said and done, found himself still at the center of the murder of his wife.

Leaving the court that day, George, who had not donned a mustache for quite some time now, was seen shaking his head in great disbelief. Not at the outcome. He was glad that his wife's murderers were convicted and would pay their debts. But more so, one source noted, at being duped so badly. It wasn't until the preliminary exam, according to that same source, when George Fulton had finally believed that his once-treasured Donna—"my life and my love"—had planned the murder of his wife.

And here was a jury and judge now affirming that undeniable *fact.*

Epilogue

SOMEONE WHO KNEW Donna Trapani very well once told me that Donna was the type of woman to either end up someone's bitch within the first few weeks of being behind bars, catering to that inmate's every need, or literally running the prison herself.

As of this writing, the latter seems to be at least somewhat true.

Same as I do in all of the cases I cover, I wrote to the major players here as well.

Kevin Ouellette never answered. He had spoken his peace, apparently, and that was it—the guy was going to let his testimony and interviews with the police speak for themselves.

Patrick Alexander was a different story. Patrick sent me what was a rather hilarious return missive. I should say that there was a part of me that expected this. Nonetheless, Patrick did his best to explain himself. The letter, to my great surprise and pleasure, like the one I would soon receive from Donna, was typed. I always appreciate it when inmates type their responses. It beats the chicken scratch I routinely receive.

Patrick told me it had taken him some time to respond (several weeks, actually) because he had thought long and hard about talking with me. He had finally come to a few conclusions he wanted to share.

This should be good, I thought while reading the opening of his letter.

Patrick did not disappoint. He said, number one, he would "not give [me] permission to use [his] name in [my] book." His "main reason" for this was that he wanted to know more about how I was "going to spin the story." Yes, *spin* the story. (He must have been watching lots of *The O'Reilly Factor.*) He said he had no problem corresponding with me, but he would have a hard time remembering various aspects of his case because he did not have any of the documents. He had been given copies of his court papers but, he added, "over the course of being locked up," he had lost all of them. Of course, he wanted me to "attain" these documents for him and send copies to the prison.

Next he apologized for asking the question before he let it rip, warning me that he was a "human being" and "*must* ask" (emphasis added). He wanted to know if there was "any possibility" for him to "get paid for helping" me with the book.

Sure, the check's in the mail, Pat.

Once again, the very thing that had landed the guy in prison—greed—was there pushing Patrick Alexander to act.

I never responded to this admitted murderer. What's the point? A guy who had pled to a murder charge in open court on the record who thinks I cannot use his name without his permission is not someone I need to be involved with. Plus, he asked for money. How could I ever trust the man's integrity? Truth be told, Patrick Alexander gave the police an entire narrative and testified in two trials. There was plenty of information about him, his crimes, and his role in Gail's murder.

I wrote to Sybil Padgett and Donna Trapani, separately. They are housed in the same facility.

Sybil did not respond.

When Donna wrote me back, I realized why Sybil had not responded.

Donna opened her letter by apologizing for not writing sooner, but she wanted me to know that she had been "spending every waking hour" preparing to meet "deadlines for appeals." This is what I admire about convicted murderers: the fact that they never give up on the appeal process; that tenacity to always believe, around every corner, that freedom awaits, if only they say the right thing and *appeal* to the right judge.

Donna thanked me for my "interest in [her] case." She did wonder, however, why I was interested. She was "open to the matter" of being interviewed, but wanted to know what had sparked my interest in her case. She claimed to be "hurt severely," as well as her "family" by all the "mass media" coverage that took place during her trial. She blamed the media for her father's death. She said Charlie, her ex-husband, regretted what he had told the media and was "still angry" about her "affair and wanted revenge at the time."

Revenge? What in the world was this crazy woman insinuating now? After all these years, was she going to blame Gail's murder on her ex-husband, Charlie?

Donna went on to say she and Charlie had "resolved everything" between them in 2003, and, sadly, Charlie died of cancer in 2009.

Ah, there she goes—blame the dead guy. If possible, they all try it.

Donna next wanted to know how I would portray her in the book. She had "moved on." She could "never" speak to me on the telephone because "all conversations are recorded."

Then came a point where Donna told me, in not so many words, how she still, to this day, controls Sybil Padgett. Donna said she *knew* I had written to her "code-fendant, Padgett," so she was not sure, she continued, if my request to interview her was about Donna or Sybil.

I wrote back. My response is worth printing here, in part—namely, because I never heard from Donna again after sending the letter:

> *Dear Donna:*
>
> *Your case interests me because I like to write about families and their struggles. . . . I would portray Gail's murder and this case—and you—as the truth emerges and I investigate the case from top to bottom, and interview all of the players involved. . . . I report the truth as I [discover] it. I didn't find "mass media" coverage of your case; in fact, there is not a lot of newspaper reporting out there today. What "mass media" are you referring to? If you have any of those stories, send them along, and we can discuss them.*
>
> *I am so sorry to hear about your ex-husband's death. I call cancer the most deadly serial killer in the world!*
>
> *You have nothing to fear from recorded phone calls. What, possibly, could the prison be interested in with you talking to me? So what if they record the calls! If you want me to tell your story, the truth is nothing to be afraid of sharing with anyone who wants to listen. . . .*
>
> *Hope to hear from you soon. . . .*

Donna Trapani's and Sybil Padgett's appeals were denied. I am sure they will continue to appeal all the way up to the

U.S. Supreme Court, as Donna contended in her letter to me. But let's be fair here. As the appeals court ruled: *The evidence was sufficient to support . . . [their] convictions.*

It's over, ladies. Accept defeat and move on.

I think I can speak for Gail here when I say, "Ask for forgiveness and repent."

Emily Fulton wanted readers to know a few things about her father. The person she talked about in this book, Emily wanted to be clear, is not the same man she knows today.

"He did get help and is a better person now," Emily said of her father. "I know that my dad is not perfect, but he is a lot better than he was so long ago when all of that stuff was happening. My dad . . . is not dark (from an energy standpoint) like he was and he is actually quite nice to be around."

George Fulton remarried in 2004. George refused to talk to me. He said, through Emily, that he is writing his own book and would rather put all of this behind him. I have nothing against George Fulton or the decisions he made. In keeping with the metaphor of the book, George's mistakes are his cross to carry. Things happen, I understand. Marriages—within the Christian community or not—go through ups and downs, fail and survive. The sad part of this, in my opinion, is that George never realized (until it was too late) that he had brought an unstable, crazy woman, with obsessive personality disorders, into the marriage in meeting and hooking up with Donna Trapani. He would have never done so, I believe, had he known the type of woman Donna was.

Then again, what's that old cliché? *You play with fire . . .*

I am indebted to Emily Fulton for sharing her side of this story with me. Emily is a courageous young woman who deserves credit for standing up for her mother. Emily asked me if she could share a few memories about her father and say some things about his life today and what she has learned from this tragedy.

"The first memory of my father," Emily told me, "was watching him jump over a chain-link fence that enclosed our neighbors' backyards. . . ."

It was the sound of his daughter crying that sent George into action.

"I was around four years old and had been riding on a bike with my older sister when I fell onto the pavement."

George was outside and heard Emily's plea for help.

"I must have howled quite loudly for him to hear me. . . . My sister had deserted me, leaving me alone in my pain, as I am sure she was scared she would get into trouble. I was a sorry mess, with bloody knees, lying in the middle of the street, when my dad came along and scooped me up and carried me home. He sat me on the toilet, and then my mom proceeded to clean and bandage my knees. I still have scars today from that fall, but I vividly remember feeling that my dad was my hero and his presence meant that everything was going to be okay—I was safe."

Thinking about it all these days, it's hard for Emily to imagine how this same man could have caused his family so much pain.

What went wrong? Emily asks herself.

"We are all human and complex creatures and each of us has unique hidden pains that will consume us if we do not heal them in a healthy manner. I think that my dad was suffering from depression from the death of his father at an early age and he lacked the knowledge to be able to process these emotions. This is not to justify his actions, but simply call attention to the fact that our hidden pains can destroy our lives, as well as the lives of those around us, if we neglect to heal those wounds. . . ."

I asked Emily if her family had moved on from her mother's murder.

"Yes," she explained, asking the question: "Do we still love and have a relationship with our father?"

That is the same question any reader of this book will ask.

"It has been a process," Emily said, "but yes."

I asked, had the fabric of her family been torn apart by irreversible damage?

"Perhaps in some ways," she added, "but we are each healing our pain in our own way and exploring the new opportunities life has in store for us. Through my mother's life and even within my own struggles, I realized there are many things that can derail us from experiencing the fulfilling lives each of us deserves. Many times I often think if my mom had only reached out for help that perhaps things could have been different. It often lays heavy on my heart that my mom essentially gave up everything for us kids and sort of lost herself amid the chaos of my father's actions and never fulfilled her *own* dreams.

"Life is a journey and the path that I chose to take to rebuild my life after this tragedy was to empower women to achieve their full potential. It is my deepest desire to share the lessons I have learned and to help women find their own path, so that no woman has to struggle alone like my mom did. This is my life's purpose now, and I feel blessed that my mom, through her death, has left this gift with me to share. . . ."

I would like to thank Colette Thatcher, Office of the Prosecuting Attorney, Administration Division; Cheryl C. Robbins (what a help Cheryl was!), Oakland County Sheriff's Office, Investigative & Forensic Services Division; Prosecutor Paul Walton; Lieutenant James A'Hearn;

Christopher Wundrach; Lynn Erickson; Thomas Tabin (you have no idea how much help you were); and reader Diane Dixon, who sent me the story idea long, long ago.

There are the usual suspects, of course. (You know who you are!) Thank you to all of you for everything you do to advance my career and see that these books get into the hands of my readers.

I also want to thank Elena Siviero, who runs the M. William Phelps Fan Club on FaceBook. I know it takes time to do those things and I greatly appreciate Elena volunteering. Please sign up on the fan club page:

http://www.facebook.com/#!/group.php?gid=52752001614

Kensington Publishing Corp.—Laurie Parkin, the Zacharius family, in particular, and my editor, Michaela Hamilton, along with Doug Mendini, and every other employee who works on my books—has been there with me for over ten years and fifteen books now, supporting me, and always trying to figure out ways to reach more readers. I am both indebted and grateful for having such a great team of publishing people behind me.

Copyeditor Stephanie Finnegan always makes me look smarter than I am.

An immense thanks to Andrew "Fazz" Farrell, Anita Bezjak, Therese Hegarty, Geoff Fitzpatrick, Julie Haire, Elizabeth Daley, Jo Telfer, Milena Gozzo, Jeremy Adair, Alex Barry, Nathan Brand and everyone else at Beyond Productions who have believed in me all these years, as well as my DARK MINDS road crew: Colette "Coco" Sandstedt, Geoff Thomas, Peter Heap, Paddy, Jared Transfield, and, of course, John Kelly. Of course, thank you to everyone else that works on the show (I know I have forgotten someone and I apologize); along with my producers at Investigation Discovery (ID): Jeanie Vink and Sucheta Sachdev. A special shout out to Henry Schleiff, President and General Manager of ID, who has been behind my show since day one. You are all some of the most professional and passionate people I have ever worked with. I am so lucky to have you on my side. I am grateful for everyone working on the series—you are all wonderful people, some of the most gracious I have *ever* worked with, on top of being great friends. I look forward to the road ahead and where we're going to take DARK MINDS!

I would be negligent not to mention all the booksellers throughout North America and beyond—those indy stores and the chains—who have supported me and talked up my books to customers (thank you from the bottom of my heart).

Lastly, my immediate family—Regina, April, Mathew Jr., and Jordon--who have stood behind me forever. I could not close any book without speaking directly to my readers: Thank you! You are the most important part of this for me. I am grateful to each one of you for coming back, book after book. You are all constantly on my mind as I write these books.

And, of course, my readers. I love each and every one of you.

Read a preview sample of M. William Phelps's
next riveting real-life thriller

Bad Girls

Coming soon from Kensington Publishing Corp.
Turn the page . . .

1

"**S**OMETHING BAD MAY have happened."

It was the only fact she was certain of. Beyond that, the woman thought the victim might be "a friend of her niece's." His name "might have been" Bob. But that was all she knew. She feared the worst, however: that Bob Something was dead. She didn't know the exact address where the police could find him, but she could explain how to drive there, and she would escort cops to the house if they wanted to meet her somewhere in the neighborhood.

On a quiet evening, May 5, 2004, forty-eight-year-old Richard "Rick" Cruz called the Mineral Wells Police Department (MWPD) and explained what his wife, Kathy, had just told him. Both Kathy and Rick were in somewhat of a panicked state. Not freaked out. But their feelings were more of a puzzled, what's-going-on–type thing they didn't quite understand.

"Have you heard anything about someone being shot on Eighteenth Street?" Rick asked the 911 dispatcher.

Rick had the street wrong. It was actually Twentieth Street. Still, dispatch wasn't in the business of sharing information with worried callers phoning in to report gunshots fired at people.

"What other information do you have?" the 911 operator asked.

Rick explained the layout of the neighborhood best he could. He said he and Kathy weren't all that familiar with Mineral Wells and this particular neighborhood where Bob supposedly lived. They had only heard about it.

The operator said they'd send an officer out to Eighteenth Street to check things out.

Rick and Kathy Cruz lived in Graford, Texas, directly next door to Kathy's mother, Dorothy Louise Smith. Graford is about fifteen miles from Mineral Wells, where the shooting was said to have occurred. Kathy and Rick had arrived home at about 4:30 P.M. Rick was driving. As they exited the vehicle after Rick parked, Kathy's mother, Dorothy, standing on her porch next door, waved them over.

"Come here," Dorothy said. She seemed frazzled and agitated, as if in a hurry to get them over there so she could speak her mind about something.

"What is it?" Kathy asked.

Dorothy was "very upset," Kathy Cruz later explained in a police report. Kathy and Rick noticed Dorothy was on the telephone. Apparently, Kathy found out after walking over and assessing the situation, Dorothy was talking to her other daughter.

Something terrible was happening.

"What is it?" Rick and Kathy asked.

A pause. Then a bombshell: Somebody shot Bob.

Dorothy got off the phone and clarified what she knew. As the story went thus far, somehow, Dorothy explained, Kathy's niece (Dorothy's grandchild)—who had been living with Dorothy intermittently throughout the past year—might be involved in the shooting. Nobody really knew how or why, or any of the circumstances surrounding the story. Just that it was urgent someone get over there to this Bob Something's house immediately.

Rick walked into Dorothy's house. Without explaining what he was doing, according to what he later told police, he headed into his niece's room to have a look around.

"You stay here," Rick said to Kathy, who was becoming more upset by the moment. Kathy's niece had lived with the Cruzes for a while as well. Kathy had been close to her.

The idea Rick had in mind was to see if he could find something in the house that might clarify just what the hell was going on. A note. An e-mail.

Anything.

There was probably a simple answer. Usually there was. People overreact. Perhaps Dorothy, in all of her excitement, had totally misinterpreted the situation and blew it out of proportion. Drama—every family, in some form or fashion, had certain members that thrived on it.

Upon immediately entering the young girl's room, Rick found an empty gun holster. Exactly what he did not expect.

Where is the weapon?

Then he found an unloaded pistol in a second holster.

This alarmed Rick. The report of a shooting. A gun missing from a holster. Another weapon on the bed in a holster. Rick wasn't Magnum, P.I., but then again, he didn't need to be a private investigator to figure out that something was up. And it didn't look good.

Rick ran out of the room, then out of the house. While outside in the front yard, Rick called the MWPD back on his cell phone.

"Have you found anything?" Rick asked the operator. He sounded more serious.

"No. The officers out at Eighteenth Street haven't located anything suspicious." The dispatcher wondered what was going on. Was this guy—Rick—playing games with the MWPD?

Rick hung up. Then he grabbed Kathy's attention. "Listen, we have to head out to Mineral Wells ourselves and find out what's going on."

Kathy thought about it.

Good idea.

They took off.

On the way to Mineral Wells, having no clue, really, where in that town they were headed, Rick phoned Kathy's sister, her niece's mother, Cindy Meyer (pseudonym), and asked for directions to a house in Mineral Wells that Kathy's niece had been hanging out at and even living in lately. There was even some indication that the niece was working with the guy, Bob, who lived there. Cindy had been to the house.

After getting more detailed directions, Rick decided that he'd better stop first at the MWPD and relay to them what he had uncovered.

"I have the gun," Rick explained, referring to the pistol he had taken out of the room in Dorothy's house. "Do you want it?"

The cop was a bit taken aback. "We need to find that house first, Mr. Cruz. And we need to see if anything happened—then we can take it from there."

Kathy's niece was young—nineteen years old. According to Kathy and Rick, she liked to "get on drugs and exaggerate things." Others had said she liked to brag about being a tough, gangsta-type chick. Although she had been in a relationship with a man, engaged to be married, and had a baby, she was an open and admitted lesbian with scores of sexual partners and girlfriends—plus, drugs had become her life. Who knew what she was into now? Could be just about anything.

They left together, the cop following Rick and Kathy.

Rick pulled onto Eighteenth Street first and didn't seem to know where he was going. He was driving slowly past each house, checking to see if he recognized any of them. In back of him, the cop became more impatient as each block passed. The officer threw up his hands, beckoning Rick to tell him what in the hell was going on here. Was this some sort of a joke?

After a time of Rick's stop-and-go game, the cop got on the telephone with Kathy's sister; she talked him directly over to Twentieth Street.

Finally they arrived at the right house.

Bob.

Patrol corporal Randy Hunter, the participating officer, got out of his cruiser and told Rick, "You stay here by your truck and wait." Hunter said he needed to approach the door by himself.

Procedure.

Hunter knocked on the front door as Rick and Kathy looked on.

No answer.

"I'm going around back," Hunter said. "Stay where you are." He held up his hand as to indicate stop. The plan was, Hunter later said, "to check and see if anybody may have been in the backyard, look around. . . ." See what he could find out.

Nobody seemed to be home, but Officer Hunter noticed something peculiar as he focused on the back door of the home.

One of the windowpanes had been smashed.

"Something may have happened inside," Hunter recalled later, speaking about that moment he spied the broken back window, "that we needed to investigate a little further [and] check the welfare of the people inside."

Several additional officers arrived. Officer Hunter approached the house slowly, his weapon drawn, reached for the knob and opened the door.

"Mineral Wells Police Department!" the veteran cop yelled as he walked in. "We're here with Richard and Kathy Cruz. We're coming in."

Not a peep.

Hunter announced himself "four or five times" before heading into the kitchen.

As he made his way through the kitchen stealthily, as if expecting to be ambushed at any moment, Hunter heard music. A radio or television was on.

Coming out of the hallway from the kitchen, Randy Hunter spied a "subject," as he described the person, "somebody lying on [a] bed. . . ."

He pointed his weapon toward the subject and shouted pointedly: "Mineral Wells Police Department!"

No response.

"The size of the body . . . it appeared to be a male," Hunter recalled.

But Randy Hunter couldn't be 100 percent certain, because the bottom half of the subject was covered with a blanket. And from his neck up, the subject's face was covered with a pillow or bag of some sort.

Randy Hunter carefully approached the subject, bent down, and placed two fingers on the man's carotid artery to check for a pulse.

No sign of life.

Then, as Hunter grabbed his radio to call in additional backup, he saw blood.

"We're going to need an ambulance over here . . . ," Hunter said into his handheld. "Send Captain [Mike] McAllester and Sergeant [Brian] Boetz, too."

Hunter worked his way around the corner from that

small bedroom and located a second back bedroom, which he also approached with caution.

The door was slightly ajar. Hunter pried it open slowly and saw a "hospital-type bed . . . with all kinds of stuff piled on it." As he walked toward the bed to check the other side, "an arm fell out from underneath a blanket. . . ."

2

SHE BELIEVED IT TO BE some sort of celestial "sign." Those incredibly vivid dreams invading her sleep were coming "for a reason," she felt. They were fuzzy images, certainly, filled with metaphors of "which path to take," she later explained. In one, Jennifer Jones believed she was setting herself up for failure simply because she had been born (as they might say in Texas) *kin* to Clyde Barrow, half of the infamous Bonnie and Clyde murderous duo. Indeed, according to her grandmother, who was said to have made a shrine in her house dedicated to the old murderer and bank robber, Jennifer had that bad blood of the Barrows coursing through her veins, and there was nothing she could do about it.

Jen's mother before her, Kathy Jones, had set herself on that same path. Kathy was tough as rawhide, a bar bruiser and career criminal, in and out of jail. Kathy had even come close to death a number of times, stabbed and beaten. Jennifer never saw herself in that manner; but coming from that sort of pedigree, a woman can't help but develop a thick exterior and disastrously unhealthy inner dialogue. She begins to convince herself that she *can't* do anything. And all of those dreams she was having lately, well, they fit right into the madness that had made up her life. She felt doomed, in other words.

Destined to fail, that is.

"I found a list once," one of Jennifer's sisters explained to me. "Jennifer was like just about fourteen. It was a list of all the guys she had slept with. She stopped at one hundred. I asked why [the list abruptly ended]. She said she lost count. The list started with names. As it continued, she dropped the names. I asked why. She said she didn't even know some of the names of the guys she'd had sex with."

Because of that Clyde Barrow connection and a mother she viewed as destructive, unavailable, and quite caught up in a world of drugs and crimes to support bad habits, Jennifer Jones obsessed over the self-prophesized fact in her head that her life had been paved by a road already chosen for her. No matter what she did—no matter how hard she tried—Jennifer believed nothing could get in the way of this tragic evolution that became her fate.

So why fight it? Jennifer decided. Why not embrace its ambiguity and dark side? Years ago, Jennifer wrote about her chosen future in a journal that had become her best friend at the time. On December 28, 2000, just five days after her sixteenth birthday, Jennifer sat down and confirmed the inevitable: *These dreams are coming to me for a reason. . . .*

The Jennifer Jones of sixteen years old had no idea how visionary—call it wishful thinking, a self-fulfilling prophecy, creating one's own reality, whatever you want—those dreams of her future were to become. The baby-faced, clear-skinned, attractive Texas teen, with long brown hair and a Colgate smile, had set herself on a dangerous and deadly course, indeed. She didn't know it, but in front of Jennifer was a carefully chosen path that her mother had tried to manage before her. It was one that Jennifer had herself predicted years before, and the new "love" of her life—a tomboyish (but deceivingly pretty), petite, butch blonde, whom friends called a "little boy"— would end up becoming the proverbial scapegoat for it.

3

IT WAS 7:30 P.M. ON May 5, 2004. By most accounts it was a quiet night in Mineral Wells, Texas. Mineral Wells is a mostly white, bedroom community of about sixteen thousand, located in the northern central portion of the state pushing up toward the Oklahoma border. Fort Worth is the closest major city; Dallas and Irving are not too far east from there.

Before Rick and Kathy Cruz had telephoned into the MWPD what appeared to be a murder, the town had enjoyed a near nonexistent homicide rate: between 1999 and 2004, for example, there had been three murders. So people killing one another was not what Mineral Wells residents worried all that much about. When the locals were asked, the main problems in Mineral Wells dated back to 1973, when the military installation known as Fort Wolters transferred its last remaining helicopters out of the popular base and began the economically devastating process of closing. At one time Fort Wolters kept Mineral Wells bustling with plenty of military money floating around in bars and petrol stations and every other type of financial mainstay holding up a small community.

During what some might call the financial heydays of World War II, some say nearly a quarter-million soldiers filed their way through the Fort Wolters base, with another forty thousand during the Vietnam War. After that last copter and soldier left, however, Mineral Wells felt the hit immediately. All that military money vanished seemingly overnight. Add to that, too, the collapse of the cottage industry of the Baker Hotel, an icon in Mineral Wells since the 1940s and 1950s. As the years progressed, Mineral Wells fell more in line with that familiar poverty-stricken, jobless brand that has become small-town America, a burg ravaged by the horrors of what meth and ice can do: robberies, burglaries, auto thefts, and rapes. Not a trade-off, necessarily, for a low murder rate, but it was a fact the locals—many of whom were born and raised in Mineral Wells—could not and would not ever deny.

"Still," one local told me, "Mineral Wells sometimes gets thrown that way"—being a bad place to live—"but it's really not. Probably just like anywhere else, we have the same problems other communities have. We're average people."

The Baker Hotel was a resort, a bona fide destination for many tourists and Hollywood celebrities and curiosity seekers from all over the world. The likes of Marilyn Monroe and FDR visited. Everyone came in search of some of that old "crazy water" said to be tapped in Mineral Wells springs. The town had been founded on a certain type of mineral water that sprung up, which was thought to have some sort of a therapeutic value. It was said to be the cure for everything from arthritis to insanity, hence the "crazy water" name. As a result, the town became somewhat of a miracle, curing destination. Everybody wanted what was in that water. The Baker Hotel, a rather large landmark in town—now run-down and about to fall in on its own building blocks—became the go-to hot spot. There in the center of town stood a high-rise establishment, with the top floor dedicated to mineral baths.

"People came from all over to soak in the baths and then profess it was a cure for anything they had," said one local. "So back in the '50s and early '60s, this was a booming town."

Throughout that time the economy was great; the military was rocking and rolling. The Baker Hotel became like a little Las Vegas, and all was copasetic in town. But then that military base closed and the bottom fell out. No sooner did the Baker Hotel implode.

Still, the one fact that MWPD officers and locals would acknowledge all day long was that, despite the downturns throughout the years, Mineral Wells had "one of the lowest, if not the lowest, murder rates in the state."

Indeed, murder was not a call the MWPD got all that frequently.

Randy Hunter and the other MWPD officers who arrived on scene to back him up weren't in the house all that long. When Hunter and the other police officers emerged, Rick Cruz heard additional sirens—other cops and an ambulance heading toward the scene. It all seemed real now to the Cruzes. Something had happened. Something terrible. Something sinister and maybe even deadly.

Officer Hunter must have found something inside the house, Rick Cruz surmised, looking on.

Hunter came out and walked over to Rick and Kathy as more cops and an emergency medical technician (EMT) van pulled up. "I'll need that gun, Mr. Cruz."

Rick handed it over. "What's going on?"

The officer didn't say anything.

"What is it?" Rick asked.

The cop said nothing.

Then again, he didn't have to. The look on his face— and all of the arriving officers and emergency medical technicians—said it all. What had started hours earlier as a "maybe" was now something much more serious. Someone had been shot. No doubt about it. And by the look of it, Rick and Kathy Cruz knew while standing there in Bob Something's driveway, sizing up the scene as it unfolded in front of them, the cop was in no hurry to help the victim out.

By now, the MWPD believed there were possibly two victims inside what was an absolute dump of a house on Twentieth Street. Inside, police had found a male and a female. Or a mother and her son, as it turned out. That first responding officer, Randy Hunter, knew the man was dead; as it turned out, the woman was alive—just barely. The MWPD had no idea what happened: how, why, when, or by whom. They only inferred that a gun was somehow involved. Hunter and his team of responding officers did a cursory search of the house, where they had found the one man—presumably Bob Something—unresponsive, lying on a bed, cold to the touch, dead as roadkill.

As Hunter walked into that second bedroom, and the arm fell off the bed, he heard a groan. And it scared him.

What in the hell? Hunter thought.

Not another DB.

There was an elderly woman awake in her bed in that adjacent room, buried under a mound of covers. The room was a complete mess. "Junked out," said one law enforcement source. There were empty Happy Meal boxes all over the place. She had been watching television, actually. And when Hunter approached, weapon drawn, ready and expecting to find her dead, too, she looked at him quizzically and wondered what in the world was going on. It was obvious she had been underfed and was perhaps suffering from malnutrition and some form of dementia.

"Out of it," one cop told me later. She was totally oblivious to the fact that the man—her son!—in the room next to her was dead. "Once she got some fluids in her, though, she bounced back quickly and was—she let us know—totally surprised that the cops were in her house."

One report had the old woman sitting up in bed at one point, saying, *"Is there anything wrong, Officer?"* as Hunter dug her out of the covers she was buried under and realized she was alive.

The responding officers were smart not to touch or meddle with the crime scene. It's amazing how many first responders muck up what can be a slippery slope when walking into a crime scene involving a potential murder victim. It's those first responders, most forensic scientists will agree, that can make or break a case depending on how they go about closing off and securing a scene. In this case the MWPD had trained its officers properly— apparently. There was a protocol, and it was followed.

Thirty-five-year-old MWPD detective Brian Boetz was at home, already done for the day, enjoying his life outside work, when he took the call.

"We have what appears to be a double homicide . . . out on Twentieth Street," dispatch said.

"Got it. On my way."

One murder in Mineral Wells on a Wednesday evening was beyond rare. But *two*? That got Boetz's attention mighty quick. He didn't waste much time hopping up out of his chair, grabbing his weapon and radio, firing up his black Yukon SUV, and kicking stone and dust from his driveway as a siren blared as Boetz found himself heading toward a possible double-homicide scene.

Inside the house Randy Hunter had made sure that the

old woman was taken out by EMTs and brought directly to a hospital.

It took Detective Boetz about fifteen minutes to get to the scene. He stepped out of his Yukon, saw Richard and Kathy Cruz standing, looking rather puzzled, and headed into the house. No sooner had Boetz arrived, did his captain, Mike McAllester, pull up.

Boetz was a Texas transplant. He, his mother, grandfather, and grandmother had moved to Mineral Wells from Denver, Colorado, when Boetz was twelve. "My dad lives somewhere in Oregon, I think," the detective told me. "I don't know for sure. I don't keep in touch with him."

Taking a look at the house from outside as they headed in, Boetz and McAllester easily determined that no one had been taking care of the place. They'd seen worse, sure. But this house was nothing more than a run-down, dirty, substandard, ranch-style box of decaying wood. It had been nearly overcome by aggressive, vinelike vegetation, with paint peeling off like confetti in droves.

The EMTs were gone by the time Boetz and McAllester arrived. A cursory review of the neighborhood and it was clear that they were looking at a cookie-cutter series of similar single-family ranch homes on postage-stamp sects of land. This was part of suburbia in Mineral Wells. Most homes were kept up as best they could be under the conditions of the economic times, and there was not much drive to fix up a community that had been falling to the ills of the drug culture for years. Drugs had a way of working themselves into the nicer communities, once the suburban partiers move on from weed and booze and into the heavier stuff, like heroin, crack, and meth. There was no defining line much anymore, separating the "hood" from the "burbs," unless one was talking exclusive areas of the town. Drugs were everywhere today.

"The town of Mineral Wells is definitely in decay," one

visitor to the neighborhood told me, "and none of the homes in that neighborhood will be in *Better Homes and Gardens*."

An understatement.

"We entered through a back door"—after reaching in through what was a windowpane of smashed-out glass with a bit of blood surrounding it, and unlatching the lock—"and found a victim deceased and an elderly female subject still alive in her bed," Randy Hunter explained to Boetz as they got together inside and talked.

"No kidding?"

"Yeah. . . ."

"So it's not a double?" Boetz asked. He was confused at first. Dispatch had called in potentially two homicides. Could there be another victim besides the old woman, who had been taken to the hospital?

"No, just the one," Hunter said. He pointed to the room where the body had been discovered.

"Thanks."

The old woman, Hunter further explained to Boetz, was unmindful of what had happened inside the home. She had no idea someone had been shot and killed.

Better yet, her son.

"There's one deceased person inside and one being attended to [at the hospital]," Boetz explained to his boss, Mike McAllester.

It was 8:23 P.M. Boetz had a look around the house before heading into the bedroom with the DB. It appeared that the old woman had lived inside her room and was being *kept*—for lack of a better term—by someone, probably her son, Boetz surmised.

The deceased victim was naked, lying on a bed, half his body covered with blankets (as if he was sleeping), a pillow or some sort of laundry bag over what was left of his face. He had been shot, apparently point-blank, several times; the right side of his jaw had been blown nearly off his face. His cheek was nothing more than ripped, torn, and bloodied flesh.

"Looks like the elderly lady has been neglected," Boetz said. Interestingly enough, there was a lock on the outside of the old woman's door. Whoever was supposedly taking care of her had essentially locked her inside her room. It was clear she hardly—if ever—left that room.

Boetz asked Sergeant Bard Belz, who had just arrived, to position himself at the front door of the residence. "Keep a log of anybody coming and going from the crime scene."

"Will do," Belz said.

Boetz asked Officer Gary Lively to do the same at the back door. "Don't let anyone in."

"No problem, Detective."

Boetz and McAllester took a moment to look around the house. A basic ranch, the front door opened into a small living room, which was "just messy . . . in somewhat disarray," Boetz recalled. There were mattresses on the floor; pillows and blankets and garbage were strewn all over, as if several people had been living in the house and sleeping anywhere they could find an open space. There was a desk with a computer and chair. "Stacked up on top of a stand, where the TV was on, was a bunch of videotapes. . . ." There was some other furniture spread throughout the room, sparse as it was, but it was old and decrepit, like the inside of the home itself. And there was a lone fan, Boetz took note of, "noisy and running," sitting on a table. This gave the inside of the house a rather eerie, creepy feel, as though the fan was the only living thing left.

Taking a right out of the living room, Boetz stared down a short hallway that went into the kitchen on the right and a sitting room (bedroom) on the left. In the kitchen there were dishes and pots and pans stacked everywhere: on counters, in the sink, on the table.

Disgusting. No other way to put it.

Heading toward the back inside the kitchen, Boetz studied the door. One of the panes had been smashed and there was some blood on the glass and door itself. Not a lot, but enough to get a sample. On the floor below were several bits and pieces of broken glass.

Boetz and McAllester walked into the bedroom where the DB waited for them. The pillow—or, as Boetz realized now, "laundry bag"—was still covering the man's face. The idea, Boetz knew, was to "back up for a moment and look at the big picture of what could have happened here." Any good cop will agree: The scene will speak to him if he doesn't stand in its way and interrupt the process.

Looking around, Boetz pointed to the wall. There seemed to be a few pictures missing. The corners of the photos or pictures were still attached to the wall by tape and staples, but the bodies of the pictures were gone. Boetz could tell by the grime and dust marking an outline of where the pictures hung that someone had removed them recently. The walls were a putrid tan color, like coffee ice cream, and smudged with filth and dirt and grease. There was a bureau to the left of the victim, a stereo on top of it. The bed itself was a mattress on the floor. The striped laundry bag covered the victim's face and upper chest area; a floral blanket, with flowery patterns of pink and green and white and yellow, covered the man from the belly button down.

"Gunshot wound on his left bicep," Boetz said out loud, noticing the wound.

"Have you looked underneath the pillow?"

"I haven't removed it, no," Boetz responded.

Both investigators had been told by then that the entire area had been searched, around and inside the house, and "no other persons had been found." The only wound visible to Boetz and McAllester was on the victim's left bicep. It was clear that he had been shot in the arm.

Boetz had Detective Penny Judd come into the room and photograph the wound on the man's bicep.

Looking closer, Boetz noticed a hole through the laundry bag/pillowcase. He could see gunpowder residue.

Judd snapped a photo. And she continued to take photos of the entire room, the victim, and anything else Boetz pointed out.

Standard operating procedure (SOP).

"That gunpowder residue," Boetz said, "means he was shot at close range."

Someone had placed the laundry bag over the man's face and fired—almost like an execution. Organized-crime figures do this. Sneak up on someone while he sleeps, place a pillow over his face, and fire a few shots into the head. Just like in a Hollywood film.

But that wound on the bicep?

Strange.

There was a pair of men's jeans on the floor by the side of the bed. McAllester walked over and, carefully, being certain not to disturb what could be an important piece of evidence, reached inside the back pocket and took out what appeared to be a wallet.

He looked for a license. Found one.

The Cruz family had it right. The guy's name was Robert "Bob" Dow. He was forty-nine, his fiftieth birthday about a month away. Bob had a potbelly stomach on him, but he was otherwise in what was average shape for an American by today's standards. He was butt naked underneath the covers. Either he had been getting himself ready for bed when someone shot him, was already sleeping, or his killer had surprised him.

As Boetz stood near Bob Dow, he looked closer at the walls, where they had spied the missing pictures.

There was blood on the wall.

"Vic's?"

Was it blood spatter from the gunshot wounds?

Boetz and McAllester didn't think so.

It appeared to Boetz that whoever removed the pictures had cut himself or herself during that process and was bleeding.

Over near the northeast corner of the room was a green chest—like a pirate's—sitting on the floor. Boetz bent down and had a look. It seemed that someone had forcefully pried the chest open. With latex gloves on, Boetz had a look inside.

And that was where, Boetz said later, "we found some ammunition and a gun."